KT-466-369

GRAND INQUISITOR

Sir Robin Day was one of the original newscasters for ITN in 1955. In 1959 he joined the BBC's *Panorama* to which he was a contributor for thirty years. From 1979–87, he presented *The World at One* on BBC Radio 4, and from 1979–89 he chaired *Question Time* on BBC 1. Awards for his broadcasting have included the Guild of TV Producers' and Directors' Award, 'Personality of the Year' in 1957, the Richard Dimbleby Award in 1975, and the RTS 'Judges' Award in 1985.

Sir Robin was knighted in 1981. He is an Honorary Bencher of the Middle Temple and an Hon. Fellow of St Edmund Hall, Oxford. He has been awarded Honorary Doctorates by Exeter, Keele and Essex Universities.

He has two teenage sons and lives in London.

GRAND INQUISITOR

Memoirs by

SIR

ROBIN DAY

PAN BOOKS
London, Sydney and Auckland

First published 1989 by
George Weidenfeld & Nicolson Ltd
This edition published 1990 by Pan Books Ltd
Cavaye Place, London SW10 9PG

9 8 7 6 5 4 3 2 1

ISBN 0 330 30787 8

Phototypeset by Input Typesetting Ltd, London
Printed and bound in Great Britain by
Clay's Ltd, Bungay, Suffolk

To my sons
ALEXANDER and DANIEL
and may they remember

'The world continues to offer glittering prizes
to those who have stout hearts and sharp swords.'

– F. E. Smith (Earl of Birkenhead)
in his Rectorial Address, Glasgow University,
November 1923

Contents

ix

Contents

Illustrations

Robert McKenzie, Election Results Night, 1970 (BBC)
With Morecambe and Wise, 1975 (BBC)
Receiving the Richard Dimbleby Award, 1975 (PIC Photos)
With Edward Heath, 1970s
Interviewing Harold Macmillan, 1976 (BBC)
Interviewing Prime Minister James Callaghan, 1979 (BBC)
Election Debate with Michael Heseltine, Jo Grimond and Michael Foot, 1979 (BBC)
With Prime Minister Margaret Thatcher at the BBC, 1980 (BBC)
Bernard Levin interviewing the author, 1980 (BBC)
The author with his sons, 1981 (*Evening Standard*)
Sir Robin and Lady Day with their two sons, 1981 (Press Association)
At the Variety Club Dinner, 1982 (BBC)
Interviewing Prime Minister Margaret Thatcher, 1984 (Topham)
With Michael Heseltine, Dr David Owen, Susan Crosland and Dennis Skinner on *Question Time*, March 1988 (BBC)
The author and his sons, Christmas 1987, photograph by Stephen Markeson (*The Times*)

Unless otherwise acknowledged the photographs belong to the author.

Author's Note

I am grateful to the Prime Minister, the Rt Hon. Margaret Thatcher MP, for permission to reproduce her letter to me on pages 293–4, and to Lord Swann, former Chairman of the BBC, for permission to include the text of his letter in Chapter 11.

I wish to thank the many friends and colleagues who have discussed parts of this book with me, in particular Sir Geoffrey Cox CBE, George Ffitch, Dr Maya Even (who first suggested that there was a book to be written about my life), Mrs Annabel Markov, and not least my admirable secretary Mrs Sheila Bailey. She not only produced the typescript but was a constantly helpful critic.

From Christopher Falkus and Candida Brazil of Weidenfeld & Nicolson I have had warm encouragement, frank criticism and wise professional advice, for which I am deeply grateful. And I have had much shrewd and friendly guidance from my literary agent, Ed Victor.

My acknowledgments are due also to those whose books, as mentioned in the text, have been helpful in supplementing my own recollection, including: Sir Ian Trethowan, Lord Briggs, Michael Leapman, Michael Cockerell, Michael Tracey, Aidan Crawley, Bernard Sendall, Ludovic Kennedy, David Butler and his co-authors of successive Nuffield College books on general elections, and Lord Donoughue. I am particularly indebted to

Dr Peter Bull and Kate Mayer of York University for their studies of political interviewing on television.

In describing early parts of my career, I have drawn on previously published material written by me when the events were fresh in my mind.

Unless otherwise stated, the source of a statement is my memory, checked and counter-checked wherever possible.

Robin Day

Prologue

The year 1955, when I joined ITN, divides my life into sharply contrasting halves. The first half, before 1955, was untouched by television. I scarcely ever saw television. I never lived in a home which possessed a TV set. I never owned a TV set. Until I went to Washington in 1954, I took no interest in television. The first time I ever saw it was in about 1937. I was in a radio shop in Romford, Essex, with my mother. The programme, on a fuzzy nine-inch screen, was Jack Hylton and his Band. I was not impressed, perhaps because I much preferred Henry Hall – on the wireless.

The second half of my life has been dominated and driven by television. Since 1955, television has brought me fame (if not fortune) and far-reaching responsibility, not least that of questioning six Prime Ministers in front of millions, with a controversial role in the coverage of eight general elections. According to a somewhat grandiloquent university Orator, television has given me 'a place on the political stage longer than anyone but the Sovereign herself'.

The twenties and thirties were innocent decades of boyhood and school – the happy pre-war time of cricket and Ovaltine and Uncle Mac and the wireless and trying on gas-masks.

The forties, for my generation, were the supremely formative years. These were the years when everything changed. The schoolboy became a soldier, the war became peace, the soldier became an undergraduate, and Oxford enjoyed its golden post-war age.

The fifties were years of struggle to make a start in the real world. They were years of setback and disappointment and, suddenly, great good fortune. The biggest of my several gambles paid of. Television journalism was born at ITN. Here was my first sweet smell of success. The television interview made front-page news, and became a talking-point for viewers everywhere. I relished the controversy which began to swirl around my head.

Then the busy, brilliant sixties with *Panorama* on the BBC, travelling the world to cover crises, trouble-spots and upheavals. This also was the time when television became a part of the political process and cast off the old inhibitions of the radio age. And a new era dawned in my personal life: I fell in love and married.

The seventies were a time of professional frustration and dispute in my turbulent relationship with the BBC. I was out of *Panorama*. But in the general elections of that decade the frontiers of television freedom were again pushed forward. I broke new ground in radio. But, most important of all, I became a father.

The eighties? No decade has been for me more dramatic and more distressing, more eventful or more exciting. I was knighted in 1981 – 'the first knight of the box'. My two young sons, Alexander and Daniel, were at Buckingham Palace to see their father receive the accolade from the Queen.

I contracted pneumonia. I fractured my pelvis in a ski-ing accident. I had a multiple heart by-pass operation. Sadly my marriage ended, in divorce by mutual consent.

My television career had 'passed its zenith'. *Question Time* had been hurriedly launched as a temporary 'filler' for a late-night gap on BBC 1. But a wheel of fortune was turning. Radio's *World at One* put me back in the forefront of broadcast journalism. And I had a bigger role than ever on both radio and TV in the two general elections of '83 and '87 – the elections in which Margaret Thatcher achieved her ascendancy and forged ahead with her revolution. *Question Time*, the temporary six-month 'filler', turned out to be a ten-year triumph.

The nineties find me in a *fin de siècle* mood. As a kind viewer recently pointed out, I have reached 'the departure lounge of life'. While my flight is happily delayed, I look back in this book at my lifetime, over half of which has been spent in the fierce floodlight of television fame.

Why, wondered a bemused lady columnist, has Robin Day become 'a late-in-life television superstar?' Recoiling from such grotesque hyperbole, I see myself as television's survivor. Ten years ago, when my career was on the way down, my morale was kept up by this devil-may-care declaration to a reporter:

> I don't come down the studio steps to the sound of the dance band. I don't tell jokes and I don't do conjuring tricks. I've never had an agent, or employed a publicity man. All I do is ask questions that ordinary people want answered – questions people would ask if they knew enough about the subject.

> Yet somehow I have continued longer than some of the more glittering people, the showbiz entertainers who may have been more popular – but have faded.

My story begins, not at the beginning, but, for reasons which will become clear, on a Sunday evening early in 1958.

1

Into Orbit

The Idiot's Lantern Is Getting Too Big for Its Ugly Gleam

The date was Sunday 23 February 1958. The interview was live. I was sitting in a small studio at Television House, Kingsway, in London. On the other side of the table was the Rt Hon. Harold Macmillan MP. TV cameras usually go to Prime Ministers at No. 10 Downing Street. On this occasion the Prime Minister had come to the TV studios, which added to the tension.

As we waited to begin, the Prime Minister derived considerable amusement from the seating arrangements. He drily complained that he was sitting on a hard upright seat, whereas I was enthroned behind the table in a comfortable swivel chair with well-padded arms. This, said the Prime Minister, seemed 'to symbolize the new relationship between politician and TV interviewer'. He felt as if he was 'on the mat'. I offered to change chairs. But the Prime Minister, keeping up the banter, said, 'No, no. I know my place.'

The occasion was a weekly interview programme put out on Sunday evenings by ITN, the news service of the commercial television network. Mr Macmillan was then in the early period of his premiership. It was just a year since he had taken over from Sir Anthony Eden following the Suez fiasco.

My interview with Macmillan lasted thirteen minutes. It was by far the most important interview I had done with a British politician. It was the moment when my life as a political journalist on TV really began. There were banner headlines on the front pages next morning.

The interview with Harold Macmillan was historic and unprecedented. No one had previously interrogated a Prime Minister in this way outside Parliament. Neither Sir Winston Churchill nor Clement Attlee would have thought of giving an interview on radio – the medium of their time – let alone on television. Sir Anthony Eden had been first to dip a toe in the water. He had used TV for addresses to the nation and in party broadcasts. He had been interviewed for TV only briefly, as at airports. Macmillan had done likewise.

This then was the first time a Prime Minister had been vigorously questioned on television. The interview was also the first in which a Prime Minister had been questioned by a single interviewer, apart from brief interviews at airports. Two days earlier, Macmillan had been questioned in an anodyne BBC programme by three newspapermen, charitably described in *The Times* as 'a restrained group'.* But the interview on ITN was, according to Derek Marks of the *Daily Express*, 'the most vigorous cross-examination a Prime Minister has been subjected to in public'.† I later heard that Macmillan himself referred to this interview as the first time he had really mastered television.

Macmillan thus became the first Prime Minister to emerge as a TV personality. He might be Edwardian in style and appearance, but on the twentieth-century box that Sunday evening he showed himself to be more than an accomplished parliamentary performer. The *Yorkshire Post* commented: 'Certainly he is no longer just a House of Commons man.'‡ Macmillan's official biographer records: 'His first breakthrough as a "television personality" had come with a full-length interview staged by a young, brash, and virtually unknown journalist called Robin Day on 23 February 1958 . . .'§

A few weeks later, having scored so brilliantly on ITN, Macmillan was able to display his screen showmanship with consummate

---

*The Times, 21 February 1958.
†*Daily Express*, 24 February 1958.
‡*Yorkshire Post*, 24 February 1958.
§Alistair Horne, *Macmillan*, vol 2: 1956–1986 (Macmillan, 1989), p. 149.

ease in a relaxed interview with Edward R. Murrow and Charles Collingwood, the star commentators of US television.

The significance of my ITN interview with Macmillan is difficult to convey today. Here was the nation's leader, the most powerful and important politician of the time, coming to terms with the new medium of television. He was questioned on TV as vigorously as in Parliament. His TV performance that Sunday evening was an early recognition that television was not merely for entertainment or party propaganda, but was now a serious part of the democratic process.

That interview, according to Martin Harrison, Professor of Political Science at Keele University, was when:

> Macmillan first grasped that television was neither a meretricious toy nor the instrument of torture he once termed it, but the means by which political leaders must henceforth reach the electorate, and through which they must now as a matter of course account for themselves.*

So that occasion in 1958 was a watershed in the premiership of Harold Macmillan and in the development of TV journalism. It was also the moment when I realized that being a TV journalist was to make me a figure of controversy at the centre of political events. I had been in television for only two and a half years. I was now into orbit.

In its newsworthiness and novelty, the Macmillan interview was a professional triumph for me. But amid the applause there was a rumbling of stern disapproval. Certain of my questions were sharply attacked by leader writers and columnists. This was the first of many such occasions during the next thirty years.

The question which provoked the controversy was about Selwyn Lloyd. He was then a much-criticized Foreign Secretary. His future was a topic of avid political speculation. Would Macmillan drop him from the Cabinet? In a Fleet Street tavern, I had bumped into John Junor, Editor of the *Sunday Express*. Referring to my forthcoming interview, Junor said, 'Are you going to ask him if he's going to sack Selwyn Lloyd?' I laughed

*Speech at Keele, 28 June 1988.

and said, 'Wait and see.' My laughter was unconvincing, I fear – because I was at that very moment thinking how to raise the question of Selwyn Lloyd without being seen as grossly impertinent. Television journalism and television interviewing were then in their nervous infancy.

The Editor of ITN was Geoffrey Cox, a seasoned political journalist who had been a 'lobby' correspondent, that's to say one of those reporters with privileged access to politicians in the lobby at Westminster. He agreed that, come what may, the question of Selwyn Lloyd's future would have to be raised. We felt that ITN's reputation for independence and integrity depended on that question not being ducked. The problem was how to phrase a question which would produce an answer from the Prime Minister without asking him outright whether he was going to sack Selwyn Lloyd.

The interview ranged over many topics of the time – the Rochdale by-election, Britain's H-bomb, Macmillan's recent Commonwealth trip. Then, towards the end, came the moment to put the crucial point. The wording had been carefully prepared:

> What do you say, Prime Minister, to the criticism which has been made, especially in Conservative newspapers, about Mr Selwyn Lloyd, the Foreign Secretary?

The Prime Minister answered quickly and calmly, and he did not express the slightest annoyance afterwards. However, a dozen years later, in the fourth volume of his memoirs, Macmillan surprisingly referred to that question as 'a somewhat truculent question from one of the new class of cross-examiners which has since become so popular'.* 'Truculent'? Macmillan's memory must have confused my delicately worded question with the over-heated reaction to it in the press.

Macmillan's reply to that question was the front-page lead in the newspapers next day:

> Well, I think Mr Selwyn Lloyd is a very good Foreign

---

*Harold Macmillan, *Riding the Storm* (Macmillan, 1971), p. 473.

Secretary and has done his work extremely well. If I didn't
think so I would have made a change, but I do not intend
to make a change simply as a result of pressure. I don't
believe that that is wise. It is not in accordance with my idea
of loyalty.

The interview continued:

Q: Is it correct, as reported in one paper, that he would like,
in fact, to give up the job of Foreign Secretary?

A: Not at all, except in the sense that everyone would like
to give up these appalling burdens which we try and carry.

Q: Would you like to give up yours?

A: In a sense, yes, because they are very heavy burdens,
but, of course, nobody can pretend that they aren't. We've
gone into this game, we try and do our best, and it's both
in a sense our pleasure and, certainly, I hope, our duty.

Some leader writers and columnists seized on this mild and
courteous exchange as if the constitution was crumbling. That
most vitriolic of columnists, Cassandra (Bill Connor) of the
Daily Mirror, lashed out fiercely at me:

If anybody wants a demonstration of the power of television
let him refer to the interview which Mr Robin Day had with
the Prime Minister on ITV on Sunday night.

Mr Day, who is a formidable interrogator, suddenly asked
Mr Macmillan how he felt about criticism in Conservative
newspapers 'particularly of Mr Selwyn Lloyd'.

At once the Queen's First Minister was put on the spot.
What *else* could he say about his colleague? How *could* he
suddenly reject him? How *could* Mr Macmillan be anything
but complimentary to his colleague – and to his accomplice
in the Suez escapade?

So here you have the ridiculous situation of how the
British Prime Minister can suddenly be put on a Morton's
Fork which forces him into defending and maintaining a
colleague who is obviously a disaster to British foreign
policy.

Mr Robin Day by his skill as an examiner has been responsible for prolonging in office a man who probably doesn't want the job and is demonstrably incapable of doing it.

The Idiot's Lantern is getting too big for its ugly gleam.*

The Editor of the *Daily Telegraph* wondered solemnly:

Should the Prime Minister have been asked what he thought of his own Foreign Secretary, before a camera that showed every flicker of the eyelid? Some say Yes; some say No. Who is to draw the line at which the effort to entertain stops?†

The *Manchester Guardian* was worried about the novelty:

Everybody wants to know what a Prime Minister thinks about his colleagues, and Mr Day asked the right questions: but Mr Macmillan is the first holder of his office to have satisfied public curiosity so bluntly. This may be judged a good or a bad development, according to taste, but it is certainly new. Could one have imagined Sir Winston Churchill when Prime Minister gossiping about Sir Anthony Eden, or Lord Salisbury?‡

Pendennis in the *Observer* speculated apprehensively:

Will the television screen begin to by-pass the House of Commons, or even (dread thought) the Press? This is the kind of question that has been sending a shiver down what's left of Fleet Street's spine.§

For the first time Fleet Street could sense a journalistic challenge, not merely a pictorial challenge, from television. Newspapers were now beginning reluctantly to devote their front

Daily Mirror, 25 February 1958.
†*Daily Telegraph*, 7 March 1958.
‡*Manchester Guardian*, 25 February 1958.
§*Observer*, 2 March 1958.

pages to reporting interviews which had been obtained exclusively by their TV competitors.

My question to Macmillan about Selwyn Lloyd had been misquoted in the *Daily Telegraph* editorial. I had *not* asked the Prime Minister 'what he thought of his Foreign Secretary'. But the effect was to give the impression that I *had* asked that question. I had learned a valuable lesson: if you are going to put a question on a sensitive or provocative subject, be sure that the question is so phrased that, when the transcript is checked, it can be defended as having been fair, proper and in the interrogative. In this way a polite and softly worded question may none the less convey a hard meaning, and may elicit a newsworthy answer or disclosure. I have spent many hours preparing such questions.

Those who criticized me for asking the question about Selwyn Lloyd were unaware that Macmillan was expecting such a question and was ready to answer it. It was *not* putting the Prime Minister on a Morton's Fork. This was not because I had forewarned him. On the contrary, he was told nothing about the questions except the main areas to be covered. But as we left the Editor's office in ITN to go up to the studio, the Prime Minister's Press Secretary, Harold Evans, took me aside. He said, 'I suppose you're going to ask him about Selwyn Lloyd?' I replied, 'No comment,' and we both laughed. But I knew then that the PM had come to the studio determined to scotch the Selwyn Lloyd speculation if he was given the chance. If I had not known this, would I still have put the question? Yes – because it was topical, relevant and based on fact: the fact of there being much speculation and criticism about Selwyn Lloyd.

Later that Sunday evening, I flew out to New York to do three more interviews for the same weekly programme, which was called *Tell the People*. The New York papers carried the Macmillan interview on their front pages, and I heard that the London papers did also. I flew down to Washington for an interview with Vice-President Nixon. This was watched with unusual interest because President Eisenhower was then an invalid. Nixon might succeed to the Presidency, or become acting President, at any moment. The Nixon interview, like that with Macmillan, was prominently reported. Once again I had the

Banner headlines after the author's ITN interview with Prime Minister Harold Macmillan on 23 February 1958

exciting sensation, immensely satisfying to a political journalist, of not merely reporting news but of *making* news, and of being more than a face on television, more than merely a 'TV personality'. After little more than two years in television, I had found a serious profession in which I could succeed. My TV work was attracting praise from influential critics. By 1958 my name and face were becoming known. As early as 1957 I had been impersonated on the screen – by Peter Sellers.

My good fortune was that my TV career began when ITV and ITN began. I was seen as a pioneer of the new TV journalism. But the thought of becoming a 'national figure' or a 'national institution' never occurred to me. These, and other descriptions (like 'grand inquisitor'), only gradually came to be hung around my neck.

I had never formed any such ambitions, if only because in the early fifties there was no such position to achieve and no such person to emulate. In Britain there was no profession of TV journalism. Before 1955 there were talented tele-politicians such as Christopher Mayhew or Aidan Crawley, who had made their names as MPs and government ministers, and who contributed occasional series to the screen. They were the only TV personalities of any significance at that time. There was no British Ed Murrow. There was not then any animal like Sir Alastair Burnet or any of the other presenters and commentators who have since become famous for their work in news and current affairs.

The most celebrated television figures of the early fifties were the over-publicized announcers like MacDonald Hobley, or panel-game personalities such as Gilbert Harding. Richard Dimbleby, of course, was already well known for his wartime radio reports and for his much-admired TV commentaries on royal occasions. But he did not become a commanding figure on television until he anchored the weekly *Panorama*. This did not begin until September 1955. Until then *Panorama* had been only a fortnightly magazine programme.

Before the mid-fifties, therefore, any young man looking for a career had no television 'giants' to emulate, no television heights to scale. The journalism of television, which is now part of daily life and of the political scene, simply did not then exist as we have come to know it.

Your young actor could aspire to be an Olivier or a Gielgud. Your young barrister could dream of becoming a Hartley Shawcross or a Norman Birkett. The Bar, the stage, Fleet Street, were long-established professional worlds with glittering prizes to be won. But one could not aspire to be a leader of a profession which did not then exist. Television journalism was undeveloped territory.

Even in the heady, pioneering atmosphere of the birth of ITN, I still came up against an occasional hankering after the traditional formality of BBC news broadcasting. One evening I had changed clothes for the transmission. I wore a bow-tie of the kind which I had often worn, like my father before me, ever since I was a student. The wearing of that particular tie, a navy-blue polka-dot bow-tie, was not an affectation, nor was it consciously flamboyant. A bow-tie to me was perfectly normal and, as my father always explained, had certain economic advantages. A two-ended bow-tie can be tied in four different ways, thus giving it a life four times as long as an ordinary tie, which tends to get badly worn in the one place where you can tie it. Another advantage was a bow-tie could hide a frayed collar.

When I came into the newsroom, unconscious of what tie I was wearing, I was surprised to be rebuked by one of the very pretty and very proper newsroom secretaries, Pamela Lyle. She later married my ITN colleague and friend, George Ffitch. In a horrified whisper, she said: 'Robin, you really can't wear a bow-tie for the news!' It was as though I was about to commit some dreadful solecism, like smoking in church. For a moment I wondered if I was doing the wrong thing. After all, her rebuke might be typical of spontaneous viewer reaction after years of formality from Auntie BBC. No sooner had that doubt occurred to me than I dismissed it from my thoughts. If ITN was to be different from the BBC, should it not *look* different from the BBC? Would not a bow-tie, of sober and conventional pattern, be a harmless distinguishing feature? But I did not ask these questions aloud. I thought it better to content myself with a polite though firm explanation that a bow-tie had always been a habit of mine, acquired from my father who had acquired it from some Victorian parliamentarian whom he greatly admired. And what, I asked, warming to my theme, was wrong with a bow-tie for the news? If the great Winston Churchill could wear a bow-tie on the most solemn occasions in our history, why could not I, a humble newscaster, wear one for the ITV evening news?

No one complained again. I have worn a bow-tie on television ever since. I had originally worn one without any thought. Then I wore one to establish my right to wear it. The tie gradually became a boon to cartoonists. So it became a uniform to which I have stuck. If I am off television, and I am not wearing a bow-tie, I am effectively in disguise, which is very convenient.

2

Boyhood

Put Those Umbrellas Down – We Can't See Mr Churchill

I was born on 24 October 1923 at No. 84 Oakwood Road, Hampstead Garden Suburb, London. There I lived until the age of seven. Only two or three happenings stand out clearly in my memory as having disturbed the tranquillity of early childhood.

The earliest memory I have is of being ill with whooping cough in 1928 when I was about five. My mother sought to cheer me up with the information that sickness was something which happened to the most important people. King George V was very ill indeed, so I was in good company. Presumably I was much consoled by this spurious argument.

The start of my education was attended by rebellion and crisis. For some reason (I do not recall what) I ran away from kindergarten on my very first day. I ran out of the school, down a hill all by myself and arrived back at home in tears. This proved only a momentary rebellion. The only other untoward incident occurred shortly afterwards when I tripped up one of the mistresses with a hockey stick. She narrowly escaped serious injury. My sense of humour had for the first time, but not for the last, led me astray.

I was the youngest of three children, and much younger than the other two. I was nine years younger than my sister, and thirteen years younger than my brother. Being the baby of the family, I was pleasantly spoilt. My father, William Day, was an

12

electrical engineer by training, and was on the administrative staff of the Post Office, which then had charge of the telephone system. I did not get to know my father well until I was in my mid-twenties. He had by then retired, and I had just been demobilized after nearly five years in the Army. My mother had died while I was overseas. My father was living alone in the house which had been their home since his retirement in 1939. This was in the Essex island village of West Mersea. We would go for long walks along the sea front. This was my first real chance to talk deeply as an adult with my father. We had lively arguments about religion, politics, politicians and the meaning of the universe.

Although he had been trained as an engineer, and had spent his career in the service of a government department, my father was a man of broad interests and outlook. He was enthralled by politics and was steeped in political biography. He read widely in philosophy. He played the piano and had been an organist in his youth.

Politically my father was a staunch Liberal of the Lloyd George persuasion. When I was quite young, he used to tell me stories about Lloyd George at the height of his power and fame. I was told of his technique on taking charge of a ministry or department of government. He would, my father said, send for every key official and ask him what his job was and how it was done. That way, my father explained, everyone was forced to justify himself. Ll. G. could soon tell who was any good and who were the dullards. Thus did he swiftly impose his authority. How true this was I have never been able to establish, but my father claimed to have employed a similar method with much success whenever he took over a new position.

My father also enjoyed telling me some of the famous examples of Lloyd George's vituperative eloquence and of his platform repartee: Ll. G. to angry heckler: 'You'll find the answer in Volume Four of my memoirs.' Angry heckler: 'I've read it.' Ll. G.: 'Oh no, my friend, you haven't, because I haven't written it yet.' My father would explain that this sort of thing was magic in a packed political meeting under the spell of the Welsh Wizard.

Politics and parliamentary performance were my father's hobbies. For several years in the 1920s he was a leading member of a then famous debating society called the Hampstead Parliament. Its members included members of the real Parliament. The proceedings were modelled on those of Westminster. Members had 'constituencies' and ministerial offices. My father was 'Member for Blackpool' and for a period was 'Prime Minister'. This Hampstead Parliament was in those pre-television years a thriving place of argument and enjoyment. So I was brought up by my father to love political argument, to revere parliamentary institutions and to admire great parliamentarians. After Lloyd George, my father's next hero was Winston Churchill, for whom he predicted greatness long before 1940. My father remained a radical Liberal all his life and regretted that Churchill had rejoined the Tory Party. But my father regarded him as a very great man, even in those 'wilderness years' when most people dismissed him as a brilliant failure or, in my history master's judgment, as 'an irresponsible madman'.

In 1933, when I was nine years old, my father took me to hear Winston Churchill speak. This was at a country meeting in Gloucestershire. Because of bad weather, Churchill had to address the meeting in a marquee. The marquee leaked. A forest of umbrellas went up against the rain which was dripping through. Our view of the great man was blocked. Suddenly, to my horror, my father interrupted him and shouted, 'Put those umbrellas down – we can't see Mr Churchill.' I sat petrified, expecting the police to arrest my dad and take him away for creating a disturbance. But my father's robust interruption brought the umbrellas down and produced an immediate response from Mr Churchill, who peered over his spectacles and asked with a grin, 'Does anybody mind the rain? I don't mind it a bit!' We all got damp, but we could all see Mr Churchill.

My only other distinct memories of my boyhood years in Gloucester are of two birthdays. On my eighth birthday I escaped death by an inch or two. Eager for school, I jumped out of my bus, rushed on to the road without looking at the traffic, and ran in front of an oncoming lorry. Its brakes were slammed on, but I was knocked over. Miraculously my injuries were slight.

On my tenth birthday I was caned by the headmaster. My

offence was being noisy and disorderly in morning school assembly. The caning (three strokes) was inflicted on the palm of the hand by Mr D. G. Williams, the much-respected headmaster of the Crypt Grammar School, Gloucester.

Apart from that painful moment, my boyhood in Gloucester, where my father was the Post Office telephone manager, was very happy. My chief pleasure was watching county cricket at the Wagon Works ground. I was not a brilliant cricket player but I loved watching. When I was given a cricket bat stamped with the signature of Jack Hobbs or Herbert Sutcliffe, it was so precious that I took it to bed with me. I queued to get the autographs of the cricketing stars of that time, notably Gloucestershire's Charlie Barnet, Tom Goddard and the great Walter Hammond.

My career as a cricket spectator reached its climax later at the Oval in 1938. I proudly showed my parents an evening newspaper which carried a front-page picture of their (unidentified) son in the early-morning queue at the Oval gates. As a boy of fourteen, I watched Len Hutton building up his record Test score against the Australians (364 caught Hasset bowled O'Reilly). In the immortal words broadcast in the deep, rich voice of BBC commentator Howard Marshall, as Hutton's record-breaking stroke was about to be played: 'The England total 707 for five, and the gasometer sinking lower and lower.'

The Crypt School, Gloucester, founded in 1539, was one of two ancient grammar schools which I attended between the ages of eight and fourteen. The second, after my father had been transferred to London, was Brentwood in Essex, founded in 1557. At both these schools the discipline was strict and we were made to work hard. Never at any stage of my life have I achieved profound scholarship or intellectual brilliance, but my academic attainments would have been infinitely worse if I had not had a solid grounding in the basic subjects at those two fine grammar schools.

In December 1936 Brentwood School was the setting of a dramatic experience in my young life. The Abdication crisis was at its climax. I was only thirteen at the time, but had been fascinated by the royal drama. It was the first public event I can clearly remember. I kept a bulky scrapbook of press cuttings about the crisis. I cut out articles which explained what a 'morganatic' marriage would mean. I memorized quite pointless information such as the King's seven Christian names (Edward Albert Christian George Andrew Patrick David) which I would rattle off to anyone interested, and can still do so.

As the Abdication crisis came to a head, Brentwood School was presenting its annual 'Winter Theatricals'. The play was Shakespeare's *Henry IV Part 2*. I was in the audience with my parents on the evening of 11 December 1936. The King had abdicated and was due to speak on the wireless at 10.15 that night. Arrangements had been hurriedly made to relay the royal broadcast in the hall, and to shorten the performance of the play. To us in the audience, the crisis gave an acutely topical significance to some of Shakespeare's lines, such as 'Uneasy lies the head that wears a crown', and 'God send the prince a better companion'.

Immediately the play was finished, a tall wooden loudspeaker was solemnly placed in the centre of the stage. Perhaps my overimaginative memory is playing tricks, but I seem to remember that behind the loudspeaker the painted stage backdrops with royal heraldic symbols were still aptly in position.

It was an extraordinary scene, a packed hall of several hundred people listening intently, some in tears, to this historic broadcast. Those who listened will long remember its opening sentence: 'At long last I am able to say a few words of my own.' To this day, more than half a century later, I cannot resist any book or article about the Abdication, though I can very easily resist reading anything about the subsequent lives of the Windsors.

The Crypt School and Brentwood School were grammar schools to which my father paid modest fees. Being in the public service, he was not on a high salary. But, through the grammar school system as it then was, he was able to give all his three children a first-class education. He considered that to be the duty of a parent. Politically he was a lifelong radical who hated privilege and social injustice. But he never believed in levelling down, or in the monopoly of education by the state. On the contrary, my father felt that there was nothing privileged or socially unjust about the payment of fees for his children's education. To pay these education bills, he had chosen to make sacrifices. He and my mother lived very simply and modestly. They never had a holiday abroad. They never owned a car. They did not drink alcohol or smoke cigarettes. 'Hence,' as my father used to say, 'I have been able to educate my children well. That was my right and my duty.'

After my second grammar school, I went to a completely different kind of school. This was largely at the insistence of my mother. She was concerned that the education I was getting was too unimaginative and too orthodox. My mother was an artistic lady. She played the violin and was a quiet, gentle person who loved embroidery and gardening and flowers.

I remember also that my mother was a person whose judgments were practical. When I was about twelve, and temporarily under the influence of a Bible-class leader, I announced my intention of becoming a missionary in the jungle. My mother patiently expressed no objection, but pointed out that I would probably get yellow fever.

She was a person of extremely good (by which I mean simple) taste in furniture and household things. She did not feel that as a day-boy at a suburban grammar school I would develop into a very imaginative or creative person. She thought the teaching was good but the education narrow.

More to the point was the fact that I was now (at fourteen) the only child at home. My sister and brother, who were both much older than I was, were away from home. I was becoming obstreperous. My parents therefore wisely concluded that I would benefit from a boarding school education. But I was not sent to an orthodox public school. I was sent to Bembridge School on the Isle of Wight, which had been founded in 1919. On the strength of an interview with the headmaster, I was awarded a bursary, or scholarship, which enabled my father to meet the extra cost of boarding school education.

Magnificently situated on the cliffs near Whitecliff Bay, Bembridge School had been founded in reaction against the conventional public school ethos, with its military overtones and classical bias. The school chapel was non-denominational. But the school was not cranky or 'progressive'. There was discipline, and there were prefects. At 7 a.m. all boys had to go for a run or, in the summer term, for a swim in the sea.

But Bembridge had a number of features which were then unconventional. There was no Officer Training Corps. Sporting prowess and academic achievement mattered less than 'creative' activities, such as woodwork, art, printing. Special features were the study of American history, and weekly sessions in 'civics' and 'current history'.

Bembridge was not then as good a school as it has become since the war. It has greatly improved under a succession of able headmasters. It is now co-educational. But in my time the education did not live up to the fine words in the prospectus which had so impressed my mother and father.

The founder and headmaster was J. Howard Whitehouse. He had been a Liberal Member of Parliament elected before the First World War. Sons of his eminent friends and contemporaries, such as Isaac Foot, were sent to Bembridge. Dingle Foot was among the first five boys in 1919. John Foot came later. Whitehouse was a Quaker, a pacifist (until 1940), and a devoted follower of John Ruskin. The school housed in its galleries a fine collection of Ruskin's drawings and memorabilia.

He was a difficult and vain character who quarrelled with many of his staff. He refused to reconsider his more eccentric educational prejudices, such as his scorn for academic excellence and for the university education which he had not himself enjoyed. But, despite his failings, Whitehouse was a considerable figure. He was a fine speaker, and an educational thinker of originality and vision.

I went to Bembridge in 1938. In the next three or four critical years my education suffered in two ways. First, the academic standards at Bembridge were less rigorous than those at my grammar schools. Second, and even more important, Bembridge was evacuated in the summer of 1940, when the Army took over its cliff-top grounds in the Isle of Wight. The school moved to makeshift premises in a hotel on Coniston Water in the Lake District. The school owned Ruskin's old home at Brantwood but that was far too small, so the Waterhead Hotel was purchased, and hurriedly converted into a temporary school.

The effect of the evacuation on the school was shattering.

Staff had left. Replacements were hard to get. Facilities and accommodation were cramped, cold and uncomfortable. The one consolation was the glorious Lake District scenery, the mountains and the walks – up Coniston Old Man, to Tilberthwaite Ghyll, and to Tarn Hows.

Towards the end of my schooldays in 1942, the privations of wartime caused me to lead a rebellion. This was in protest against the school's failure (as it appeared to several of us) to give us our due ration of Spam. This tinned meat from America was an item of rationed food under the monthly 'points' system. We knew that there were many large tins of Spam on the shelves of the school foodstore. This was a reserve for emergencies, but we who were about to leave at the end of that term saw no justification in storing for others Spam which was ours. It had been supplied on our ration points. I went to the headmaster's study and claimed our rights. He was furious and threatened me with expulsion. I politely pointed out that I was leaving anyway in a fortnight's time at the end of term. As Head Boy, I had a duty to speak up for the Spam rights of the others. The rational force of my protest must have impressed him. Though he remained angry, our Spam appeared in the refectory next day.

I am not without gratitude for my four years at Bembridge School, despite its shortcomings. I owe a special debt to two senior Bembridge masters, Ernest Baggaley and Tom Stedman. Both took special and encouraging interest in my progress. But for them, I would not have got my Higher School Certificate or entrance to Oxford. From the headmaster I absorbed a healthy lack of reverence for people in important positions. Looking up from his newspaper, or on return from a visit to London, he would sound off with contempt for a Cabinet minister, or for the government in general. To hear some eminent figure, such as the Chancellor of the Exchequer or the Home Secretary, described as 'a fool' or as 'crackbrained' was a refreshing reminder to a schoolboy that those in the highest authority should not be regarded as all-wise.

But, if we were encouraged to be sceptical of our political leaders, we were taught to revere parliamentary institutions. In our 'civics' lessons and 'current history' sessions we were given loving explanations of the traditions of Parliament, and stories of Westminster dramas in the past. On more than one winter Saturday evening we were told the story of George Archer Shee, the thirteen-year-old naval cadet who was (wrongly) sacked from Osborne in 1908 for stealing a five-shilling postal order. The story and the constitutional principles involved were told us by the headmaster. He had been an MP when the case was raised in Parliament thirty years earlier. So the Archer Shee story was not unfamiliar to me when it was brilliantly used in 1946 by Terence Rattigan as the basis of *The Winslow Boy*.

My last four years as a schoolboy were dominated by war or the approach of war. I and every other boy knew we would soon be in one of the fighting services. In September 1938, we were fitted with gas-masks at school. On 3 September 1939, I sat in the garden on holiday making a model boat, and listened to Neville Chamberlain's broadcast on the declaration of war.

For the next few years, the wireless was to be our prime medium of news and entertainment. I heard all of Winston Churchill's historic broadcasts on my bedside headphones at school, or later in the Army. Churchill's oratory never failed to thrill me. To this day I cannot play a recording of one of his speeches without feeling all over again the fierce sense of excitement and pride in that rasping, growling, declamatory voice with the rolling sentences and the marvellous mixture of noble rhetoric and the plainest of plain English.

Churchill's leadership and his imperishable words require no eulogy from me. I merely wish to record the personal effect they had on me as a schoolboy and as a soldier. I felt then, and I have felt ever since, that my liberty, and that of all in these islands, would have vanished but for his courage and eloquence.

3

Army

Hired Assassins of the State

Young people are mystified when told by me that I am of that generation which enjoyed no youth. By that I mean no youth as it has been enjoyed since the 1950s. From my sixteenth year, when I was fitted with a gas-mask at school, until the age of about twenty-eight, we lived under the shadow of war, through war itself, and its aftermath. Our lives were deprived and restricted by the rigours of war, which continued long into peacetime.

For a dozen years from the age of sixteen, in my so-called youth, my generation lived under conscription, food rationing, petrol rationing, clothes rationing and innumerable other shortages and restrictions. Not many people remember (or if they remember they can hardly believe it) that strict food rationing and clothes rationing continued in force until about six years after the war ended.

Of course there were pleasures, and the camaraderie of shared discontent. The austerities were cheerfully endured. But the pleasures of today's youth were denied to a generation whose only foreign travel was by courtesy of HM forces.

On leaving school in the summer of 1942, I enlisted in the Royal Artillery. For men with appropriate educational qualifications, the Army ran short courses at universities in mathematics and science as part of a potential officer's training. There was some weeks' delay before my course began. I joined my local Home Guard in West Mersea, the little island in Essex which was where we had spent many happy family holidays. The West Mersea Home Guard was a coastal unit intended to repel invasion by Hitler. Fortunately that danger appeared to have receded since 1940. But this experience meant that for me *Dad's Army* was no situation comedy. It was a nostalgic documentary.

During those few months in the winter of 1942–3, I also became a temporary teacher in two local elementary schools. There was an acute teacher shortage. If you had passed certain examinations, you could be employed as an 'uncertificated' teacher. Getting up at 6 a.m., I went by bus and bicycle from my home at West Mersea to a school at West Bergholt, and later to another school, also near Colchester, at Wivenhoe. I had a huge class of boys and girls from about nine to fourteen. Most of them did not have the slightest idea what I was talking about. Nor, for much of the time, did I.

The Army course was at Queen's University, Belfast. There, in between academic lectures, we did parade-ground drill and had small-arms instruction from a sergeant-major of the Royal Ulster Rifles. He would remind us that, when the German bombs had fallen on loyal Belfast, the Luftwaffe had been guided by the lights of neutral Dublin.

In 1943, loyal Belfast looked much like any other big British city in wartime, except for the Royal Ulster Constabulary with revolvers in their black leather holsters. Other signs that this was not mainland Britain were the sectarian graffiti scrawled on bridges and walls, such as the mysterious message which I remember seeing in huge letters as we docked in Belfast: 'The blood of the Pope be on McGinty.'

Our course at Queen's University was the first stage in the process of becoming a gunner officer. But there were many hurdles to be surmounted along the way. Satisfactory marks had first to be achieved at the University in mathematics and science. After passing the University course (the standard was inter-BSC) we were sent back to the Army for primary training – seven or eight weeks of square-bashing and basic weapon training – such as every soldier went through. This was at a barracks in Lincoln. It was tough and hard, especially so for us; we were potential officers. It was those first few weeks in the Army which taught me that what seems a grim experience now may seem hilarious, or ridiculous, in a few years' time. I have tried to remember this at low points or black times in my life. I've asked myself at such moments: 'In five years' time, how will I describe this hell which I'm going through now? What humour will I extract from it?' A joke, even a bad joke, can help to put pain, even tragedy, in perspective. Our sense of humour is our sense of proportion.

To keep that sense of proportion, it is only fair to say that we suffered neither pain nor tragedy during our weeks of primary training. But a sense of humour was an essential item in the kit of 1151266 Gunner Day R. For one thing, there was Sergeant Mason. Or Sahnt Mason, as we came to call him. He was in charge of us. He was a small, energetic man who reminded you of Arthur Askey until he opened his mouth. Rarely can a man have held a group of his fellow human beings in such contempt. We were the lowest of the low. We were a 'shower'.

Sahnt Mason knew exactly how to horrify us. In his first talk to us he said, 'Why do you think you're here? I suppose you think you are here to defend freedom and democracy? Well, I will tell you why you're here. You are hired assassins of the state. That's what you are.' Several of our group winced noticeably. One, an elegant aesthete from one of the more exclusive public schools, who had the habit of reading a slim volume of Ezra Pound before turning in, was narrowly persuaded not to desert.

Our weeks of primary training, of gruelling hard labour, were clearly intended as a short, sharp shock (a phrase which had not yet acquired a penal significance) to our sensitive systems. The parade-ground rang with barking and stamping and shouting as young men were knocked into military shape. Sahnt Mason took pleasure in making his group of over-educated, would-be officers understand what war was about. We were being trained to kill. During bayonet practice, with sandbags in lieu of human beings, he would recite with gusto the words of the drill: 'Point, pass through, withdraw.' He watched for any delicate stomachs turning. During Bren-gun instruction he would declaim the weapon parts with a sexual relish: ''Ere we 'ave the body locking-pin. And 'ere the barrel nut retainer plunger.'

Sahnt Mason came from a famous infantry regiment. He saw his duty as not only to teach us simple soldierly discipline, but also to initiate us into the brotherhood of warriors willing to kill at close quarters in cold blood with cold steel. In our case he performed the former duty better than the latter.

He would also exhort us to support the war effort in every patriotic way – especially by not wasting paper, such as lavatory paper. 'Never,' he sternly instructed, 'never use more than four pieces of lavatory paper per sitting.' 'But only four, Sergeant? Only four?' 'That's the drill, only four: one up, one down, one anti-splash, and one polisher.'

He was a first-class NCO and deserved better material than the group of which I was one. It became evident that Sahnt Mason had never seen a more miserable bunch of effete, cissified drips. How anyone imagined that we were fit to be trained as potential officers, he could not conceive. Nor, I am bound to say, could some of us.

After Sahnt Mason, we went to a Royal Artillery training regiment at Marske-by-the-Sea, near Middlesbrough, for two or three months. This was more interesting than the square-bashing at Lincoln. We learned something about guns and gunnery, before beginning our training as officer cadets. That would be at 123 OCTU (Officer Cadet Training Unit) at Catterick Camp in Yorkshire. But before OCTU there was pre-OCTU.

That was at Wrotham in Kent, where we learned to drive three-ton lorries, then a week on motorcycles. Practising at high speed on one of these machines was the nearest I came to violent death during my Army service. At any stage during our training we were liable to be 'RTUd' – Returned to Unit. Several of my comrades suffered this fate. I could not understand why it never happened to me.

Apart from several weeks at the pre-OCTU and the six months at OCTU, there was a critical weekend at a WOSB, a War Office Selection Board. This, known as the Wosby, was to assess our psychological and (it was said) social suitability as officers. A group of us went to a requisitioned country house near Selby in Yorkshire. The atmosphere was dignified and comfortable like an officers' mess in a regimental HQ. There were several senior officers, a psychologist and a psychiatrist, who was known in those days (his function being then somewhat novel and suspect) as the trick-cyclist. We dined in style with our red-tabbed hosts, taking care to eat our peas with the correct implement. We had discussions, TEWTS (Tactical Exercises Without Troops) and hypothetical situations to analyse.

Rumour had it that special attention was paid to the psychological 'word tests'. These were to detect temperamentally unsuitable or unbalanced candidates. A word was flashed on a screen momentarily. You had to write down the first thought which that word put into your mind. If the word BREAD came on the screen, your first thought might be BUTTER or DRIPPING or WINE or DAILY. The Army psychologists might deduce from BUTTER that you were normal or dull, from DRIPPING that you were honest but proletarian, from WINE that you were a regular communicant, and from DAILY that at least you knew the Lord's Prayer. The word was flashed on the screen for only just long enough for it to suggest more than one thought. You had to take care not to be too clever, or unspontaneous. I mastered the art.

One word on the screen was BEAT. This was an obvious trap to detect perverts of one kind or another, in case one's instant reaction was PLEASURE or CANE or BUTTOCKS – not that any of these were my first thought. DRUM would seem too military to be true. RHYTHM might be too jazzy. So, as my thought-reaction to BEAT with only half a second to spare, I put POLICEMAN. A good, wholesome, robust reaction with undertones of law and order. Nothing too clever about it. And virtually spontaneous.

LOVE was another of the words flashed on the screen. I don't remember what 'first thought' was suggested to me by LOVE. Presumably I rejected as too obvious, or as dangerously significant, PASSION, SEX, KISSES. But I remember what I eventually wrote down. I played safe with MOTHER. This seemed reasonable, if not original, for a young man of twenty. At the subsequent interview, the trick-cyclist, who in a film should have been played by Peter Sellers, said suspiciously, 'I see you are very fond of your mother. What does that mean?' Silently I retorted, 'It's your bloody job, chum, to find that out.' Aloud I said, 'Nothing abnormal, sir.'

I sailed through my Wosby. Then to OCTU at Catterick for

twenty-four weeks. In one week we went to firing camp to practise using 25-pounder guns with live ammunition. The 25-pounder's bang was a very fierce crack, liable to damage the eardrums of anyone close by. This happened to me. I was left with permanent high-pitched ringing in the ears, and a slight deafness which the ear specialists call 'loss of high tone'. This means I cannot hear high-pitched sounds properly, especially against a background of noise. Hearing aids do not help. They merely amplify the background noise. I do not notice the ringing in the ears except if I am in conditions of absolute quiet. Deafness and damage to eardrums, in many cases much worse than mine, have long been suffered by artillerymen and naval gunners. The minor damage done to my eardrums at practice camp, though permanent, is fortunately much less severe than that suffered by many servicemen from the blast of guns in battle.

A climax of our training to be commissioned in the Royal Regiment of Artillery was the battle-camp week. For this we went to the Lake District near Ullswater. A different cadet each week was put in charge of our troop. I was in charge of troop C29 for the week at battle-school. Live ammunition whizzed and hissed just over our heads as we splashed through mud and water or wriggled on our stomachs under barbed wire. In our climb up Helvellyn I carried, in addition to my own, the rifles and packs of two older or weaker men who had become exhausted. Ascending Helvellyn that day in 1944 at the age of twenty, I was in a state of physical fitness and energy which I have never since surpassed or equalled.

One of my more endearing comrades, right through from primary training to the passing-out parade at octu, was an eccentric Old Harrovian character called Hugh Robert La Touche Corrie. He shared my sense of the ridiculous, and was even scruffier and more argumentative than I was. I dare not go further. Hugh Corrie, who became a barrister, has been for many years a most formidable expert in the law of libel.

In the summer of 1944, I was duly commissioned Second-Lieutenant ra with the number 334866 on my black tin kit-box. There followed several specialized courses on matters such as motor transport, gas warfare and gunnery. My first posting as an officer was back to Northern Ireland, to 109 Field Regiment stationed on Downpatrick racecourse. Where would I be sent next? To Northern Europe possibly, where the Allied armies were about to triumph. In fact we sailed for the East on VE-Day at the very moment of victory in the West. After weeks of waiting in an Egyptian transit camp we sailed on to East Africa. We were to be part of the build-up from there of our forces in Burma against Japan. Having left the UK on VE-Day, we arrived in Kenya in time for VJ-Day. The atomic bomb had ended the war against Japan. So there I was, with many others, having been through tough and intensive training, dumped in the colony of Kenya with nothing much to do except wait for demobilization. I learned some Swahili, which came in handy when I was a *Panorama* reporter covering the Uhuru (Independence) celebrations in Kenya and Tanganyika in the sixties.

Nairobi, still agog with talk of the Earl of Erroll's murder, was the centre of a raffish settlers' community. The decadent 'Happy Valley' set, with their adulterous, hedonistic lifestyle which had made wartime Kenya notorious, was no longer in full swing, but the Kenya settler community had not yet realized that their world had gone forever. On the day of the news of Labour's election victory, in July 1945, I was walking in Government Road, Nairobi. I saw a European in civilian clothes reading the newspaper placard which said 'Socialist landslide majority'. The man turned to his companion. I heard him say, 'I suppose they'll give Kenya to the bloody Germans now.' If that was typical of the settler reaction, few in the forces, except for some officers, were horrified.

A government headed by Attlee, with Ernest Bevin and Cripps and Morrison, all of whom had been loyal and patriotic colleagues in Churchhill's wartime coalition, seemed to be what was needed for post-war reconstruction. But I myself had not voted Labour. By the proxy process for servicemen I had voted Liberal. Despite my great admiration for Churchill I doubted if he, at seventy, would be a good reforming leader in peacetime. But I was not persuaded that post-war reforms could be achieved only through Socialism.

I spent two years in the Army in Kenya, doing practically nothing useful. I was fortunate in having as my Commanding Officer, who became a good friend, Lieutenant-Colonel Harry

Withers OBE, MC, RHA. He was a tremendous personality, a gallant veteran of the desert war, and was the brother of the film star Googie Withers, then at the height of her fame.

There was no soldiering. The East African Artillery, to which I was posted, had no significant place in our imperial strategy. My four-and-a-half years in the Army seemed a pointless waste of time. The intensive training, those technical courses to become a gunner officer, that physical fitness which enabled me to stroll, heavily laden, up Helvellyn, all that had been to no purpose. I saw no action during my Army service. Not until I was a civilian, as a TV reporter, did I go into any theatre of war or revolutionary upheaval such as the Congo, the Borneo 'confrontation', Vietnam and other uncomfortable situations.

My final two years, hanging about in the Kenya sun, were mostly spent in administrative duties, and in attending and recovering from the riotous fortnightly parties which were held as each 'demob' group left for home. I do not recall what or whom I was administering, except for helping to close down units.

The number of paper-pushing officers in post-war Nairobi who had been over-promoted in phoney or unnecessary units amounted to a scandal. One day a staff major, a veteran of the Fourteenth Army from Burma, arrived at East Africa Command Headquarters. This dynamic officer was appalled by the 'Nairobi Warriors' and their luxurious living. He immediately asked some embarrassing questions. Within a few days of his arrival, dozens of officers lost rank. Superfluous units were unceremoniously shut down, including the large depot at Athi River of which I was, very briefly, the Adjutant. Captain Day had to remove a pip from his shoulder – a demotion which was wholly justified.

Towards the end of my service in East Africa I made one decision of great personal importance. I decided that I wanted to be a barrister. I had intended to become a teacher, mainly because there were state grants to pay the university fees for teachers in training. But a wider choice of career was open when it became known that every ex-serviceman with university entrance qualifications would be entitled to a government grant.

The Bar attracted me for several reasons. It appeared to be a career in which a young man without influence or connections could make his name and his fortune, if he had luck and ability, like Sir Edward Marshall Hall and Sir Patrick Hastings, about whom I had read. I did not know whether I had the ability, but I thought I might have the luck. And was not the Bar a springboard to a career in politics? This was something I was beginning to think about.

I wrote to my father, who was surprised but delighted. A man of energetic decision at moments of importance, he rushed up to London next day to see Neil Lawson, a junior barrister whose family had been a neighbour of ours in London. From Neil Lawson (later Sir Neil Lawson, a judge of the High Court) my father received excellent advice. I should join the Middle Temple, which I did. But I was to realize that beginning at the Bar could be a slow and dispiriting process. My father put down Lawson's advice in a long letter, but wrote that if I wanted to go to the Bar I should do so. He was glad and proud that I had set my sights with courage on a fine but difficult profession. With a characteristic flourish he added that 'a budding barrister must read *The Times* every day so as to keep in touch with the Law reports and other public matters. I am having the airmail *Times* sent to you.'

My father added that my mother would have shared his pride in my ambition. My mother died soon after I was posted to Kenya. She had wept when I left in my new Second Lieutenant's uniform to go overseas, saying, 'I never thought you would have to go away like this.' I did not see her again.

During my last few months in Kenya, as I waited for my turn to board a troopship for home, I fell in love for the first time. I was a shy twenty-three. I had known other girls at home in England, in Belfast and in East Africa. But I had never fallen in love. I was well and truly smitten. She was an Army nurse, stunningly pretty, with a golden tan, blonde hair and dream figure. Wherever she had been stationed men had fallen head-over-heels for her. She was older than I was. As is not unusual for nurses, she was in love with a doctor. She tolerated my youthful adoration very kindly. We played tennis and went for jeep drives on the tracks up Mount Kenya. It took me quite a long time to get over her.

I mention this episode not to pander to the fashion for personal revelations, but simply because it has a place in my life story. I must disappoint the reader who wants to know more about this or any other romantic attachment of mine. I have an old-fashioned belief in decent reticence, in respect for other people's privacy, and in consideration of the feelings of others, especially my family.

Also I cherish fiercely what is left of my own privacy. For almost thirty-five years I have been in the public eye. My work has been public. My face has been public. My marriage, my divorce, my children, my illnesses, my accidents – all these events have been public. I make no complaint about this. If you join in a hazardous game of your own free will it is your own fault if you get hurt. Or as the lawyer's Latin more elegantly and succinctly puts it: *Volenti non fit injuria*.

But where it has been possible, for the sake of others as well as myself, I have kept these things private, and will continue to do so. In particular, my marriage, my divorce, my family, my friendships, will continue to be treated by me as private and not for the gratification of public curiosity.

When, therefore, should an autobiography of a public man reveal details of his private life? My answer is only if the revelations are directly related to his public position or career, or are relevant to an understanding of his work, of his art, of his music, of his writing. In writing about himself he is, of course, free to disregard his own privacy. But he should still respect that of others who may be concerned.

Some people win praise for honesty and frankness in writing their life stories. But there are some allegedly revealing autobiographies which omit or conceal certain personal matters which may have been profoundly significant in the author's life. Such matters are understandably omitted out of consideration for others, or because they would amount to indecent exposure. Autobiographical 'candour' is liable to be selective and deceptive. Better to be openly reticent than spuriously candid.

But I have digressed. A twenty-three-year-old subaltern was about to leave Kenya and the Army to become an undergraduate in the golden age of post-war Oxford, there to enjoy the most privileged, the most memorable and the most exciting time of his life so far.

4

Oxford's Golden Age

This House Wants to Have It Both Ways

In October 1947, on my first morning in St Edmund Hall, Oxford, I sat down to a breakfast of porridge and kippers. This was simple but nourishing, and preferable to dried egg. On my right sat a grizzled twenty-eight-year-old lieutenant-colonel who had been wounded at El Alamein. I did not learn of his rank or record till later. On my left was a nervous eighteen-year-old boy of scholarly appearance. He had come up straight from school. By reason of his academic ability, his military service had been postponed. I was twenty-four that month. It was that mixture of ages and backgrounds which gave post-war Oxford its unique character. After six years of war, a backlog of three or four generations merged into one great influx. It was Oxford's golden age.

There have doubtless been other golden ages, with their glittering collections of brilliant youths fresh from school. But in contrast to the normal peacetime intake of schoolboys, 75 per cent or more of the post-war undergraduates were ex-servicemen on government grants.

Oxford was a broader, less exclusive place. It was a classless Oxford. No one cared, no one asked, which school you had been to, or what your father was, or what rank you had held in the services. Such irrelevant details emerged by accident, if at all, and only in conversation with close friends.

There was a marked absence of snobbery. Decadence was not in vogue. Brideshead was not revisited by the ex-servicemen of the Second World War. But the atmosphere was not earnest or humourless. Post-war Oxford sparkled and bubbled with talent and originality. A brilliant array of characters went up during those years 1945–50. But only in later years, as reputations were won, did one begin to realize what an abundance of talent had been gathered together at Oxford after the war: in journalism, politics, drama, literature, history, philosophy, law – in every field. There were aesthetes and athletes, playboys and poets, scholars and sportsmen. There were entertainers, egg-heads, wits and war heroes. There were men who had been up before the war and had come back to complete their degree courses, like Anthony Crosland and Ludovic Kennedy.

Fortunately there were also more than a few undergraduates who were not brilliant, not remarkable and not overly ambitious. Without them the theatre which was post-war Oxford would have had no backcloth against which the stars could glitter, and no audience to whom the prima donnas could perform.

Paradoxically, in an Oxford where the average age was twenty-five, and the majority of undergraduates were ex-servicemen, the most celebrated personality of the time was not a rugged war veteran, but a thin, pallid, twenty-year-old aesthete with long hair, a purple suit and gold satin shirt: the phenomenon called Kenneth Peacock Tynan.

By his outrageous clothes, his notorious reputation, his originality with words, Tynan fascinated and conquered post-war Oxford. He personified another Oxford which the ex-servicemen thought had gone for ever. Tynan was the antithesis of austerity, of drabness, of earnestness. His electrifying talent was displayed not only in theatrical production and in literary criticism. He took the Oxford Union by storm. A speech by Tynan would always pack the Debating Hall.

The Union was then a men-only institution. The visitors' gallery upstairs would be filled with women eagerly leaning over the edge, seemingly hypnotized, as Tynan made one of his legendary Union speeches. He had transmuted his stammer into an asset which kept his audience on tenterhooks. One of his memorable Union performances was a speech opposing the motion 'That this House wants to have it both ways'. Tynan was against the motion because it 'clearly implied there were only two ways of having it. And I personally know', he went on, leaning languidly on the despatch box, 'that there are at least forty-seven different ways of having it, not including the one on the gr-gr-grand piano.' Today that may not sound particularly shocking or sophisticated. But in 1948, humour with a sexual flavour was less acceptable in mixed company than it is now.

Ken Tynan was elected Secretary of the Union in 1948. He defeated me in that election, which was not surprising. He had been a star performer in the Debating Hall, and he was the most celebrated undergraduate of his time. I had been up for only a year. Tynan wrote me a note thanking me for my congratulations, saying that my time would soon come.

Apart from Tynan, the Union stars were the Hon. Anthony Wedgwood Benn (as he was then known) and Sir Edward Boyle Bt. Benn displayed the natural eloquence and polished wit which forty years later still made him the most brilliant debater in the House of Commons. Boyle, at twenty-three, already had an elder stateman's gravitas, with the ability to make any platitude seem profound. Other union notables were Kenneth Harris, Godfrey Smith, Peter Kirk, Jeremy Thorpe, Dick Taverne, William Rees-Mogg, Ivan Yates, Keith Kyle and Stanley Booth-Clibborn. Stanley was the only one of my undergraduate friends to become a bishop. About to shine as Union stars of the early fifties were Patrick Hutber, Peter Blaker, Patrick Mayhew, Bryan Magee, Peter Tapsell and Michael Heseltine.

The Union was only one stage on which talent could be displayed. In my time, the Editor of the magazine *Isis* was Robert Robinson. Bob recalls meeting me one morning in the autumn of 1951. We were on the steps of the Radcliffe Camera to read belatedly for our degrees. Our respective periods of power and glory were over. According to Robert Robinson, I said to him, 'We will never rise to such heights again.' He thought I was joking. But when he recalled it thirty-five years later, Bob declared, 'You were absolutely right!' He added, with that literary scholarship he wears so lightly, 'Thus the whirligig of time brings in his revenges.'

Alan Brien was another brilliant columnist-critic in the

making. And a young ex-cavalry officer of virile appearance from the magazine *Cherwell* called James Morris came to interview me in the President's office. He later reported the ascent of Everest for *The Times*, and later still went to Casablanca and changed sex.

The most celebrated female undergraduate of the time was Shirley Williams (Shirley Catlin as she then was). She had tremendous charm, and was the daughter of a famous mother, Vera Brittain. According to one historian of post-war Oxford, Shirley had 'most of male Oxford in love with her'.* I was never one of Shirley's escorts. But I did touch the hem of her duffel-coat once or twice. And I recall the pleasure of listening with her in my room to the 1950 General Election results on the radio.

One undergraduate with more than his fair share of talents was Peter Parker. He played King Lear in the OUDS. His Cordelia was Shirley Catlin. He was Chairman of the Labour Club, was a considerable rugger player, and had had a good war. He was handsome, dynamic and persuasive. Peter Parker was the only Oxford undergraduate known to me who became a top industrialist.

I have mentioned about twenty names or so. But to mention two hundred names would not do justice to this multi-talented Oxford generation.

Undergraduate women were, of course, in a minority. These were young girls fresh from school. Suddenly they had found themselves (this was how one of them described it to me) 'surrounded by scores of men aged about twenty-five, magnificent men, sophisticated men, experienced men, men who would not take "no" for an answer'. A girl who had never previously been alone with a man would find herself entertaining one of these demigods to tea and crumpets in front of her gas fire in her own room.

That was one girl's eye view of the scene. If the ex-servicemen saw these eager, innocent maidens as delicious fruit, ripe to be plucked, there were not enough of them to go round. But there were, of course, the 'camp-followers', the many ladies who were

*David Walter, *The Oxford Union* (Macdonald, 1984), p.129.

not undergraduates. They were not *at*, but *in* Oxford, studying or training. They tended to be intellectually less demanding than female undergraduates. This made them relaxing company for male undergraduates under academic stress, a condition under which I occasionally found myself.

My studies of the Law were not as profound nor as thorough as they should have been. I went to tutorials, read in libraries (I was incapable of studying law books in my own room) and wrote my essays. But most of my time, until the final panic-stricken six months, was spent in talking, arguing, gossiping, flirting and politicking. Thus was the mind broadened, the wit sharpened, the eyes opened and friendships made for life.

I envied those of my contemporaries who had the greatest gift of all – the ability to organize their time. Anyone who could do that, who could work at their books for three or four hours every day, would have plenty of time left for socializing, for girlfriends, for squash, for politics, for acting, for journalism, or anything else. Given a bit of luck, just a little bit, he could even get a First.

It was important for me to get at least a Second, because this would give exemption from Part One of the Bar Examination. In the end I managed to achieve this due to the immensely stimulating law tutor I had for several terms. St Edmund Hall did not then have a law tutor, so I went to one at Oriel College. He was Zelman Cowen, a brilliant young Australian who had been a Rhodes Scholar and he won that most distinguished Oxford prize, the Vinerian fellowship.

Hitherto I had found academic law dry and heavy. No longer was this the case when I was a pupil of Zelman Cowen. It was when studying Constitutional Law and Jurisprudence with him that I first was fired with intellectual enthusiasm for the subject I was reading.

My tutor also gave me advice about a major personal decision which faced me in my third year. Should I interrupt my law studies by going on an Oxford Union debating tour of United States universities for which I had been selected? The tour would take three or four months. I would have to delay my bid for the Presidency of the Union, and I would have to delay my final examination for a year. Zelman, my tutor, urged me to take the risk, to go to the United States, to enjoy a new dimension of experience outside Oxford.

I am grateful for his sound advice. Zelman and his wife Anne have remained my good friends ever since. He is now the Rt. Hon. Sir Zelman Cowen, AK, GCMG, GCVO, CBE, QC, Governor-General of Australia from 1977 to 1982, and Provost of Oriel College from 1982–90.

As things turned out, I won the Presidency easily on my return from America, and I got a better degree by reason of the extra year. But to go off on that tour of the United States was the first of several gambles I was to take at critical moments in my life.

Your Election, Sir, Was as Clean as Any in American History

The debating tour of the United States was in the autumn of 1949. This was my first visit to the USA. It was also to give me my first experience of appearing on television. I had been chosen as one of a two-man team to represent the Oxford Union. Since the 1920s there had been a tradition of sending such teams to American universities and colleges. The previous Oxford team, in 1947, had been Sir Edward Boyle, Anthony Wedgwood Benn and Kenneth Harris.

My co-debator from Oxford, Geoffrey Johnson Smith, was well-dressed and good-looking. He was a Socialist. At the end of our tour he took a job in San Francisco, and married a beautiful American psychiatrist who was a Republican. Soon afterwards Geoffrey became a Conservative. He has been an MP since 1959 and was a junior minister in the Heath administration. He was knighted in 1982.

A few hours after we landed from the *Mauretania* we debated in front of 3,500 people at the University of Pennsylvania in Philadelphia. We were in an auditorium normally used for basketball, like a vast aircraft hangar. The opening speeches were called 'constructives'. We then paused for 'intermission' during which we prepared our 'rebuttals', which were considered the real part of the debate. The judges gave the Oxford team the decision. The British Consul told us we were a credit to the Empire.

The next night, at Yale, we lost the debate, deservedly. The Yale team was led by the formidable William F. Buckley, subsequently famous as a brilliant right-wing writer and TV personality. He and his Yale colleague wiped the floor with us. Mostly, however, the Americans were rather heavy going. Their idea of proving a point would be to quote an eminent person. Their idea of humour would be to tell a story which might or might not be funny, but which had no relevance to the subject under discussion. The idea of wit as a weapon of argument seemed unknown to many of them. But our hosts were charming, generous, hospitable and very pro-British.

For me it was an unforgettable first visit to this glamorous, prosperous land. Austerity Britain was still struggling to recover from six years of war. Because of the war and the dollar restrictions, hardly any of our generation had ever been there.

Apart from our university debates we spoke at Rotary clubs and businessmen's luncheons. We were entertained in American homes, and went to the ball games. It was in Philadelphia in October 1949 that I first appeared on a television programme. This one, in the American style, was relaxed and informal. So much so that our interviewer did not have the slightest idea who we were or why we were on his show, except that we were from 'Oxford college'. The experience made no impact on me.

We also met several eminent Americans privately, including Mrs Eleanor Roosevelt and General Eisenhower. Mrs Roosevelt invited us to lunch at her Hyde Park home near New York. In her reminiscences of the White House, she quoted a remark by her husband about Churchill during the war. 'The trouble with Winston', FDR had said, 'is that he enjoyed the old world too much to understand the new.'

General Eisenhower was then President of Columbia University, where we had one of our debates. Ike was interested to hear that one of our subjects was the public ownership of basic industries. 'Y'know,' said the General, 'I've just set up a panel of the finest brains here in Columbia to work on that very issue – in an entirely non-political way of course. I've asked them to draw the line,' and he repeated those words emphatically, 'to *draw the line* between public and private enterprise.' I politely suggested certain difficulties. 'Oh sure,' said Ike. 'It won't be a *straight* line.'

Johnson Smith and I polished up our act as our tour proceeded. One little piece of Oxford cut-and-thrust was used by us as one of our routines in the debates when we were against each other. It was pinched from Dick Crossman and Bob Boothby, who were favourite visiting MPs for Oxford debates. After one such debate which had clearly gone against him, Boothby declared triumphantly to tremendous cheers, 'I have an overwhelming sense of having won the argument.' Whereupon Crossman leaped to the despatch box: 'Mr Boothby says he has an overwhelming sense of having won the argument. Ah yes! Ah yes! But won it for whom? Won it for himself, or won it for me?' More loud cheers.

One night in the Middle West Johnson Smith and I were tired. We had been getting on each other's nerves. I seized my opportunity. Knowing that Geoffrey was not listening to a speech he had heard from me many times before, I maliciously left out my routine 'Boothby' line about having won the argument. When Johnson Smith spoke in rebuttal and did his usual 'Crossman' bit about 'winning the argument for whom', I intervened icily. 'With great respect, I never said anything about having won the argument.' Geoffrey was furious, but he forgave me my mischief as soon as he realized what a good story it made to tell against both of us.

Our debating tour took us to about forty-five universities, colleges and academies. We went to Yale, Columbia and Chicago Universities, and to West Point and Annapolis. We debated at huge state universities in Illinois and Virginia, and at small colleges like Wabash College, Wabash, Indiana. Our travel schedule was hectic; a different place every night, by plane, railway and Greyhound bus, in the East, the South and the Midwest. We slept in student hostels, fraternity houses or in overnight trains. When we first landed in New York we stayed at the YMCA, and sent home postcards of the Waldorf Astoria.

Our tour was self-financing. Each host college paid $100 to the Educational Institute which was arranging the visit. The Americans took their debating very seriously. Many of those with whom we debated were studying for Degrees in Speech. We were surprised to find Professors of Speech, Faculties of Speech and Coaches of Debate. The debates were sometimes judged not by vote but by a points system. Points would be awarded for logic, style, presentation, humour, persuasiveness, argumentation and even gesture. A Faculty member at the University of Illinois came up to me and said, 'Those gestures of yours were terrific. I made a careful note of them.' At one college points were also awarded for dress. Fortunately my companion, Geoffrey Johnson Smith, was always immaculate.

For several weeks on our tour we had been hearing of the great plans for our visit to Wabash College, Wabash, Indiana. 'Operation Oxbash' it had been brightly designated by an ex-Merton Rhodes Scholar. Wabash went English for the day. A bagpiper preceded us on campus to make us feel at home. Jellied eels were on sale. Austin A40s, bought as novelties by rich students, drove us around. Wabash men wore gowns and scarves, and rode bicycles. We played cricket with baseball kit. For the evening's debate, an overflow crowd packed the chapel, fortunately unconsecrated. Our Merton friend had coached the whole of Wabash in Union etiquette. Our opponents congratulated the first President of the Oxbash Union on his magnificent victory over non-existent candidates in an imaginary election. Former Oriel Rhodes Scholar Byron K. Trippett was touched by these tributes. 'Your election, Sir,' opened Geoffrey, 'was as clean as any in American history' (prolonged applause).

To Speak Like Gentlemen and Not Like Hooligans

When I returned to Oxford I moved a motion in the Union to thank our American hosts. This gave me an opportunity for a *tour de force*, a speech packed with wit and anecdote, recycled from the debating tour. It made a big impression, particularly among the freshmen of that year. A few weeks later I was elected President by an enormous majority. Sadly, my father, who would have been proud of his son at this moment, was not alive to share in it. He had died during my first year at Oxford.

The vote for me was 263, more than all the other candidates

put together. They were Peter Emery, 93, Jeremy Thorpe, 89, and John Gilbert, 23.* To be fair, none of them was a serious threat. Thorpe was making a premature bid to fly his flag. He was duly elected President the following year, when he defeated Dick Taverne and William Rees-Mogg.

I heard of my Union victory from Michael Summerskill and Shirley Catlin, who had dropped in at my John Street rooms to tell me the result and to congratulate me. My pleasure was enhanced by the fact that I was the first undergraduate from St Edmund Hall to have been elected President of the Union. This, I was pleasantly surprised to find, was a source of quiet pride to my fellow Aularians, whose interests mainly lay in fields other than the Union.

In every Oxford generation there are many to whom the Union and its Presidents are pretentious, boring and pompous. During the 165 years of its history, the Oxford Union has often been over-publicized. Yet it is simply a place where young men and (since 1963) women can practise the art of public speaking, in front of a large critical audience. They have a chance to debate with Cabinet ministers and leading parliamentarians. They learn to keep their tempers and to cope with hecklers. They learn to debate with tolerance and humour. These things are not to be dismissed as trivial. Many famous public figures happily testify to the value of the experience they had as undergraduates at the Oxford Union.

Oxford offers many prizes to be won. There are scores of Blues and Firsts each year. There are only three Presidents of the Union, one per term. To have been elected President has given greater satisfaction to some eminent men than their other achievements. To have been defeated has sometimes seemed a devastating setback. Perhaps the intense disappointment felt in 1940 by Roy Jenkins,† who was twice defeated for the Presidency that year by only a few votes, was assuaged nearly half a century later by his election as Chancellor of Oxford University in 1987.

---

*Subsequently Sir Peter Emery, Conservative MP; Rt Hon. Jeremy Thorpe, Leader of the Liberal Party 1967–76, MP 1959–79; Rt Hon. John Gilbert MP (Labour) since 1974, Minister of State for Defence 1976–9.
†From 1987, Lord Jenkins of Hillhead.

In his foreword to David Walter's admirable history of the Union Society, Harold Macmillan, first Earl of Stockton (who was elected Librarian of the Union in 1914), wrote: 'The Oxford Union is unique in that it has provided an unrivalled training ground for debates in the Parliamentary style which no other debating society in any other democratic country can equal.' In the same book Macmillan is quoted as saying rather less grandiloquently: 'But of course by far the best thing it did was to teach us to treat each other properly . . . to speak like gentlemen and not like hooligans, to try and get some shape and system into a speech and to behave.'*

For the eight weeks of his, or her, term of office and for the preceding vacation, the President of the Oxford Union Society enjoys a position of prestige and patronage unique in the University. Indeed he will probably not enjoy such a position again for many a year after he goes down. Like an impresario or business executive, he has a large booklined office, a vast desk, a private telephone, headed stationery and a hospitality allowance. The President's favours are continually sought by ambitious undergraduates. He decides which undergraduates are called to speak in debates. He chooses the motions for debate and invites the distinguished visitors. He selects the main speakers, known as 'paper' speakers because the names are billed on the printed order paper which is posted throughout the University.

In my time it was also the President's duty to write a review of each debate in the University weekly, the *Oxford Magazine*, with judicious comments on the debaters. The speakers whom I noted as 'very able' were 'Mr Gerald Kaufman (The Queen's College), who expressed a Socialist's contempt for the Labour Government', and 'Mr Patrick Mayhew (Balliol), who rolled out picturesque metaphors in an impressive voice'. I delicately reported that 'Mr William Rees-Mogg had made a thoughtful speech which improved as it proceeded.'

To give an aspiring Union member his first 'paper' speech was patronage which had to be carefully exercised. I well recall the thrill in 1948 of an invitation from the President to make my first 'paper' speech. This threw me into intense excitement.

*David Walter, p. 12; p. 206.

The motion I was invited to propose demanded reform of the system of Oxford education. What on earth was I to say? Far from wanting to reform it, I was only too pleased to be at Oxford at all after four and a half years in the Army. But, after a week of careful preparation, my nervousness was gone. The speech was well received. I scored a minor triumph. The *Isis* called me 'smooth and witty and a master of the art of quotation'. The comment which encouraged me most came from John Owen, the reporter of the *Oxford Mail* who has regularly reported Union debates for the local and national press for over forty years. Owen said to me after that first paper speech in 1948. 'You're all right. You'll be President.' I was astounded, and kept quiet about his prediction.

During the latter part of my time at Oxford I had my first experience of journalism. I even earned some money to supplement my government grant. The political journalist Honor Balfour, who was then on the London bureau staff of *Time* magazine, asked me to be their Oxford 'stringer'. News about eccentric dons, scholarly disputes or undergraduate pranks – these might tickle *Time's* fancy.

Any material from me, if it ever appeared, would be rewritten in Timese and ruthlessly cut. But on one occasion a story based on my report ran for a column and a half. It concerned a stormy Oxford Union debate over which I presided in June 1950. My eyewitness material was extensively used, but with much additional decoration in typical *Time* style:

Heading for Hell?

In 1933, sparked by Guest Speaker Cyril Edwin Mitchinson Joad, a bearded posturing professional pundit, the famed old Oxford Union voted 275 to 153 'that under no circumstances will we fight for King and Country'. When graduate members, led by Winston Churchill's choleric son Randolph, tried to expunge this from the record, they were swamped 750 to 138. In his history of World War II, Winston Churchill sombrely wrote: 'It was easy to laugh off such an episode in England, but in Germany, in Russia, in Italy, in Japan, the idea of a decadent, degenerate Britain took deep root and swayed many calculations.'

Last week ex-pacifist Joad and Randolph Churchill squared off over another provocative Union resolution: 'That this House regrets the influence exercised by the US as the dominant power among the democratic nations.'

'Money is the sole American standard of value,' said Joad. 'The nations are heading for hell and it is America which is leading us there . . . [American influence] corrupts, infects and pollutes whatever it touches.' Angry shouts of 'Shame' greeted Joad's remark, 'What a genius the Americans have for coming into a war late, on the winning side.'

Other shouts drowned out Randolph when he said, 'Back the professor comes after 17 years, with his rotten advice, trying to lure yet another generation along the wrong path.' Union President Robin Day rang the bell for silence, but Randolph soon brought another uproar by saying, 'It may be just a joke for the professor, this third-class Socrates,* but he is corrupting, infecting and polluting the good relations between Britain and the US . . .'

But when the shouting had died down, and the vote was taken, Joad had won again, 224 to 179.*

That asterisk after 'third-class Socrates' was for a footnote explaining Randolph's jibe, proudly rehearsed to me over dinner, which was intended as an allusion to Joad's court conviction for travelling on the railways without the necessary ticket.

For his contribution to that report, *Time*'s Oxford stringer received fifteen guineas, a fee which was not to be sneezed at in 1950.

A minor interest during my final year concerned Norman St John Stevas,† who had come to Oxford from Cambridge as a postgraduate student. An accomplished speaker, he had been President of the Cambridge Union when I was President in Oxford. His ambition was to become the first man to be elected

Time, 1950.
†Since 1987 Lord St John of Fawsley.

President of both Union societies. Though this was within the Oxford Union rules, I and others considered this to be pot-hunting. We felt that a Cambridge graduate who had had three years' debating experience at the Cambridge Union culminating in its Presidency would have an unfair advantage over the under-graduates of Oxford. Our rules did not forbid it, because no one had ever imagined that an ex-President of our sister society in Cambridge would stoop to attempt a second Union career in Oxford. I mounted a Stop Stevas campaign. This was equally within the rules, as it was openly conducted by ridicule and interruption. The Union historian records how in one of his speeches Stevas remarked that I seemed surprisingly silent. I was in fact dozing off. With a show of reluctance, I lumbered, amid loud cheers, to the despatch box: 'I am willing to go to any lengths in order to make the speech of the honourable gentleman memorable.'

Norman managed to get himself elected to the junior office of Secretary, but that was as far as he got. I regretted, in a way, having to put a spoke in his wheel. Much later his ability and wit made him a memorable Leader of the House of Commons. But for his wit his Cabinet career might not have been cut short.

When St John Stevas was my opposite number in Cambridge our relations were cordial. He accepted my challenge that our two Unions should have a boat race. This was one of the most spectacular and enjoyable events of that era. It took place in Cambridge on the Cam during May Week 1950. Stevas and I, in full evening-dress, were the coxes of our respective boats. I then weighed over seventeen stone. The oarsmen were in dinner-jackets. The Oxford Union boat included Peter Emery, who was the stroke, Jeremy Thorpe (already the rising Liberal star), who was number seven, and Godfrey Smith (already a brilliant writer), who was at number six. Stanley Booth-Clibborn was number four. Numbers three and two were Keith Kyle and Dick Taverne, a pair of brilliant brains.

Our Union boat race was conducted with dignity, except when May Week crowds on the bridge bombed us with tins and apples as we passed underneath. Halfway down the course, stewards of the Cambridge Union came out to us in a boat to serve us sherry. At the end, St John Stevas was ceremonially ducked. I begged to be excused this honour for fear of damaging my tail-coat. The occasion was filmed for BBC Television Newsreel and has been screened many times on documentaries about the various participants. I do not remember if either boat won.

At first in Oxford I was active in the Liberal Club. But I lost interest. The central argument of the time was clearly between Socialists and Conservatives. The Liberal Party did not matter much. Most of the Liberal speakers who came to Oxford meetings were dreadful bores. Undergraduate politics involved tedious activity. Far too much time was wasted in canvassing and membership drives. What could be more pointless than a political punt-party?

I did not switch political parties. I simply had other more enjoyable things to do. There was my increasing activity in the Union, its debates and its committees. The debating tour of America took up several months out of my third year. After that, when I held the office of Union President there was spare time for little else.

Eventually I had to concentrate ferociously on my neglected studies of the law. In the event my degree, though not of the very highest class, was much better than I had expected. There were, as the saying went, touches of alpha. My Jurisprudence paper was even marked alpha minus. This was due not to any scholarly analysis but to a last-minute flash of inspiration. There was an essay to write, with a choice of subjects. All were completely beyond me, except one at which I thought I could have a shot: 'Whom do you consider to be the greatest jurist in English law?' Some names quickly sprang to mind – Bracton, Edward I, Henry II, Blackstone, Coke, Mansfield CJ, and one or two others. I included for fun the name of one whose dissenting judgments had begun to excite admiration in academic circles, Lord Justice Denning as he then was. Even as I jotted down the names, in no particular order, I realized that my knowledge would not extend to more than a few lines on any of them. Time was running out. I had to put something down on paper. So I began to answer the examiners' question.

I wrote all that I knew about each of the great men on my list, only to comment in each case that, great as he was, he was not the greatest. I knew that King Edward I had often been described as the 'English Justinian', but incorrectly because he did not codify our law. After about half-a-dozen such vignettes of scholarship, I was stumped. I had written about several figures in English legal history only to dismiss them as not relevant to the question. A fat lot of good that was. I was seized with panic. Then, as the hands of the clock signalled the approach of doom, a flash of inspiration came. I wrote it down even as it occurred. None of the above-mentioned was the 'greatest jurist' in English law because English law had never been the creation of jurists. There had been outstanding legal or political figures who had made great contributions, but we had had no code-makers like Napoleon, or Justinian. The common law had not been enshrined in a code of principles. It had been handed down from precedent to precedent, case by case.

By now I was warming to my theme. As I reached the climax, I was almost writing to music. My memory of the words I wrote is as fresh as if I had written them yesterday:

> So if there is a great jurist in English law, it is no judge or king or scholar. It is he who has fashioned the principles and set the standard in cases for a thousand years. In other words, the Reasonable Man, the man on the Clapham omnibus, the man who mows the lawn in his shirt-sleeves on a Saturday afternoon. It is he from whom the judges have sought guidance, into whose mind they have peered. It is the Reasonable Man whom juries have been instructed by judges to emulate.

I concluded, to a flourish of trumpets, with seconds to spare,

> Undoubtedly the greatest jurist in English law is the Reasonable Man.

I hoped the examiners would have a tolerant sense of humour. Apparently they did.

I had achieved one personal reform at Oxford. In my twenties I had become enormously fat. This had been due to various causes – ceasing to take the vigorous exercise of my Army years, three months' over-eating on the US tour, and a family tendency to put on weight. Whatever the excuses, I weighed over seventeen stone in 1950. For a young man, six foot in height, aged twenty-seven, this was dangerous.

Under medical supervision, as an out-patient at the Radcliffe Infirmary, I took off about four stone – over fifty pounds – during my final Oxford year. This was the first of several huge weight losses I have achieved during the last forty years. In fact I can claim to have lost more weight in my life than anyone I know. Unfortunately I have also managed to *put on* more weight than anyone I know.

The problem became more acute, and very hard to control, after I stopped smoking in 1982, and harder still in 1984 after my heart-by-pass operation. This invigorated me and increased my appetite. The prospect of what remains of one's life without cigars, without alcohol and without eating any of the food one enjoys most is bleak. But, I suppose, marginally less bleak than premature death.

Be that as it may, and to resume my story, I moved to London in the summer of 1951 to study for the Bar Final. I took a bed-sitting room in the house of a barrister and his wife, David and Jean Moylan. Mrs Moylan had answered my 'Wanted' advertisement in the agony column of *The Times*. They were very civilized to their somewhat troublesome lodger. The rent was thirty shillings a week. There was a gas-ring, but usually I had my breakfast in the Lyons' tea-shop at South Kensington tube station. My room was tiny, but the location, Walton Street, Chelsea, was ideal. Nearby, my fellow Bar student, Ronald Waterhouse, shared a flat with his enchanting sister Sally* in Cadogan Lane. There, for many months, they dispensed continuous hospitality to a brilliant circle of friends who had come down from various universities to launch themselves upon the metropolis. I was one of the least distinguished but most frequent members of their *salon*.

In December 1951 I took the Bar Final examination and passed. I was called to the Bar in the new year.

---

*Later Mrs John Thompson, a gifted bbc radio producer. In 1978 Waterhouse himself became Sir Ronald Waterhouse, Judge of the High Court.

5

The Bar

***My Client Has Used Less Violence This Time Than in the
Past***

I was wearing my barrister's wig and gown in court for the first
time. The date was 6 February 1952. I was seated behind the
barrister with whom I had just started my pupillage. Unusually
for him, because he was more often at the Old Bailey, we were
in one of the Chancery Courts across the Strand. The judge was
Mr Justice Harman, one of the old school, whose manner could
be intimidating. He had a military moustache and wore a mon-
ocle slung on a length of fishing line. He was hearing argument
in a case which had begun a few minutes previously when the
Court sat at 10.30 a.m. The Court official in front of the judge's
desk stood up, turned and handed him a note. My master
stopped speaking. Mr Justice Harman, whose height was six
foot four, stood up, straight as a ramrod. He adjusted his mon-
ocle and spoke: 'Gentlemen, I have an announcement. The King
is dead. Long live the Queen! This Court is now adjourned.'
There was a moment of shocked murmur in court as the judge
left.

So ended, after ten minutes, my first day as a barrister in
court. We disrobed and went out to the Kardomah café in Fleet
Street. Over coffee we chatted. Those ringing words, 'Long live
the Queen', had not been heard for over half a century, not
since Queen Victoria was on the throne. Now it was Queen

Elizabeth. Queen Elizabeth II. Were we at the beginning of a new era? Did the death of a monarch make as much difference now as in the past? I pointed out one small difference to my pupil master – that when he took silk, which would be fairly soon, he would now be a QC instead of a KC. A day or two later, the workmen in the Temple who were painting the names of barristers on the boards outside chambers were also changing KC to QC after the names of the silks.

That night I listened to an emotive broadcast by the Prime Minister, Winston Churchill, who had been born in 1874: 'I, whose youth was passed in the august, unchallenged and tranquil glories of the Victorian era, may well feel a thrill in invoking, once more, the prayer and the anthem "God Save the Queen".'

The previous night had been my 'call-night' in Middle Temple Hall. I was called to the Bar by Earl Jowitt, the former Lord Chancellor, a stately figure with high wing-collar and magnificent voice. It was said that Lord Jowitt owed more of his success in the law to his voice than he realized. Those called to the Bar with me that night in Middle Temple Hall included future silks and judges, such as Ronald Waterhouse, and a future Foreign Secretary, Geoffrey Howe.

My 'master' was Fred Lawton, who had one of the busiest practices at the Common Law and Criminal Bar. He went to the High Court Bench in 1961 and became a Lord Justice of Appeal in 1972. One of his later pupils, a couple of years after me, was a barrister by the name of Margaret Thatcher. Over thirty-five years later, a dinner was held in the Inner Temple at which the Prime Minister was guest of honour. The dinner was given by Sir Frederick Lawton to mark his retirement from the Court of Appeal. He was kind enough to include me among the guests.

During my pupillage in No. 5 King's Bench Walk, I shared a basement room with another barrister, who had just completed his pupillage with Fred Lawton. This was Caesar James Crespi, now a Queen's Counsel and a Recorder. James Crespi was a legal scholar of deep learning and great distinction. He had achieved a 'starred First' at Cambridge. In his company I felt sure I was with a future Lord of Appeal. But James chose to concentrate on practice at the Criminal Bar. He became a prominent figure at the Old Bailey, noted for his forensic skill and for his vast size.

Crespi is reputed to have been the model, or one of the models, for that fictional star of the Criminal Bar, John Mortimer's marvellous 'Rumpole of the Bailey'. I would doubt if this is true. James Crespi has only two or three things in common with Horace Rumpole: he is a heavyweight, enjoys his food and wine, and would not claim to dress with elegance. Otherwise Crespi is not in the least Rumpolian. He is a fine lawyer. Rumpole prides himself on knowing more about advocacy than about law. Crespi prefers prosecuting to defending. He is not married. His conversation is more likely to be laced with quotations from Archbold or Halsbury than from Wordsworth or Shakespeare. My view is that Rumpole was modelled on more than one Temple character, but that the chief model was Mortimer himself.

In 1952 Lawton's practice took him to every type of court. I accompanied him to the Old Bailey, to Bow Street Magistrates' Court, to Assizes and Quarter Sessions on the South-eastern Circuit, and to the Law Courts on the Strand. To work with such an able barrister and to study his techniques of advocacy and cross-examination was an invaluable experience.

As Lawton's pupil, I would study his papers, attend his conferences with clients, draft opinions for him and help him by taking a full note in court. In the civilized tradition of the Bar, a newly called pupil is encouraged to put forward ideas and suggestions. These are heard with elaborate courtesy. Fred Lawton would listen to a point of mine and then would gently explain that my argument, though flawless in theory, was demolished by some simple practical point which I had overlooked through inexperience of the courts.

I soon came to realize that, to be a first-class barrister, a combination of several different qualities is needed. It is no use being an impressive speaker if you do not have a clear mind. It is not much use having a clear mind if you do not have in it a strong grasp of the law. And it is no use being the most learned legal scholar without some knowledge of human nature, and some common sense.

The old story was told to me, and by me often to others, of

the young barrister who had carried off every academic prize and distinction; a Double First, a fellowship of All Souls and so on. His carefully prepared cross-examination of a police witness went like this:

'And how far were you, constable, from the accused when he first caught sight of you?'

'About fifteen yards, sir.'

'About fifteen yards. And were you in uniform?'

'I was, sir.'

'And you were wearing police boots?'

'That is correct, sir.'

'Policemen's boots have big iron hob-nails on the soles, do they not?'

'They do, sir.'

Then leaning forward intently, with a confident hitching up of the gown over the shoulders:

'And hob-nailed boots make a loud crunching noise on the ground, do they not?'

'That is so, sir.'

'Then perhaps you will explain how the accused failed to hear you until you were only fifteen yards away from him?'

'I was riding my bicycle, sir.'

Fictitious, perhaps, but questions as silly, or sillier, have been asked by incompetent cross-examiners in court, and (I regret to say) on television.

Sometimes I was able to slip away from chambers, as pupil barristers often did, to be a spectator at the sensational murder trials of the time. The death penalty was then in operation. I watched the Lord Chief Justice, Lord Goddard, presiding over the trial of Craig and Bentley for the murder of a police officer. I saw Mr Justice Finnemore, with the black cap upon his bewigged head, pass sentence of death upon John Reginald Halliday Christie for the Rillington Place murders.

Among the celebrated barristers who appeared in big cases in which I was involved as a pupil or with a 'noting' brief were Sir Hartley Shawcross QC and Gerald Gardiner QC, two brilliant advocates then at the top of their profession. To sit in court with them was an education and an entertainment. Shawcross, the former Attorney-General, debonair and supremely confident; Gardiner, the future Lord Chancellor, undramatic but coldly incisive.

While still in my pupil year, I began to get a few briefs of my own, in small cases which would come into my master's chambers at No. 5 King's Bench Walk. These cases would include lesser driving offences, petty theft, and some County Court cases. Like other newly called barristers, I would also be sent to make a 'plea in mitigation of sentence' when the accused had pleaded guilty. A relatively simple matter, it might be thought. I found it intensely difficult. I remember racking my brains for anything plausible to say on behalf of a man who had pleaded guilty to his eighth conviction for robbery with violence. In the end the only thing I could find to say to the judge was: 'Your Lordship will note that my client has used rather less violence this time than he has in the past.' The judge, Mr Justice Hilbery, was a senior judge who was capable of being very difficult. He looked sour as I made my little speech in Court No. 1 at the Old Bailey. When I sat down he said to the man in the dock, who must have been very disappointed with his counsel: 'Mr Day has said the only thing which can be said on your behalf.' He then gave the man five years.

There were some less depressing moments, as when one's client was acquitted in spite of what had seemed a strong prosecution case. I was particularly glad to have persuaded a bench of magistrates in a Surrey town to dismiss a charge of indecent exposure which had been brought against a young lorry driver. The prosecution witness, a schoolgirl of fourteen, alleged that the man had been waving himself at her. Our defence was that he had been relieving himself by the side of the road during a long journey, and that he was merely shaking off the drops.

Fortunately the young lorry driver had brought his sexy young wife with him to court. As the firm of defending solicitors had not sent a representative, I was permitted by Bar etiquette to see a witness myself. I talked to the wife briefly. Would she be prepared to go into the witness-box and answer questions about their sex life? What would she say if asked whether her husband enjoyed normal, satisfying sex with her? She would say 'Yes, definitely.' I had no difficulty in believing her, although whether I did believe her was beside the point. I suggested that her evidence might be even more impressive if she took off her mackintosh and testified in her sweater. Whether her evidence was strictly admissible I was not sure, but it seemed relevant. Anyway there was no objection when she testified.

I rose to address the three magistrates, a colonel and two ladies. I warmed to my theme which was that it was quite customary, as the bench would of course be well aware, for members of the male sex to shake the drops off their person after urinating. The two lady magistrates were for some reason looking down at their papers, so I concentrated on the colonel, who was chairman. The colonel appeared to be nodding. I hoped he was indicating his awareness of the custom to which I had referred.

The charge against my client was dismissed. Back in chambers the clerk, Stanley Hopkins, was pleased but surprised. He had not expected a 'win'. I was elated, convinced that I was now on my way to becoming standing counsel for the Transport and General Workers' Union, whose solicitors had sent the case to our chambers. The brief fee was two guineas.

Such moments of glory were infrequent during my short time at the Bar. I was now twenty-nine. I had started late at the Bar, having been four years at Oxford and even longer in the Army. With luck, I could hope to earn a moderate living at the Bar by the time I was thirty-five. Meanwhile, my contemporaries were settling into other occupations with reasonable salaries.

As a barrister, I earned about two hundred guineas in my pupil year, 1952. That was relatively high, much higher than some who had been called with me. I had won two Middle Temple Scholarships – one, the Blackstone, which helped with some of the capital payment required for entrance to the profession, and the prestigious Harmsworth, which was two hundred pounds a year for three years. So at first I felt able to stay at the Bar. But after my contribution to the rent of chambers, rail fares, hotel bills, circuit fees, legal textbooks, my fees of five or six guineas a week were reduced to nothing. At the age of twenty-nine I was impatient for something better than a bed-sitting-room existence with a student's standard of living. Even so, at the end of my pupil year, I still intended to persevere, with the aid of my Harmsworth Scholarship and by earning money in other ways.

One way of earning extra money was by writing articles about how young barristers needed to earn extra money. Through the good offices of my friend Godfrey Smith, who had succeeded me as President of the Union at Oxford, and was now doing well on Lord Kemsley's *Sunday Times*, that newspaper published an article for which I was paid twenty-five guineas. I wrote under a pseudonym because of the Bar's rules against advertising. My pseudonym was Stuffgownsman, an old name for a junior barrister, whose gown is made of 'stuff', not of silk like that of a Queen's Counsel. My twenty-five-guinea piece came to a moving climax in this final paragraph:

In the meantime, observe that prosperous-looking fellow with a First in his Tripos, thoughtfully pacing the Inner Temple lawns; he is wondering how he is going to pay his next week's rent. That ex-President of the Oxford Union with the carefully pressed striped trousers and a bowler from Lock's, accompanying his master across to the Law Courts, lives in a tiny bed-sitting room at thirty shillings a week and cooks his own meals on a gas-ring. They are hoping it will all be worth it. They work hard in their chambers, they watch the performances of the fashionable silks and they read Lord Simon's memoirs. They observe the comparative affluence of their salaried contemporaries with envy and good-humour, typified the other day by the struggling young barrister, who, too poor to attend his college reunion, wrote that he was compelled to decline 'owing to the pressure of my hope of work'.*

By the spring of 1953 I had begun to doubt not only whether I could financially keep going at the Bar, but whether I really wanted to be a practising barrister. Why was it that I was about to abandon the profession on which I had set my sights six years previously as a subaltern in Kenya? My friends were puzzled by my thought of quitting. Had I not made an excellent start, with

Sunday Times, February 1953.

work beginning to come in? To have been a pupil of Fred Lawton with his thriving practice in crime and the common law was surely a tremendous advantage? Would I have been given a seat in Lawton's busy chambers unless they thought me to have shown some promise? Why throw all this away? Surely, with my Harmsworth Scholarship and with briefs trickling in, I could hold on financially?

I endured a long period of uncertainty, which lasted through the summer of Coronation Year, 1953. In the end, despite the urging of my friends, the brutal truth was that I did not want to be a practising barrister. I had become convinced that, even if I could hang on and build up a practice at the Bar, I would not become more than a run-of-the-mill hack. I did not have the qualities which a top-flight barrister should have, namely a first-class brain, a mastery of the law and an infinite capacity for long hours of hard, concentrated work.

Nor did I think I would ever acquire that cold professional detachment which would enable me to bear the strain of a busy barrister's life. I used to go through agonies of doubt about the relatively trivial cases which I handled, particularly those of a squalid or tragic nature. Once I was briefed to prosecute a poor old man for stealing half-a-crown (or some such sum) from a Rowton House, one of the hostels for London's down-and-outs. I have long forgotten the details, but I have not forgotten the anxiety this wretched case caused me. There was more complexity to the matter than at first met the eye. I was relieved when a more experienced barrister in my chambers was brought in to take over.

All these considerations for and against my quitting the Bar weighed heavily on me. What tipped the scales was the simple fact that I was more interested in politics and politicians than in the law and in lawyers. During the general election of October 1951 I had been studying for the Bar Final, or rather trying desperately to do so. I was incapable of concentrating on anything but the election. The climax came on polling day itself, when Winston Churchill issued a writ for libel against the *Daily Mirror* for their sensational front-page spread: 'WHOSE FINGER ON THE TRIGGER?' At least this was a political distraction which turned my mind swiftly to the law of defamation. I wondered if there would be a topical question about it in the Bar examination: 'What advice do you give the *Daily Mirror*?'

I was not yet thinking of a political career, nor, at that stage, of standing for Parliament, but politics was my addiction. The talk I most enjoyed was the friendly, argumentative conversation I often had with the one barrister in our chambers who was a Parliamentary candidate, and who won a by-election that summer. He was Airey Neave, a much decorated wartime intelligence officer.*

By midsummer 1953 I had decided to quit the Bar. But my time had not been wasted. A knowledge of the courts and our system of justice would always be a useful background. The ordeal of my early court appearances had been a toughening and testing experience. Television has never been as nerve-racking.

From my pupillage with Fred Lawton, I had learned the simple, but too often neglected, lesson that a good cross-examination in court depends on a thorough mastery of the facts, and on the ability to anticipate almost any answer. This, as I was later to appreciate, was a lesson with equal application to the interviewing of politicians on television.

In the thirty years or so since I began to become well known on television I have been continually asked, 'Don't you regret leaving the Bar?', and 'If you had stayed at the Bar what would you be now?' The answer to the first of those two queries has always been 'No, but I'm glad to have had the experience.'

The second question is usually coupled with flattering but unrealistic suggestions that I would have become a judge or a great advocate. The answer is that the most I could have become would have been a Rumpole of the Bailey without his genius. Instead, as a kind wit put it, I ended up as a Rumpole of the Beeb.

I was certain that somewhere, somehow, I would be able to make good use of my eighteen months as a barrister in chambers. But I could not see where or how. Television never crossed my mind. I was attracted by journalism, but enquiries showed that Fleet Street editors were not interested in giving jobs to

*See below, pp. 299–300.

failed barristers. I did not wish to drift into a business office or a government department as a 'legal eagle'. That would mean all the drudgery and none of the drama of practice at the Bar. I remembered a phrase of my father's when we were discussing careers open to lawyers. He had urged me against becoming a 'house' lawyer or legal adviser. A lawyer in that position, he would say, 'is always on tap and never on top'.

So I had no further use for my black jacket and striped trousers. I gave up my Harmsworth Scholarship which I had been so proud to have won. My barrister's gown, and my wig in its black tin box with my name in gold letters, were sold to a friend. That friend was Ivan Yates who was also reading for the Bar at that time. Ivan had been President of the Union the year after me at Oxford. Having purchased my wig and gown, he never wore them. He went into journalism and became one of the *Observer*'s most valued writers. But Ian kept my wig and gown in some upstairs cupboard. After I married, he unexpectedly presented my wig and gown to my wife when she was called to the Bar in 1968, fifteen years after I had sold them to him.

On 27 August 1953, Ivan was one of the dear, good friends who came to see me off on the boat train at Waterloo Station. He had written me a letter the night before:

> As you well know, I've grown up with a peculiarly English and wholly wrong-headed habit of not expressing anything I feel deeply – but hide it, pretend it isn't there. It must be a very tiresome habit for one's friends; it's a very tiresome one for oneself – but it has just one advantage, that when one does say what one feels it means something.
>
> I want to say just two things. First, to thank you for your friendship – not ending, I know, but entering a new phrase. We shall all miss you; and you'll miss some of us, I expect, for no one I know lives more for his friends before himself and does it without fuss. You have a right to know that. I'm sure others feel the same. I'm grateful for so much you've said and done from time to time, sometimes openly, always tactfully, that I wouldn't wish to particularize. . . .
>
> Count on me for anything I can do – always. As the Welsh say, strangely beautifully, I think – go well. Keep in touch!

I quoted from that letter when giving the address at the memorial service for Ivan Yates in 1975 at St Bride's, Fleet Street. He had been killed in a road accident.

On that August day in 1953 at Waterloo station, the girls in the group which had come to say goodbye to me were in tears. My emotions were held in check by a show of bravado and bluster which served only to emphasize the melancholiness of the occasion. I was sailing to the United States. I had failed. I was quitting. It was a miserable moment in my life. I could not see a glimmer of hope. I was taking a reckless gamble, much riskier than my gamble four years previously in going to America on the Union debating tour. The possible rewards of that gamble had been clear to me. But I was now going to a badly paid and inferior job in America with no prospects and no future.

6

Washington

***The Truth Comma the Whole Truth Comma and Nothing
But the Truth***

The chance of a job in the United States had arisen from my
Oxford debating tour four years earlier. At that time I had met
Charles Campbell, head of the Washington office of British
Information Services. He had heard me debate before a large
audience at a Washington university in 1949.

If any man earned the nickname of Mr Anglo-American,
it was Charlie Campbell. He was a legendary figure among
newspapermen on both sides of the Atlantic. His very British
appearance, with a florid face and walrus moustache, concealed
a shrewd understanding and deep love of America. He had been
a reporter and an editor on a New Orleans newspaper.

His BIS post in Washington was that of Press Officer to the
British Embassy. His office was in the National Press Building
in downtown Washington at 14th and F streets. Campbell gave
help and guidance to correspondents both American and British.
He was trusted by journalists as few press officers are. If Charlie
told a newspaperman that there was absolutely no truth in some
rumour or other that would kill the story.

My job in Campbell's office was called Assistant to the Director, British Information Services, Washington. In plain language, it was a minor public relations job. One of my duties
was to be liaison officer with Washington TV and radio stations.

59

I had to study the programmes, make contact with the producers and arrange for appearances and broadcasts by visiting British MPS or VIPS, or by the British Ambassador. British visitors would sometimes have preferred a higher level of programme than that which I was able to arrange for them.

Canon John Collins, then Dean of St Paul's, was touring America with the St Paul's Cathedral Choir. He was interviewed between commercials on a breakfast-time TV programme. In 1953 Britain had not yet experienced either TV commercials or TV at breakfast-time. He was asked how long the St Paul's Cathedral choir had been going. Canon Collins replied: 'Eight hundred years.' 'Gee, Canon, that must be the longest run in show-business.'

There was no career, no future in this post. It was a low-grade, locally recruited, temporary, unpensionable government job, without diplomatic status. I was recruited and appointed in London because Charlie Campbell heard that I was leaving the Bar and looking for something else to do. He was looking for an assistant. So he arranged for me to be seen in London by a senior Foreign Office official, Paul Gore-Booth. As the post was classed as 'locally-recruited', I (and not the Treasury) was responsible for paying my transatlantic fare.

I had about a hundred pounds in the bank, an emergency reserve fund which was all that remained of the small sum which my father had left me and which had helped me through Oxford and my year at the Bar. This hundred pounds was enough to buy my boat ticket (a single ticket) and to cover other expenses of emigrating (if only temporarily) to the United States.

When I arrived I felt immediately that I had made a terrible mistake. After qualifying to enter an élite profession I had thrown it all up. My first few weeks in Washington were the blackest period of my life.

I suffered acutely from loneliness. I missed my friends in London. I was unused to the sweltering Washington heat, for which I had only the English idea of tropical clothing. I was living in a hurriedly rented and uncomfortable room. Worst of all, my work seemed neither interesting nor significant. I loathed working in a government office, with office hours. I longed for what I had just abandoned – the civilized, gentlemanly lifestyle of a barrister in the Temple.

My morale was touching rock-bottom. I was thirty years old and had got absolutely nowhere in life. I had a new job, but that job was a non-job. If I gave it up, what would I do then? How many more times could I chop and change jobs at my age? I might be forty before I achieved anything. Achieve? Achieve what, for God's sake?

I ran into someone I'd known at school, Richard Parsons. He was a third secretary in the British Embassy. It was humiliating for me that this young man, four years my junior, was on much higher pay than I was. He enjoyed full diplomatic status and allowances, and had a large and elegant apartment. Richard Parsons was on his first posting in a high-flying diplomatic career. At school he had been one of the obstreperous small boys in the dormitory of which I had been the prefect in charge. Now, twelve years later in Washington, I was one of the lower orders, and he, like George Nathaniel Curzon, was a most superior person.

Happily this was a situation from which we both extracted much humour. My sense of humiliation evaporated. Richard was extremely generous with his introductions and his hospitality. In later years, he became Sir Richard Parsons KCMG, British Ambassador in Budapest, in Madrid and in Stockholm.

Then, by good fortune, one of my oldest Oxford friends appeared on the Washington scene. This was Keith Kyle, who had been appointed Washington correspondent of *The Economist*. He was my first undergraduate friend at Oxford. He had been reading History at Magdalen where he was one of A. J. P. Taylor's ablest pupils. I can see Keith Kyle, more than forty years ago, in the High, talking to himself, gesticulating enthusiastically and striding absent-mindedly in the wrong direction.

I always thought Keith's destiny was to be an Oxford don. But he was as eloquent as he was erudite. He was determined not to have a cloistered, academic life. He became, first, a BBC radio talks producer. Then that great Editor of *The Economist*, Sir Geoffrey Crowther, discerned his outstanding ability.

As a correspondent in Washington, Keith Kyle was to win high respect for his knowledge and his integrity. Three years later, at a moment during the Suez crisis when Anglo-American relations were down to freezing point, Keith was one of those used by HMG and the State Department as an unofficial go-between in Washington.

With two such stimulating and congenial friends in Washington my spirits began to rise. I could have arguments again, and sharpen my wits. I got rid of my self-pity. The overpowering summer heat was giving way to the more English temperatures of the fall. I found that my relatively low pay was enough to live on simply. I was able to rent an apartment. My job began to be more interesting. It brought me into contact with the different worlds of Washington DC, the politicians, the officials, the diplomats and the journalists. Keith Kyle and Richard Parsons were two of my personal links with these intermingling worlds. Another Oxford friend who was also to arrive was Howard E. Shuman, an American who had been elected President of the Oxford Union shortly after me. Howard, who was from Illinois, came to Washington to work for the respected Democratic Senator Paul Douglas. For over thirty-five years he and his wife most generously entertained and advised me during my frequent visits to the American capital.

I got to know leading British correspondents, such as Henry Brandon of the *Sunday Times*, Bruce Rothwell of the *News Chronicle* and Max Freedman of the *Guardian*, all of whom became good friends of mine. I was fortunate also to make the acquaintance of a young British correspondent with an elegant manner and a name which struck Americans as strange, Peregrine Worsthorne. Perry does not, I think, remember meeting me in those days, which is not surprising. I then kept a relatively low profile, if only because I had nothing to be high-profile about. But Peregrine Worsthorne was, even then, an attention-catching personality, with style.

I studied the way these British correspondents covered the Washington news. When their newspapers arrived in Washington a day or two later, I would compare their interpretations, their angles and their exclusives.

My job in BIS did not, I was glad to find, imprison me in my office on a telephone every day. I made several speaking tours to talk about Britain and British life to schools and other institutions. I would also appear on the local radio or television. My broadcasting experience was increasing.

The Washington social round of cocktail parties and dinner parties was exciting to a newcomer. The parties I went to were not at the highest level, but the talk and the drink and the women were to my taste. The talk was invariably about Washington events and personalities. The social round was like a crash course in American politics.

By the summer of 1954 one man was the dominant topic of Washington conversation. Senator Joseph McCarthy, the Communist-hunting Republican from Wisconsin, was then at the height of his influence. American politics was going through a shameful phase.

For weeks during the spring and summer of 1954 the notorious Army – McCarthy hearings were televised live from Capital Hill. McCarthy had been slinging mud at the US Army department. Hour after hour I watched, hypnotized by the extraordinary spectacle of this thug McCarthy, arrogant and unscrupulous, strutting contemptuously in the centre of the Washington stage. But those hearings did more than produce hours of compulsively watchable television. They demonstrated the power of television to destroy that which it had helped to create. Television enabled the American people to see McCarthy (together with his odious henchmen Cohn and Schine) challenged and exposed by Joseph Welch, the courteous Boston lawyer with the old-world manner.

Welch was counsel for the United States Army. Rarely have I seen a more dramatic moment on television than when Welch turned on McCarthy because of a hurtful smear which McCarthy had made about the student activities of one of Welch's Harvard assistants. This had nothing whatever to do with the hearings. It was just another sickening example of McCarthy's technique, of McCarthyism in action.

This time the Senator did not go unanswered. Lawyer Joseph Welch turned on McCarthy with a cold fury and a noble eloquence:

Until this moment, Senator, I think I had never gauged your cruelty or your recklessness. . . . If it were in my power to forgive you for your reckless cruelty, I would do so. I like to think that I am a gentle man, but your forgiveness will have to come from someone other than me.

The utter contempt with which these words were delivered cannot fully be appreciated from the printed record. But on television their impact was devastating.

The cross-examination of McCarthy by Welch gave me my first sight (which I was never to forget) of how televised interrogation of a politician can, if skilfully and fairly conducted, be an instrument of vital importance in a democracy, and particularly so if the interrogation is conducted under oath.

When McCarthy gave evidence on oath, the cross-examination by Welch exposed him for the thug he was. Some cross-examinations have been more brutal. Some have been more sensational. But no cross-examination has given me more pleasure. Here is a small part of it:

> Q: The oath included a promise, a solemn promise by you to tell the truth comma the whole truth comma and nothing but the truth. Is that correct, Sir?
>
> A: Mr Welch, you are not the first individual to try to get me to betray the confidence and give out the names of my informants. You will be no more successful than those that have tried in the past, period.
>
> Q: I am only asking you, Sir, do you realize when you took that oath that you were making a similar promise to tell the whole truth to this Committee?
>
> A: I understand the oath, Mr Welch.
>
> Q: And when you took it, did you have some mental reservation, some 5th or 6th Amendment notion [laughter] that you could measure what you would tell?
>
> A: I don't take the 5th or 6th Amendment.
>
> Q: Have you some private reservation when you take the oath that you will tell the whole truth that lets you be the judge of what you will testify to?
>
> A: The answer is there is no reservation about telling the whole truth.

Q: Thank you, sir. Then tell us who delivered the document to you.

A: The answer is 'No'. You will not get that information.

Q: You wish to put your own interpretation on your oath and tell us less than the whole truth?

A: . . . I repeat, you will not get their names. . . . You can go right ahead and try until Doomsday.

Television coverage of those hearings began the downfall of a demagogue. Edward R. Murrow, on CBS, was to accelerate that process with his magisterial programme *See It Now*.

An historic event of that year 1954 in Washington was the last visit to the US capital as Prime Minister of Sir Winston Churchill. Minor duties were given to me in connection with the press arrangements for the visit. These included an on-the-record press conference and a small briefing for invited members of the British press corps. Churchill was then seventy-nine. The previous year he had suffered a stroke, which had been kept a close secret.

I had to inform the British correspondents of the time and place for Sir Winston's private talk to them. I never expected to meet him, but I was detailed to attend the briefing. The small gathering of newsmen – there were about a dozen – waited in the sunshine on the garden steps of the British Embassy on Massachusetts Avenue. They were conscious that they were being accorded an exceptional privilege. In those days a British Prime Minister, certainly not Sir Winston Churchill, rarely gave press interviews or briefings. He occasionally gave an audience to an Editor or an eminent columnist. TV interviews of course had yet to raise their ugly heads.

The great old man, in a light tropical suit, came walking slowly out through the French windows, steadying himself with his walking-stick. He looked somewhat exhausted after his meetings with the President. He was shepherded on to the patio by the Ambassador Sir Roger Makins, who towered above the Prime Minister and above most of the newsmen. Sir Winston beamed broadly as he shook hands with each of us. I treasure among my most precious memories his opening words to that gathering of journalists, all hard-boiled professionals, all trying not to show their excitement, all hanging on Sir Winston's every word. He began to speak, hesitantly and gravely, but with just the hint of a twinkle in his eye: 'Gentlemen, I wonder if you will permit me to take up a few moments of your valuable time, so that I may tell you about my talks with my old friend President Eisenhower?'

There was a pause. Glances were exchanged. It seemed to be generally agreed that their valuable time was at Sir Winston's disposal. I find it difficult to imagine any Prime Minister of more recent times greeting journalists with such an impish mixture of courtesy, flattery and mockery.

By September 1954 I had spent a year in Washington. I had recovered from my gloom. The year had gone quickly. I had enjoyed a romance, deeper than most of my attachments in Oxford or London, or perhaps it seemed deeper because it happened when I was downcast. It was, as the song says, a trip to the moon on gossamer wings.

I was tremendously attracted to America and Americans. The efficiency, the vitality, the dynamism of the American way of life were much needed in Britain. I was increasingly drawn to the world in which many of my Washington friends worked, the world of political journalism and broadcasting. I had become a critical student of American television and its programmes.

That year, the British Parliament had passed the Television Act to launch commercial television financed by advertisements. This would break the BBC's monopoly. A new field of opportunity was said to be opening in British broadcasting. I booked a return passage. I had been able to save enough dollars for that, and to tide me over while I looked for work in London. What had my gamble in going to Washington achieved?'

I was certainly no nearer to finding a career. But I had learned much about the media and about America. I had come to think that my future should be in broadcasting. At least I now had some idea of where I wanted to go.

It seemed the time for another gamble, to take a chance on finding a way into broadcasting. There must be something for me in the BBC, or in this new commercial set-up. There were, of course, absolutely no grounds for any such hopes. But I could try. Only one thing was certain. Time was not on my side. I was now thirty-one, whereas I had been only thirty the year before.

4

Broadcasting House

In Talks We Like to Wear Suits

By nature I am an optimist. Why else would I take one gamble after another? But in September 1954 there seemed to be practically nothing going for me. I had no money, neither capital nor income. I had no influential family connections. I did not bear the name of a famous father. I did not wear a famous old-school tie. I was not distinguished. I had not done anything. I had not run the mile in four minutes, as my Oxford contemporary Roger Bannister had done that year. I had not had a glamorous war. I was nothing but a failed barrister who had been (big deal) President of the Oxford Union. And I was thirty-one. Harold Wilson was in the Cabinet at that age.

So when I returned from Washington to London that autumn, my chances of making a new start, finding a new career, two years after coming down (rather late) from Oxford, were not good. I soon found that those much-mentioned new opportunities in television dissolved in a series of polite refusals: 'Your name will be kept in mind, but at the moment we need people with experience.' I was up against a familiar problem. How do you get experience if the only way you can get it is in the job you need experience for?

I was unemployed for about four months, except for irregular jobs which earned me a few guineas – such as lectures for the Workers' Educational Association, and the odd radio talk for the BBC. I was desperately hard up, and my lifestyle was uncomfortably austere. Luckily I was able to share a flat very cheaply with Ivan Yates and Ronald Waterhouse. Ivan was himself now reading for the Bar. Ronald was beginning to build up a promising practice on the Welsh Circuit.

This was a most agreeable ménage, probably because we were rarely in the flat together. We were old friends, with much in common. We were all impecunious bachelors. Our tastes in women were happily different. We had all read Law, though with varying degrees of dedication. We had each been President of the Union (in Ronald's case at Cambridge). We shared a lively interest in politics. Ivan was staunch Labour and stood for Parliament in 1955. Ronald had been a Liberal at Cambridge, but joined the Labour Party and was a candidate in 1959. They were firmly of the Gaitskellite tendency and were both founder members of the Gaitskellite Campaign for Democratic Socialism having attended its inaugural meeting in the Princess of Wales public house in Chelsea. Unlike them I was not a Socialist but I argued that I was much more radical than either of them.

British politics was entering a new era. Churchill was soon to retire. Anthony Eden was about to begin his ill-fated eighteen months as Prime Minister. Attlee would go after fighting one more general election. Hugh Gaitskell and Aneurin Bevan personified the growing ideological conflict which was to keep Labour out of power for another ten years.

My personal preoccupation, however, was not with the changing political scene but with my unchanging lack of work. I made innumerable applications and enquiries, but drew blank after blank.

I decided not to pursue one possibility to which my attention had been discreetly drawn. This was for 'something interesting in the government service'. I was asked to go to a curious address in SW1. When one of my more sophisticated friends explained what this meant, I decided not to go for interview. I do not know whether it was for MI6 or MI5. I may be unduly modest, but it is doubtful whether my talents, such as they are, would have been suitable for a career in espionage or in counter-espionage.

I also pursued my enquires in Fleet Street – without much success. I did earn ten guineas from the Editor of the *Daily Mail*, William Hardcastle, for giving him a political scoop. I wrote him an exclusive story about how my Oxford contemporary, Anthony Wedgwood Benn, MP, then twenty-nine, intended to bring forward a Bill to enable him to renounce the viscountcy which he would in due course inherit from his father. Bill Hardcastle was impressed, and made quite a splash with it. But he did not offer me a job. Nor did any of the other Fleet Street editors to whom Charlie Campbell had given me a glowing introduction.

Most discouraging of all was the continuing failure of my approaches to BBC Television. I applied for a BBC Television training course, but was rejected. I applied to Peter Dimmock for work in Outside Broadcasts. The reply, via Aubrey Singer, was negative.

More hopefully, I wrote to Leonard Miall, the new Head of Television 'Talks', as TV current affairs were then quaintly known in the BBC. I had met Miall in 1949 when he was the BBC's celebrated Washington correspondent and I was on the Oxford Union debating tour. He had then interviewed me for *Radio Newsreel*. We got on well. But in 1954 Leonard Miall merely referred me to his assistant, Mrs Grace Wyndham Goldie. She, in turn, merely referred me to her opposite number in the Radio Talks Department at Broadcasting House.

Nothing materialized from BH until a senior talks producer, Stephen Bonarjee, tried me out as one of the panel of freelance broadcasters on a programme called. *Topic for Tonight*. My name had been mentioned to Bonarjee by one of his regular contributors, Honor Balfour of *Time* magazine, for which I had been the Oxford 'stringer' during my undergraduate years.

Topic for Tonight was a four-minute explanation of a subject in the news. *Topic* was excellent experience, because all my talks (I did about five) were on matters about which I was ignorant. The subjects about which I broadcast talks of trenchant analysis and confident authority included: the rising price of tea, Mau-Mau surrender terms, the situation in Formosa and Mr Malenkov's resignation.

Topic was abysmally paid. The fee was eight guineas, if my recollection is correct, for researching, writing and broadcasting a 600-word piece. But I had no complaint about the money. I was lucky to get whatever the BBC, which had a broadcasting monopoly, cared to pay. I had no contract for this freelance broadcasting. It was casual labour, but it brought me into personal contact with the broadcasting world and, above all, with the people who wielded the patronage, the talent-spotters, the BBC producers.

Stephen Bonarjee produced a current affairs radio programme with the dignified title *At Home and Abroad*. He offered me a temporary contract as a producer. This vacancy came because Jack Ashley was off on a university fellowship in the United States for a year. I had known Jack, who had been a trade union shop steward, when he was President of the Cambridge Union. He had a warm, gutsy personality. He has since won widespread respect for soldiering on as an MP in spite of the total deafness which struck him in 1968. He is now the Rt Hon. Jack Ashley and a Companion of Honour. I stepped into Jack Ashley's place, and thus became a temporary producer in BBC radio. This meant not only that I received a salary, but that I was entering the priesthood of broadcasting.

My salary (wage would be a more appropriate word) was £875 a year. After tax and other deductions, the net amount each week was just over £14. I would draw this amount in a small brown envelope from the Langham branch of Barclays Bank. I immediately deposited three pound notes in the Post Office Savings Bank and spent the rest. This was not affluence but it was an improvement. And my feet were planted on the bottom rung of what I wittily called Jacob's ladder, in honour of the General who was then DG.*

My introduction to the BBC bureaucracy was somewhat formal. I was summoned by the administrative officer of the Radio Talks department. He was a brisk, well-turned-out fellow with a double-barrelled name, whose public school manner suggested that he could have been an estate agent or something in Lloyd's. Our dialogue is engraved on my memory:

*Lieutenant-General Sir Ian Jacob GBE CB, Director-General of the BBC 1952–60.

'Ah, Day! Good morning. Welcome to Talks.'

'Thank you very much. It's nice to be here.'

'Now, to give you some advice: I want you to see yourself as – well – as having become an officer in a rather good regiment. Please regard John Green as the Colonel, and myself as the Adjutant. Do you follow?'

'Yes, indeed. Actually I was in a rather good regiment myself.'

'Oh really? Which?'

'I was a gunner. Very exclusive. What were you in?'

The double-barrelled admin officer did not seem to relish being interviewed by me. He had been, I later discovered, in the Grenadier Guards. He continued:

'Now, I expect you'd like some advice about dress.'

'That would be most helpful.'

'I see you're wearing a stiff collar.'

'It's a habit I got into at the Bar.'

'Well, you may be glad to know that here we do not insist on stiff collars. But in Talks we like to wear suits.'

'Of course.'

'In Features they wear sports jackets, and I have to admit that in Drama they even wear corduroys. But, as I say, in Talks we like suits.'

Thus imbued with the appropriate *esprit de corps* I threw myself into the genteel battles of Broadcasting House. There were programmes to be organized, ideas to be proposed, contributors to be suggested, and above all meetings to attend – departmental meetings attended by all the Talks producers, many of them formidable women. I was amazed to see them all crowded into a conference room. I had never imagined that so many talks were produced.

Then, one day in July 1955, I started a small battle of my own. I put up a revolutionary idea. In those days BBC radio gave the listener no choice at breakfast-time. From 6.30 a.m. on the Home Service there was mainly light music, with news at 7 a.m., 8 a.m. and 9 a.m. But on the Light Programme there was nothing on the air until 9 a.m., when there was news followed by *Housewives' Choice*, a popular record programme. So on a typical morning in early 1955, between the 7 a.m. news and the 8 a.m. news the wretched licence-holder could get nothing on the BBC except, for example, *No No Nanette, Lift Up Your Hearts* with a reading from Ezekiel, and the weather forecast.

I drew my colleagues' attention to this lamentable gap in our radio service. I referred to the increasing number of car radio licences, indicating a vast captive audience of motorists, unable to read newspapers at the wheel, but ready to hear radio.

I urged that BBC radio should accordingly transmit an early morning topical talks programme. I predicted that the audience for such a programme would be enormous, and that whoever was the presenter would become a national figure.

A copy of the memorandum which I put up is still in my possession:

7 July 1955

FROM: Robin Day, Talks Department, 207 B.H.
SUBJECT: NEW MORNING TALKS PROGRAMME
TO: Chief Assistant, Talks (Mr John Green)

I have already discussed with Mr Bonarjee, Mr Macdonald and others the idea of an early-morning Topical Talks Programme. Mr Bonarjee has asked me to put it forward in writing together with my reasons.

In the morning Sound Radio has the public all to itself, and listening figures for that time of day are impressive. The 8 a.m. News has an average audience of 13%. Can we not offer this large and constant audience something intelligent and lively by way of Topical Talks, something more than the present succession of routine items, service talks and light music?

I therefore suggest a new daily morning programme under such a title as 'Morning Review'. . . . Presumably this would be on the only Service at present offered to listeners in the early morning, the Home Service. 'Morning Review' would give intelligent, pithy comment, and description of the sort found on the feature-page of newspapers and in the more serious diary column. . . .

The following are some of the things that might be included:

Comment on some event due to occur that day or week. . . .

Footnotes to the news (historical, personal, legal, humorous, etc.) similar to items in Pendennis or in the *Manchester Guardian* London Letter. *Not* gossip, or tittle-tattle.

Comment on a notable new book published that morning, or on last night's new play, film, or other event in art or entertainment.

Comment on a sporting news item.

Talk on an event occurring late the previous evening or some important news released overnight and heard for the first time on the morning bulletin.

I realize that this proposal may mean radical departures from existing practice with regard to the BBC's morning output. It also raises difficult questions of staffing and organization. But the magnitude of these obstacles is surely the measure of the opportunity open to Radio at this time of day.

As Television advances, Radio will find more and more that early-morning programmes command its big audience. These are now its big opportunity. This is shown by listening figures for the various news bulletins. In the last three years the average audience for the 7 a.m., 8 a.m. and 9 a.m. bulletins has remained constant at 10%, 13% and 9% respectively. Yet for the evening bulletins over the same three years the figures have dropped from 18% to 15% (6 p.m.), 13% to 12% (7 p.m.), 10% to 7% (9 p.m.), 14% to 9% (10 p.m.). This trend will obviously be intensified.

Another point is that there is a steadily increasing

audience to car radios. This element must be particularly large first thing in the morning when people are motoring to work. These people cannot read while driving. Why should we not offer them comment and description that the rail or 'bus traveller can read in his newspaper?

As regards contributors, 'Morning Review' could draw on the younger journalists and broadcasters, anxious to make their names, who ought not to mind getting up for an early programme easily fitted in before their day's work. . . .

I envisage 'Morning Review' as a *daily* programme (Monday to Friday). This is because its principal feature will be its up-to-date quality – overnight comment on things which people may not have yet read about in their morning papers. The programme would thus have the unique advantage of giving a large number of people the first available comment on some late-night news item. . . .

I think this could prove an imaginative enterprise for Radio at what is now a bleak and barren time of day. If something is launched on these lines, I am sure that before long we would look back to the present morning programmes with the same incredulity with which we now regard pre–1939 days, when there was nothing, not even a news bulletin, until mid-morning.

(Signed) Robin Day

A week later, I returned to the attack with another note to John Green:

Room 207 B.H. 14 July 1955

May I back up my memo outlining the suggestion for an early morning topical talks miscellany? It may help you if I give two examples of the character and content that I have in mind for the programme . . . I have taken two days at random during the last fortnight. . . .

Friday, 1 July

1)   Comment on Wimbledon.

2) A note on Evelyn Waugh's newly published novel *Officers and Gentlemen*.
3) A note on the Russian oarsmen at Henley, their style, etc., their lack of boat.
4) A note on the new film starring Elizabeth Taylor.
5) A background comment on the announcement made the previous afternoon about talks on Cyprus.

Thursday, 7 July

1) Note on prospects for third Test Match beginning that morning.
2) Comment on the position in the case of Mrs Sispera.
3) A note on the Royal Agricultural Show.
4) Background comment on previous day's announcement of a round-table conference on Malta.
5) Note on the previous evening's announcement about prospects for colour television.

My proposal was put on the agenda of the monthly meeting attended by scores of producers. The chairman was Andrew Stewart, Controller of the Home Service: 'The next item on the agenda,' (and his voice did not conceal his distaste), 'is a proposal for an early-morning talks programme from Mr-er-' (he managed to find the name) 'Mr Day.' He then summarized my idea and asked, 'Mr Day, do you really think there is a public demand for this sort of thing *in the morning?*' I stood up and responded to his question. After many discussions with colleagues, my answer was ready:

Of course not. But there's never a public demand for anything. There was no public demand in 1939, before war broke out, for early-morning radio news. There was nothing then on national radio until the daily religious service at 10.15 a.m.! But when the public were given their early-morning radio with news, they wanted it. Surely the job of broadcasters is not to decide what the public want, or should want, but to decide what the public should be *offered* so that the public can choose.

I doubt if the solemnity of a massed gathering of BBC Talks producers had ever been disturbed by such an utterance, and from a new boy too, on a very temporary contract.

Shortly afterwards I left BBC Radio to join ITN. I told the producer with whom I shared an office: 'Don't let them forget that morning programme idea. Keep at them. It's got to come.' My colleague's reply shocked me. 'Nobody will pursue it,' he said, 'because it was your idea, and therefore no one else will get the credit. Anyway, it would be far too much work – all that early rising.'

Two years later, radio's *Today* programme was launched. It is now the jewel in Radio Four's crown. In the eighties the programme has been much sharper and harder than in its early years. The golf-club, bar stool manner of Jack de Manio proved inadequate for a programme which, even at breakfast-time, had a duty to cover serious topics seriously. Jack de Manio may have been a popular 'character' in his time, but Brian Redhead, John Humphrys and Sue MacGregor are accomplished radio journalists.

That revolutionary proposal of mine in 1955 had an interesting sequel twenty-five years or so later. This was when Julian Holland, the gifted Editor of *The World at One*, had been appointed to take over and improve *Today*. Julian invited me to come with him to the *Today* team. I enjoyed telling him about my 1955 proposal. But regretfully I felt much too old for 'all that early rising'. In any case, for people with delicate stomachs I would have been rather strong meat for breakfast.

8

ITN

Mr Crawley Will Tell You Something to Your Advantage

In 1955 Eden succeeded Churchill as Prime Minister and won a general election. This was also the year when commercial television was to open. That summer, BBC staff were being lured with lucrative offers. For the first time since the birth of radio in 1922, employees of the BBC would have the chance of an alternative career. The BBC's monopoly was ending. It was a time of conspiratorial excitement in the broadcasting world.

One hot afternoon in June 1955 the telephone rang in my small office on the second floor of Broadcasting House. It was my friend and former flat-mate Ronald Waterhouse. Unlike me, Waterhouse had stayed in practice at the Bar. He knew that I was not content to remain a BBC radio producer. He was telephoning to tell me about a job he had seen advertised at lunchtime on the noticeboard of Gray's Inn. 'I thought you might be interested in this one,' he said. I listened, just in case.

Independent Television News Limited invites applications for the post of 'newscaster'.

What did that mean?

The job would involve helping to prepare, and appearing on

Election results night, June 1970. The puppets of Heath and other Tories were a Labour gimmick to launch the derisive slogan 'Yesterday's Men'. But Labour lost and the anti-Tory slogan rebounded sharply.

The King of Swing: Professor Robert McKenzie of the LSE with his beloved swingometer on election night, 1970.

An election night marathon in the seventies, before the author gave up smoking.

The zenith of the author's career – his appearance on *The Morecambe and Wise Show*, 1975.

HRH Princess Anne, President of the Society of Film and Television Arts, presenting the author with the Richard Dimbleby Award in 1975 'for his enormous contribution to political journalism on television'.

With Edward Heath at a Conservative conference in the '70s.

The author interviewing Harold Macmillan, October 1976, for his first intervention in British politics since he was Prime Minister. He called for a coalition government 'of men of goodwill'.

Interview with Prime Minister James Callaghan during the 1979 election campaign.

Chairing *Election Debate* in the 1979 campaign – with Michael Heseltine, Jo Grimond and Michael Foot

ime Minister Margaret Thatcher, escorted by BBC brass, visits the *World at One* office in Broadcasting
)use, 1980.

rnard Levin asking me (BBC2, 1980) whether it was not rather odd that whereas he was hired to express
; opinions, I was hired not to express mine.

The author with his sons Daniel (left) and Alexander (right) at Buckingham Palace after his investiture, February 1981.

The author, after receiving his knighthood at Buckingham Palace in 1981 with Lady Day and their two sons, Daniel and Alexander, then aged five and seven.

At the Variety Club Dinner, July 1982, to celebrate the sixtieth anniversary of the BBC televised live from the Dorchester Hotel. Laughing on the left, Sir Ian Trethowan.

e author interviewing Prime
nister Margaret Thatcher live from
10 Downing Street for *Panorama*,
ril 1984.

Around the *Question Time* table with me (from left to right), Michael Heseltine, Dr David Owen, Susan Crosland, Dennis Skinner in March 1988.

The author with his sons Alexander (thirteen) and Daniel (eleven) by the sea in Dorset, Christmas 1987.

The author in the Chair at a public meeting (of the legal profession) 1989.

the screen to deliver, the daily news bulletins for the new Independent Television service due to start next Autumn.

This sounded more interesting than I had expected. I wanted to hear more. I suggested to my secretary that it was a convenient moment for her to go for tea. This telephone conversation was not one which should be overheard in Broadcasting House.

I had tried and failed to get a BBC television training course. So to a lowly radio producer, on a temporary BBC contract, the possibility of a job with the new commercial television network was incredibly exciting. With my secretary safely out of earshot, I listened avidly to the rest of the ITN advertisement:

No previous broadcasting experience necessary.

As it happened, I could claim to have had considerable broadcasting experience.

Requirements: sound knowledge of current affairs, ability to think on feet, good presence.

Well, I thought, that's put pretty broadly.

The work might appeal to a barrister thinking of giving up practice. The post would carry a good salary.

It was two years since I had given up practice as a barrister, and the job appealed to me. I had heard little about ITN. I knew that it had been formed by the commercial programme contractors to provide their network news service. I knew also that ITN's Editor was Aidan Crawley, a former Labour MP who had established himself as a TV commentator with his BBC series *Viewfinder*.

I did not hesitate a single moment. By the time my secretary returned from tea I had already written a brief letter of application. I enclosed a list of my qualifications and experience. The letter was in the post within an hour.

A few days later there was an interview and preliminary camera test. That summer scores of would-be ITN newscasters were going in a steady stream for five-minute tests in a closed-circuit TV studio in Hampstead. Some three hundred names were weeded down to six. I was one of the six. We were then summoned for final auditions which were held in Highbury. Not being sure where the place was, I arrived much too early at Finsbury Park tube station. At a wine-merchant's I bought one of those miniature bottles of brandy. I walked into a Lyons tea-shop in the Seven Sisters Road, hoping no one would notice me take the bottle from my pocket and pour the brandy into a cup. It seemed an odd thing to be doing on a sweltering July day. I don't usually feel the need for a drink at a moment of stress. On this occasion I felt a definite need for the fortifying comfort, real or imaginary, of hard liquor.

Sipping that brandy in a Lyons tea-shop in the Seven Sisters Road, I read and re-read the notes of the 'dummy' newscast we had been instructed to prepare. It had to cover the main points of the previous evening's news – about four minutes' material.

We had been sent a summary of the news and told to put it into our own style, choosing our own order of items. The only requirements from Aidan Crawley were that the facts should be clear and that the style should combine the responsibility of the *Manchester Guardian* and the vigour of the *Daily Express*! This was aiming wide and high – typical of Aidan Crawley's approach. This tall, rugged man, with his jutting chin and warm, expansive manner, exuded energy and optimism.

Outside the recording studio I was surprised to meet Cyril Ray, a well-known journalist from the *Sunday Times*, whom I knew as a contributor to the BBC programmes on which I was a producer. We were both embarrassed at meeting. He was one of the final six and had just been tested, so he knew what I was doing there. I begged him not to breathe a word to my superiors at Broadcasting House. As I later discovered, this would not have done my position with the BBC any harm – rather the reverse. He told me how his test had gone. 'Bloody,' he said.

Inside the studio I was told to sit at a table and deliver my newscast straight into the lens of the camera. Only two or three studio technicians were present. Aidan Crawley was in another room to watch the recording being made. The camera lined up its shot. The floor-manager explained the winding-up signals he would give me: 'one minute . . . thirty seconds . . . fifteen seconds . . . out'. He told me to watch for these signals out of the corner of my eye without ever looking away from the camera. I must end exactly on time. This was a vital point of the exercise. Fortunately my piece had been timed carefully.

A message was passed from Aidan Crawley. I was to speak to the camera as if it were a person sitting at home. The camera stood cold and inhuman ten feet away. At first I could hardly pick out the lens because I was dazzled by the fierce battery of lights blazing down upon me. After a few minutes, my eyes adjusted themselves. I fixed my gaze on the small circle of thick glass, hooded by a black tube, like the end of a powerful telescope. It did not seem a very friendly object.

I was ready to go. But there was a little more delay. The lighting was causing trouble with my spectacles – reflection flashes from the lenses and shadows from the heavy hornrims. An engineer climbed up ladders to adjust the arc-lamps until the director in the control room was satisfied. It seemed to take a very long time. I began to sweat under the heat of the lights.

We had been asked to memorize our material so that we would not have to look down. They wanted to see us looking full-face into the camera. I took a final look at my notes. The phrases which last night were crisp and bright seemed limp and dull, but it was too late to make any changes.

'Are you ready?' called the floor-manager. I nodded.

'Stand by.' He stood to one side of the camera, and raised his arm above his shoulder.

'Thirty seconds to go . . . fifteen seconds.'

Suddenly the floor-manager jabbed his hand down towards me. A red light glowed on top of the camera. This was it.

Immediately I found that the last few seconds of studio tension had communicated itself to me. I felt a sudden burst of vitality and a compelling urge to give out the news items I had prepared. No longer did they seem stale or dreary. They were fresh, exciting and charged with vital significance. I rapped out each item with a mounting sense of urgency and crisis. It must have sounded as if I was reporting the end of the world.

I ended exactly on time. I flopped back against the chair. Though at this moment nothing was further from my mind, that working-up, second by second, to the tense climax of transmission was to be part of my daily life during the next few years. Lights, cameras, clocks, signals, were to form the ritual setting for the culmination of a day's work.

'Mr Crawley says thank you very much.'

Aidan Crawley met me outside the studio. He was friendly but non-committal. My spectacles still bothered him. 'Could you get some lighter spectacles?' Crawley enquired.

'Of course,' I replied, sensing that he might still be interested.* We shook hands and he promised to let me know.

Shortly afterwards, Aidan Crawley's secretary rang me at Broadcasting House with the cloak-and-dagger message: 'If you will come to see Mr Crawley tomorrow, he will tell you something to your advantage.' I went, and he did.

As soon as I received Aidan Crawley's offer to join ITN I went to inform John Green, the head of my department in BH. Three weeks previously he had read out to me a somewhat tepid departmental report on my progress. Now, he immediately became effusive. Holding up a bundle of files from his pending-tray, he said: 'But your name is very high on the short-lists for these vacancies on our permanent staff – very high indeed.'

I replied that it was a bit late to tell me that. Green commented: 'I suppose we aren't paying you very much?'

'No,' I said.

'Well, then,' said John Green, 'would it help if I were to ask the Director-General for an immediate and special increase in your salary?' I had a hilarious vision of General Sir Ian Jacob solemnly considering a little memorandum headed, 'The Case of R. Day – Urgent', and weighing in his precise mind the sum appropriate in the circumstances. I was almost struck dumb by this sudden interest towards someone who had battered at the BBC's door for months. For the first time in my life I really understood what competition meant. I was no worthier of the BBC's interest than I had been a month previously. It was simply that someone else was after my services. I had a choice of employer and a chance of earning more.

Suppressing my amusement, I murmured something about it

---

*The lighter spectacles, with half frames, were later obtained but were generally disliked, so normal spectacles were resumed.

being more a question of opportunity. This was true, because my initial salary from ITN was to be only £1,000, hardly more than my BBC pay. I then brought the discussion to a head.

'What would you do if you were me?'

'Do you want me to answer personally or officially?'

'Personally,' I replied hastily.

'I would go,' he said. 'It is obviously a big chance for you.'

A big chance, yes – but a big challenge. Aidan Crawley had offered me only a three-month trial. I might be an abysmal flop. Everyone would know about it. The first efforts of commercial television were bound to come under a fierce spotlight of publicity. Criticism would be merciless. If ITN dropped me, what then? I could hardly go crawling back to the BBC for a nice safe job, rising by increments of fifty pounds a year. But I was not in the mood for 'safety first', I would not be the only new boy at ITN. I liked Aidan Crawley. I felt that I could do the job.

I had taken another gamble.

A Rather Eccentric Choice

When Aidan Crawley chose me to be one of ITN's first news-casters I grasped the offer with both hands and hung on like grim death. That is what many people thought I looked like in my first few months as an ITN newscaster.

Not until years later did I learn the inside story of the battle which Crawley had fought against the ITN Board about my appointment. There was no opposition to his other choice, who was the twenty-four-year-old Christopher Chataway, the star athlete and holder of the world three-mile record. But Crawley had to threaten resignation in order to keep me in this team.

My final newscaster test was seen by several members of the ITN Board. In his autobiography *Leap Before You Look*, Crawley writes:

Sidney Bernstein, head of Granada Television, for whom I had great respect, did not like Robin Day's appearance or manner. . . . I realized that Day's rather acerbic tone and aggressive manner might irritate some people, but to me he

was the ideal antidote to Chataway's film-star looks and
boyish charm . . . and when Sidney seemed adamant and
said he would have to raise the matter at the board, I said
that in that case he would have to find another Editor.*

Within a year or two, Sidney Bernstein (later Lord Bernstein)
was enthusiastically employing me as the chairman of his weekly
audience show *Under Fire*, and in other Granada ventures.

Was Crawley's resignation threat to demonstrate his confidence in me, or to demonstrate his independence as the Editor?
I never had the nerve to ask him. All I know for certain is that
I owe my career to Aidan Crawley's courage. But I do not hold
him in high regard for that alone: Aidan was one of the most
talented all-rounders of his time – cricketer and politician, Fleet
Street journalist, early television star, wartime fighter-pilot and
prison-camp escape leader, Member of Parliament, Minister of
the Crown, President of the MCC, and not least (in my book)
the founding Editor of ITN.

At Oxford in the late twenties, he was the finest all-round
sportsman of his generation. Not only did he play cricket for
Oxford University and for Kent, but (and this was in the days
before limited-over cricket) he hit ten sixes in one innings of a
first-class match. Less than a dozen batsmen in history have
done better than that.

After his Hurricane fighter had been shot down in the North
African desert in 1941, he spent four years in German prisoner-
of-war camps. His escapes, and his exploits as an escape organizer, are legendary. He escaped four times and was recaptured
four times, once near the Swiss border and freedom. He resigned
as founding Editor of Independent Television News because the
ITV contractors refused to give the infant news company
adequate air time or adequate money. Aidan's courage and
vision in that crisis ensured ITN's survival. ITN was the most
important new national organ of news since the war. It went on
to revolutionize TV journalism, and knocked the BBC News for
six in the process. Tragedy befell Aidan in his old age. His gifted
wife, the author Virginia Cowles, was killed in a car crash. Then

---

*Aidan Crawley, *Leap Before You Look* (Collins, 1987), p. 307.

in 1988 his two sons, Andrew and Randall, were killed together when their aeroplane crashed.

On my very first day at ITN in August 1955, I was greeted in a way which did nothing to boost my self-confidence. The half-empty newsroom was being organized in Television House, Kingsway. Desks and typewriters were being put in position. Telephones and tickertape machines were being connected. People were shaking hands and introducing themselves. The atmosphere was one of amicable chaos. Transmission was a month ahead.

I entered the newsroom to report for duty. No one appeared to be in charge. No one paid any attention to me, until a redheaded girl who had been sorting some papers at a desk got up and came over towards me. She was a gorgeous creature, pleasingly plump, and wearing a low-cut summer frock. She exuded (all at once) sex-appeal, authority and humour. She spoke with a pronounced Welsh accent, with every word lovingly articulated. She was obviously rather irritated by the preparatory chaos in the newsroom. I was closely inspected:

'Who the bloody hell are you then?'
'My name is Robin Day.'
'God Almighty! You're one of the newscasters?'
'That's right.'
'Christ! Can't Aidan do better than that?'

This remarkable lady, then aged twenty-three, was Miss Diana Edwards-Jones, who had come from being stage-manager in Swansea Rep to being floor-manager in ITN. 'Floor-manager' is a title which does not convey the importance of her position. She was a key personality of the operation which (eventually) put ITN's programmes on the screen. She was prodigiously efficient, outrageously funny, and her language was legendary. My first fumbling performances on television were made under her guidance. I have been devoted to her ever since. She became ITN's senior director, and has directed NEWS AT TEN, together with ITN's election results and other big programmes, during the last thirty-five years. In 1987 Diana Edwards-Jones was appointed OBE.

I duly appeared on the screen, along with Chris Chataway, as one of ITN's first newscasters. The official historian of Independent Television, Bernard Sendall, wrote in 1982:

> Robin (now Sir Robin) Day was a young barrister whom Crawley had personally selected for the job. Some people at the time thought it was a rather eccentric choice. . . . After 25 years in television and radio journalism, Day is now the acknowledged leader of his profession in Britain.*

In 1955 I knew that many people disliked my style. I tried not to let this rattle me. My most difficult time was before ITN's transmissions began. The three weeks before opening night were a hectic shakedown operation. Camera teams were sent out to cover stories as if news bulletins were already going on the air. People were asked to give filmed interviews that no one would see, for a news service that did not yet exist. Film was rushed back to be developed and cut. At transmission times, the film was screened on the bare newsroom wall by a portable projector.

For these mock news programmes, the producers, newscasters and sub-editors practised their jobs with the real news as it came in on the tape machines. The studio was not operational until twenty-four hours before ITN first went on the air. The mock newscasts had to be done in the newsroom. The producers cued in the film shown on the wall. The newscasters spoke their material to a wooden stand, which was meant to be the camera.

To give some sense of reality, Aidan Crawley assembled the whole of the ITN staff – about a hundred and fifty people – to be an audience. Editorial and production staff, cameramen, technicians, secretaries, despatch-riders, office boys – everybody came crowding in to watch those trial newscasts at fixed 'transmission' times. Five minutes before time all these people would pack the newsroom, standing on tables and chairs, waiting for the newscaster to begin. They were a far more unnerving audience than ever the unseen millions were to be. They were curious to see what it was they were all going to be working for

---

*Bernard Sendall, *Independent Television in Britain*, vol. 1: *1946–62* (Macmillan, 1982), p. 124.

– this television news. They usually went away bewildered and depressed. These newsroom try-outs were invariably a shambles, and bore no noticeable resemblance to a television programme.

. The ITN staff audience focused their cold and critical attention on the newscasters. These were the men whom the public would see. These were the men on whose personalities and performances the whole ITN operation would depend. These were the men whose names and faces would become famous, while the rest of the staff would work anonymously behind the scenes.

Were they up to the job, these two, Chris Chataway and – who was the other? – Robin Day? The ITN staff were not very impressed. Chris and I hated these mock newscasts. We were far worse at them than ever we were when real transmissions began. We fluffed and fumbled. Morale dropped several points after each dummy run.

The staff audience was less hostile to Chris than to me. They had all heard of him and understood his celebrity value. But this fellow Day – who on earth would switch on to watch him? Maybe ITN wasn't looking only for glamour boys, but – well – there were limits, weren't there?

As I waited to begin one of these dummy newscasts I would look round at the unenthusiastic faces of the secretaries. I knew what they were thinking. I was not their idea of a popular audience-winning TV personality. I was quite different from the smooth announcer idols built up by the BBC in the early fifties: McDonald Hobley or Peter Haigh. But I also knew that Aidan Crawley was not looking for announcers. There were to be no announcers or news*readers* in ITN, only news*casters* – television journalists who were to develop their own professional skill and authority. Exactly why Aidan Crawley had chosen me, I must admit I did not fully understand. Mine was not to reason why. I knew it was not because of any potential as a pin-up boy. All I could do was to ignore the hostility, forget that most of my colleagues couldn't stand the sight of me, throw myself into the job, and hope for the best. It was an uphill fight.

My belligerent interpretation of the newscaster's role in preparing the newscasts had made the sparks fly more than once. But I had clear instructions from Aidan Crawley: a straightforward attacking style, whose keynotes were to be clarity and authority. Several ITN colleagues later told me that they pressed Aidan Crawley to get rid of me. I was too unsympathetic, they argued, too harsh in manner.

Three things saved me. One was that Crawley was convinced that I would get over the awkward stage before long and that I had the ability to cope with big news in the way he wanted. Secondly, the ITV audience was very small when we started. Only a very small proportion of the total TV audience saw our early efforts. When ITV opened on 22 September 1955, not more than about 200,000 homes had sets which could receive the new programmes. So I had the chance to dig myself in before the ITV network had begun to spread to the whole country. It could be said, without much exaggeration, that I survived those early weeks because hardly anyone was watching.

My third piece of good fortune was that for the first few months of ITN the newscaster upon whom public attention centred was Chris Chataway. He was an instant success as a personality – partly because his fame as a runner had already made him a national figure (his dramatic victory over Vladimir Kutz in the 5,000 metres was fresh in the public mind), and partly because of his easy, unaffected charm.

With Chris Chataway getting all the limelight during ITN's first few months, my own efforts were spared too much attention. But I was still too intense and aggressive for many people's taste. This description, by Denis Thomas, a television critic, was enjoyed by friend and foe alike:

So unequivocal is Mr Day's relish for his job that he seems at times to be daring you to contradict him. He treats the news with an air which I can only describe as proprietorial, as if he had been out and got it all himself. He hunches forward, often into full close-up, narrowing his eyes meaningfully behind glinting spectacles. Or, withdrawing a foot or two, he bites off some item of less than front-page news with an unspoken hint of deeper significance. When a snippet of film shows him conducting an interview, as at Smithfield during the bummaree dispute, he is practically at his man's lapels. In the studio he puts his blunt, loaded questions with the air of a prosecuting counsel at a murder trial. As he swings back to face the cameras, metaphorically blowing on his knuckles, one detects the muffled disturbance as his shaken victim is led away.*

Aidan Crawley had taken a considerable risk in choosing Chris Chataway, though not so big as the risk he had taken in choosing me. In my case, the risk of whether my forbidding appearance and fierce approach would ever have any appeal to the mass audiences which commercial television was out to capture. In the case of Chataway, the risk was that by choosing a young athletic star as its leading newscaster ITN would be accused of a publicity gimmick and would forfeit any claim to be a serious news service. Aidan Crawley's boldness paid off. The determined intelligence behind Chris Chataway's deceptively casual manner soon showed itself in his handling of the newscaster's job.

Six months after ITN began, Chris moved over to the BBC's *Panorama*. As a young man whose face was recognized wherever he went, he felt that his nightly TV appearances were exposing him to excessive personal publicity in addition to his athletic fame. He wanted to continue on television but less often. Chris would warn me that a television face 'wears out'. To which I would mutter about dealing with that problem when it arose.

As a weekly survey of current issues, *Panorama* was an ideal programme for him to join. Chris was now keenly interested in politics. He entered Parliament, as did Margaret Thatcher, in 1959, and began a promising ministerial career. But for his decision to leave politics in 1974, Chris Chataway would surely have achieved high Cabinet office. Admittedly he was a Heathite Tory, but then so were some of Mrs Thatcher's most valued Cabinet colleagues of recent years.

The first four years of my television career were in ITN. As one of ITN's original newscasters, my starting salary was £1,000 a year. Chris was paid £1,500, which he persists in maintaining was an appropriate differential. But within three months I was appointed ITN's parliamentary correspondent, and was given a longer contract – this time at Chris Chataway's salary level. In

Truth, 22 June 1956.

1957 I began *Roving Report*, a weekly film documentary, in addition to regular newscasting. This took me, within eighteen months of ITN's foundation, to America, Russia, Europe, Africa and Cyprus, and to many crisis areas and trouble-spots of that time.

There was an atmosphere of adventure and experiment in Television House. The newscaster system, which ITN was to launch in British broadcasting, was the most adventurous and experimental feature. 'Newscasting' was explained by Aidan Crawley at a press conference shortly before the start of ITV. The point seized on by the press was that the newscaster was to 'inject something of his personality'.

Veterans of BBC radio news were at first appalled by the idea that a 'newscaster' was not merely to be a newsreader or announcer with a beautiful baritone voice, but a journalist with personality and authority, who was part of the editorial and reporting team. The newscaster was not only to present the news on air but to help write the words to be spoken. To those brought up in the solemn tradition of the announcer-read BBC radio news, this was heresy of the most dangerous kind. It proved, however, to be a heresy which gave ITN distinctive personality from the outset. It also proved (and this was the greatest of ITN's early triumphs) that TV news could be dramatic and vivid and amusing, without being sensational or biased or trivial.

That was Aidan Crawley's simple but revolutionary concept, developed and refined by Crawley's successor, Sir Geoffrey Cox. The newscaster system, coupled with incisive interviewing and imaginative use of the 16 mm sound camera, reached its culmination in 1967 with the brilliant success of *News at Ten*.

To have entered television in 1955 was my great good fortune. Not only had I at last found a profession, but it was a *new* profession, in a new field. Those of us who helped to found television journalism in the mid-fifties were not following an established profession. We were creating a new one as we went along. That was so in Independent Television News. We were a motley, multi-talented crew. Some of us were from Fleet Street, some from what passed for TV news on the BBC of those days. Some were from BBC radio news, some from the cinema newsreels. Others, like myself, were lucky enough to have no directly relevant experience. We were unhindered by long-formed habits in other professions.

Veteran cameramen of the cinema newsreels were irked by having to waste their skill on 'talking heads'. 'What we want is moving pictures, not yakkity-yak.' This was how they contemptuously dismissed the TV interview which was soon to become one of the most important instruments of the new TV journalism. Old hands from Fleet Street found it hard at first to grasp that whereas a page of words can be compressed, footage of film can only be cut. The TV reporter had to be his own sub-editor, by asking crisp, incisive questions to elicit (he hoped) crisp, incisive answers.

In the judgment of Lord Annan's Committee on Broadcasting in 1977: 'the greatest of all changes in the nation's broadcasting system took place when commercial television was born in 1955'. Thirty-five years later it may be hard to realize how revolutionary was the coming of ITV. The BBC had achieved a position in British life which was apparently impregnable. The Conservative government's decision to set up a rival television service, financed by commercial advertising, was taken in the teeth of fierce opposition, much of it within the Conservative party. The establishment was split wide open. On one side was the Labour Party front bench, allied with Lord Hailsham, Lady Violet Bonham Carter and *The Times*. On the other was the Conservative Cabinet, supported by City investors who, urged on by Norman Collins* and others, were ready to risk their capital.

The mid–1950s ushered in a revolution in the social and political life of Britain. Since 1954, television had been spreading at the rate of over a million new homes each year. By 1955 the five-million mark was passed. BBC television transmissions were then already within reach of 94 per cent of the population. In that year, 1955, as Britain was moving towards mass viewing on a nationwide scale, the BBC television monopoly was broken. Under the last administration of Sir Winston Churchill, Parliament had set up the Independent Television Authority 'to make

---

*A former Controller of BBC Television who lobbied for commercial competition. and who did more than anyone else to achieve the creation of ITV.

provision for television broadcasting services in addition to those provided by the British Broadcasting Corporation'. ITV went on the air for the first time on 22 September 1955.

A great gust of fresh air had blown into British broadcasting. Nowhere were the healthy effects of competition more evident (or less expected) than in the coverage of news and current affairs, especially politics. ITN set new standards of vigour, enterprise and pace for television news, making the BBC version look stiff and stuffy, which it was. Ludicrous taboos and restrictions were swept away by the post–1955 wind of change. The notorious 'fourteen-day rule' was dropped. This absurd dictat banned discussion on TV or radio about anything due to be debated in Parliament within a fortnight.

Another post-ITV development was the coverage of TV of elections. Extraordinary though it may now seem, the 1959 general election was the first time a general election campaign had been reported on television like any other news. 1959 was also the first time there were any broadcasts about the election, apart from the parties' own election broadcasts. Radio and television coverage of elections by the BBC had been ludicrously unworthy of a mature democracy. It is an incredible fact of broadcasting history that in the very year that ITN began (1955) there had been a general election in which there was no coverage by BBC broadcasters of the campaign, *not even in the news bulletins*.

The post-1955 wind of change had other effects. Political interviews became less sycophantic. Politicians were asked questions which the public wanted them to answer. Impartiality, for long a fundamental principle of broadcast journalism in Britain, was interpreted more actively. The duty to be fair was seen as enhancing, and not restricting, the right to enquire.

All this did not happen overnight. But television began to be a part of journalism and a part of politics in ways that it never was before 1955. My own entry into television coincided with the enormous impetus which competition gave to the growth of television as a new branch of journalism. The effect of competition, and the BBC's response to it, was to transform the atmosphere in television, to extend the boundaries of freedom, and to begin making television's coverage of politics more appropriate to the second half of the twentieth century.

This is not, however, to belittle the pioneering efforts of BBC television in current affairs, if not in news, before 1955. Notably there was Mrs Grace Wyndham Goldie, who tried hard to free television from the inhibitions inherited from radio. Christopher Mayhew and Aidan Crawley had made television reputations with their BBC documentaries.

But the brutal truth is that many of the famous topical programmes for which the BBC won high prestige did not come into being until after ITV (and especially ITN) started in 1955. *Tonight* did not begin until 1957. *Monitor*, the arts programme, did not begin until 1958. John Freeman's *Face to Face* interviews did not begin until 1959. This was a year after ITN had run the first regular series of lengthy interviews with eminent people. *Panorama*, that flagship of the BBC fleet, was not launched in its weekly form until the same month that ITV first went on the air. (There had been an earlier version of *Panorama* in the period 1953–5, but this was a fortnightly 'magazine' and was shaken up under new management in 1955.)

The BBC, at first stunned, was invigorated by competition and hit back boldly. In May 1956 Chris Chataway was taken on by *Panorama*. But for Chris having emerged as ITN's star personality, *Panorama* would never have looked at him. I recall Chris saying to me: 'All the BBC would offer me before ITN started were sports programmes and *What's My Line!*'

Talented BBC producers such as Michael Peacock and Donald Baverstock had their salaries jacked up to prevent their leaving the Corporation. When ITV began, many BBC people had seized the chance to move over. Some of these had already made a name on the BBC. Others were unknown people who had not been able to find an opening in BBC Television. I was one of those.

To begin in television when competition began in 1955 was a golden opportunity.

From the Sewers of Port Said to the Studios of ITN

The creation of ITN in 1955 was a landmark in British journalism. A new organ of national news appeared as a daily challenge to Fleet Street and to the BBC. The style and character of ITN, soon established, was in sharp contrast to the BBC's television news. ITN was attempting something entirely new in British journalism and broadcasting. Our aim was to combine the punch and sparkle of Fleet Street with the impartiality and accuracy required by Act of Parliament. We were determined to present the news with humanity and humour, and a spirit of enquiry. Newspapers had long been free to do this. But Fleet Street could brighten its pages by crusading, campaigning and attacking. ITN had to obey Section 3(1)c of the Television Act 1954, which laid down that any news should be presented with 'due accuracy and impartiality'.

This statutory requirement denied to ITN the freedom of Fleet Street. But it was also a guarantee to ITN's Editor of his independence and integrity, of non-interference from proprietorial prejudice or political influence. Sir Geoffrey Cox, ITN's Editor for twelve years, had previously experienced the problems of a journalist working for newspaper proprietors. In his enthralling book, *See It Happen: The Making of ITN*, Sir Geoffrey explains why, for him, Section 3(1)c of the Television Act was an advantage to be profoundly welcomed, rather than a restraint to be chafed at. Sir Geoffrey relates that when he read the clause in the Bill requiring accuracy and impartiality, he realized at once that this would free an editor of television news from proprietorial pressures, and 'would give him the freedom to create something new in popular journalism'.*

Geoffrey Cox, a New Zealander, had first come to Britain as a Rhodes Scholar. In the thirties he became a foreign correspondent (that was in the age of the great foreign correspondents) for the *Daily Express* and the *News Chronicle*. He covered the Spanish Civil War (narrowly escaping execution by a firing squad), the Anschluss and the Finnish War. In the Second

---

*Geoffrey Cox, *See It Happen: The Making of ITN* (The Bodley Head, 1983), p. 47.

World War he was a soldier in action in Africa and Italy. Earlier in the war, a spell as New Zealand's Chargé d'Affaires in Washington gave him, at the age of thirty-two, the heady experience of representing his country on the Pacific War Council at the same table as President Roosevelt and Winston Churchill.

Before becoming Editor of ITN, Cox had been on the *News Chronicle* as lobby correspondent and assistant editor. There has been no other television executive with his rich experience, in war and peace, of newspapers, soldiering and diplomacy. In my judgment, Sir Geoffrey Cox is the greatest television journalist we have known. His tremendous achievements should be more widely appreciated. He built up ITN during his twelve years as Editor into a highly popular and respected success. He proved that television journalism does not have to be trivial or yellow to win an audience. He created *News at Ten* (against stiff ITV resistance), thus proving that the public may not know what they want until it is offered to them. Cox implanted in younger generations of TV journalists his profound belief that truth and fairness are principles which do not inhibit but inspire great journalism. He brought into TV journalism many new recruits whose talent and potential he had shrewdly discerned, such as Ian Trethowan, Alastair Burnet, Sandy Gall, Nigel Ryan, Peter Sissons, Andrew Gardner, Julian Haviland and David Nicholas.

To a young man entering this new profession, there could not have been two finer editors under whom to work than Aidan Crawley and Geoffrey Cox. To Aidan, I owe my original chance. He also gave me time to come through. Geoffrey Cox gave me my first major reporting assignments and encouraged me to develop the arts of interviewing and film reporting.

ITN gathered momentum swiftly. The atmosphere was one of creative tension. Rival enthusiasms clashed. Cameramen would fume about the film editors. Film editors would curse the cameramen. Reporters would grumble that their most brilliant question had ended up on the cutting-room floor. Newscasters, particularly myself, were a target of abuse on all sides. The subeditors would complain that the newscasters had mauled their copy. The Editor would rebuke the newscasters for not mauling it enough.

The individual styles of the newscasters were to be a central feature of ITN's image. My style was a minority taste. Fortunately the Editor was among that minority. There was more than one deputation to Crawley urging him to remove me from the screen. Four months were to pass before I won acceptance from my ITN colleagues.

My breakthrough to their confidence came on the night of 13 January 1956, which was the day that Aidan Crawley's resignation as Editor was announced and accepted. He had been fighting a battle with the ITN Board (whose members were tycoons of the entertainment world) against cuts in money and air time. The Independent Television authority, whose Chairman was then Sir Kenneth Clark, ruled that there must be at least twenty minutes of news per day. This was to be the sheet anchor of ITN's existence. Crawley's fight saved ITN. But he and the ITN Board had lost faith in each other, so he resigned, feeling that he had won his battle and that ITN's future was safe.

Aiden Crawley's resignation turned out to be a professional milestone for me. I was newscasting that night. I suggested to Crawley that we should invite Kenneth Clark to be interviewed in the late bulletin about the ITN dispute. But Crawley feared that to ventilate the ITN dispute in this way might look like grinding his own axe. I argued that Sir Kenneth Clark should be interviewed just like any other public figure at the centre of an important news story. Then Crawley, who had been doing some of the important interviews for ITN, said he could not do this one because he was personally involved. So I offered to do the interview myself. To my surprise, Crawley agreed. To my even greater surprise, Sir Kenneth Clark agreed. I prepared to question him on the late news that night. It was my first 'live' television interview.

I was in a delicate position. I was subject to the Editor's control. Aidan Crawley tried to persuade me not to put questions which might give the impression that he was using me for his own purposes. However, with the Editor personally implicated as the subject of a major news item, this was a unique situation. The Editor was manifestly not the best judge of what questions were to be put. With some relish, I reminded him of ITN's statutory duty to be accurate and impartial. I told him that

I could not skate over anything vital, and would have to use my own judgment.

It was a crucial moment for me and for the staff of ITN. My ITN colleagues – whether on duty or at home – would be watching anxiously. Aidan Crawley's vision of ITN's future had led many of them to join. Was the news company for which they had such high hopes on the brink of extinction? Were their jobs in danger? These fears, justified or not, existed. Now was the time to clear the air. The *Evening News* TV critic, Kendall McDonald, described the interview as a 'dramatic end to the evening's viewing', and reported: 'Robin Day hammered at Sir Kenneth Clark so hard that at one stage a definitely worried look came into Sir Kenneth's eyes. Full marks.'* I was not consciously 'hammering' Sir Kenneth. I was merely putting simple, straightforward questions to which answers were anxiously awaited.

Here was the chairman of a public authority being cross-examined on TV about his responsibilities by one of the employees. This was unprecedented. I had no option but to put the relevant questions, as in any other news interview. Was Aidan Crawley right to resign? Did Sir Kenneth agree with Crawley that news was not getting its right place? Did he think that programme companies whose main business was light entertainment were the right people to provide news? What was his answer to criticism that the ITA was 'becoming weak-kneed, and losing control'? The interview continued on these lines for several minutes and overran the bulletin time.

The interview drew from Sir Kenneth important declarations of ITA policy, in particular that 'the Authority believes that a full and responsible news service of at least twenty minutes a day is essential'. From the start, Sir Kenneth declared, the Authority's policy had been that news should be one of the principal items, and 'We intend to uphold that.' These answers, obtained from the Chairman of the ITA, did much to raise the morale of the ITN staff.

The official historian of Independent Television writes that this interview 'was a milestone not only for Day but for ITN and

*__Evening News__, 14 January 1956.

for the ITA itself'.* It was not only my first live television inter-view; Kendall McDonald's report in the *Evening News* was the first favourable press notice I had received, after four months of regular TV appearances. Most important of all, the interview won respect from my ITN colleagues. The questions I had put to the Chairman of the ITA were the questions which they wanted answering. A veteran sub-editor, who had clashed sharply with me many times in the newsroom, was good enough to greet me the next morning: 'I take off my hat to you.'

There were no more deputations from my colleagues to the Editor to demand my removal from the screen. The reaction was so friendly that I had a sudden feeling of shock at having asked questions which had apparently been so daring. Yet there was nothing outrageous or impertinent in what I had asked. They were simply questions that needed answering. That this should have made such an impression is a significant reflection on what had been the traditional style of broadcast interviewing. It even impressed a person rarely given to compliments, Michael Peacock of the BBC. He was then beginning to establish his reputation as the tough young producer of *Panorama*. 'Your interview with Sir Kenneth Clark,' he said bluntly, 'was the first time you made any real impact on me.'

It was just as well for commercial television that its news service was not allowed to be mutilated or trivialized. Within a year of Geoffrey Cox taking over from Aidan Crawley any notion that the television audience was not interested in news was shattered by world events: Nasser's nationalization of the Suez Canal, the Hungarian uprising crushed by Russia, and the Suez fiasco, leading to Eden's resignation and to Macmillan's surprise appointment as Prime Minister.

The momentous year 1956 was a fascinating first taste of what was to be my working life in television. For the next three decades, as a film reporter or interviewer, I was to cover politics and politicians at home, and the conflicts, crises and upheavals of the post-imperial world.

First, there burst upon us the supreme crisis of the fifties. All that summer I had witnessed the political drama of Suez at

*Sendall, *Independent Television in Britain*, vol 1: *1946–62*, p. 144.

Westminster. I reported the tempestuous and impassioned scenes in the House of Commons. Sir Anthony Eden came under furious attack. He was amazingly calm and courteous at the despatch box, if not in private.

One Conservative MP on whom the Suez debates made a deep impression was the barrister Peter Rawlinson.* He had been elected only the previous year. In his memoirs he describes the Suez scenes at Westminster as 'sensational parliamentary theatre'. Lord Rawlinson adds:

> No parliamentarian who did not live through those weeks can really claim to understand the nature of the House of Commons. In few other national assemblies could the leader of a nation be confronted daily, and for weeks on end, by nearly three hundred shouting and jeering political opponents.†

I, alas, have never been a parliamentarian, except in spirit. But I lived through those momentous weeks, and witnessed Eden's ordeal from the press gallery. There has been no parliamentary spectacle in my time to compare with it.

On 12 and 13 September 1956, Parliament had been recalled in mid-recess for an emergency debate on the Suez crisis. As ITN's parliamentary correspondent it was my job to report the two-day debate. In those days there were no radio broadcasts of Parliament from which could be taken key passages of sound to be played behind 'stills' of those speaking. Television could present only a verbal summary by the reporter, illustrated where possible by pictures, maps and so on. Normally a seven-hour debate would be summarized in about one-and-a-half or two minutes. But on these nights I was allowed, and encouraged, to take whatever time I needed. This came to about seven or eight minutes, which was an unheard-of length for a report to camera in a news bulletin.

My reports were delivered live to camera in the ITN studio after I had rushed back from Westminster by taxi. My material

---

*Later Sir Peter Rawlinson QC, Attorney-General 1970–4, now Lord Rawlinson of Ewell.

†Peter Rawlinson, *A Price Too High* (Weidenfeld & Nicholson, 1989), p. 68.

was unscripted, and ad-libbed from notes, which I had made as the debates proceeded. I doubt if any parliamentary report had ever before been broadcast without having been pre-scripted. Nor, I think, had any broadcaster been permitted, let alone encouraged, to mix (as in a sketch) colour and comment with his factual report of a debate. ITN's Editor, Sir Geoffrey Cox, himself an experienced parliamentary reporter, writes of my 'mingling description with an element of evaluation which was then rare, if not unknown, in political broadcast reporting'.*

ITN's late bulletin then went out, as the final programme of the network, at 10.45 p.m. Thus we could overrun in emergencies, and overrun we did on these two nights. The debate was an historic parliamentary occasion, charged with great political and personal drama.

The political drama at Westminster centred on whether force should be used against Egypt's President Nasser. In July 1956 Nasser had suddenly nationalized the Suez Canal in defiance of the international convention which guaranteed free and open navigation through it. For over eighty years the Canal had been a vital lifeline of the British Empire. Deep-seated emotions were aroused. On the right, resentment over the loss of imperial power, the rise of third-world nationalism, and the American take-over of world leadership. On the left, passionate opposition to the use of force by Britain. Hugh Gaitskell, the Labour leader, demanded that Eden should not use force except in accordance with the UN Charter. Sir Anthony Eden responded that there must be no abject appeasement of a dictator, as in pre-war years. And in the debate on 2 August Gaitskell himself had compared Nasser to Hitler and Mussolini.

The excitement of being at that moment of history may be apparent from these verbatim, unrevised excerpts from my ad-libbed reports – rough, repetitive and unpolished though they read today:

Well, at 2.34 precisely the cry went up in the corridors of Parliament, 'Mr Speaker in the Chair,' and the Commons were sitting again. Because the debate was to begin

*Cox, *See It Happen*, p. 74.

straightaway, without Question Time, the House was completely crowded out for prayers, which is extremely unusual. The Speaker rose and spoke in his deep Scots voice. He said, as he always says, but this time he seemed to say it with a special sense of occasion – 'Order, order.' And there was silence. The House was on tenterhooks for a minute while a couple of formalities were dealt with. Then the Speaker called: 'Sir Anthony Eden.' A long, loud, deep-throated cheer came up, not just the murmured 'Hear, hear, hear, hear,' which normally passes for cheering in the House of Commons, but something much more. Sir Winston Churchill joined in as hard as he could go, his head jutting forward in time with the cheers.

The Prime Minister began calmly and deliberately. He said he had to remind the House first of what was at stake in this Suez business. More than half Europe's oil passes through the Canal, and it was beyond dispute that any prolonged interference with traffic through the Canal would be a grievous blow to the economy of Western Europe. . . .

Then Sir Anthony sprang his surprise on the House, his surprise plan. Britain, France and America are to set up without delay this new organization, this 'Users' Association', to enable countries who use the Canal to exercise their rights. . . .

. . . Sir Anthony added: 'I must make it quite clear that if the Egyptian government does not co-operate with this Users' Association, then we will be free to take such further steps as seem to be required, either through the United Nations, or by other means.' This brought a loud chorus of protest from the Opposition, shouts of 'What do you mean, "other means"?' and 'What a peacemaker!'

Referring to the United Nations, the Prime Minister said he had reported the position to the President of the Security Council, but he reminded the House that the Security Council had not proved very effective over Abadan. Then he spoke of the use of force. 'It is ludicrous,' he said, 'to charge me with sabre-rattling.' Egypt was the first to use force. The Canal Company's offices had been seized by armed agents of Egypt. . . . The government, he said, had no intention of relaxing our military precautions, and when he said that the cheers were such that it was some time before he could continue.

'I would like to finish,' Sir Anthony said, 'on a personal note. Once again as in the pre-war years, we are faced with an act of force, which if not checked, will lead to others. There must be no abject appeasement. We shall work by peaceful negotiation as long as possible, but if that should fail, the government must be free to take whatever steps are open to it to restore the situation. That is the policy,' and the Prime Minister raised his voice to a shout, 'that is the policy I am asking the House to approve.'

Sir Anthony sat down. The terrific din of cheering for him mingled with the Labour Party's reception for Mr Gaitskell. He moved in straight to the attack. 'I am sorry to say,' he said, 'that what the Prime Minister has told us cannot but divide the nation even more deeply.' He said things have changed quite a bit since the debate of August 2nd. . . . Mr Gaitskell said either the Government did seriously intend to use force, and what the Prime Minister had said this afternoon seemed to suggest that, or of course they may be simply bluffing.

Mr Gaitskell attacked the Prime Minister's new plan for a Users' Association. 'That seems to me', he said, 'dangerously like a thoroughly provocative step.' He went on: 'What happens if we go to war with Egypt? The Russians may not come in. Russian volunteers probably would. Are the government prepared to risk a general war over this issue? Why,' he asked, 'why should the dispute not go to the Security Council at once?' Mr Gaitskell summed up: 'We must press our case through the United Nations. Force would be justified in self-defence, but it is not justified as a solution to this problem.'

Well, through these two opening speeches, the House and its galleries were absolutely chock-full, not a seat anywhere. Members were sitting on the floor and had overflowed into the galleries. The Diplomatic Corps was there in full force in the gallery – twenty-seven ambassadors, five high commissioners, and thirteen chargés d'affaires.

The blunt fact is that there is now a clear clash of parliamentary opinion between Government and Opposition on how to deal with Colonel Nasser. The unity which appeared to pervade Parliament on August 2nd has now completely evaporated.

May I sum up this clash of opinion. The Opposition say we must not take the law into our own hands. The Government say, in effect, if Nasser gets away with this, then it will be like Hitler all over again. And the surprise development tonight is that the government are going to ask for a vote of confidence tomorrow, and the Labour Party have tabled a censure amendment to the government motion.

The following night, 13 September 1956, I reported the second day of this emergency debate. Its final moments were tumultuous and impassioned. Eden gave a qualified assurance about the use of force. My colleague Ludovic Kennedy was the ITN newscaster, and gave the news of what Eden had said. Then, tremendously excited, I delivered my unscripted seven-minute report, or sketch:

First let me remind you of what the Prime Minister said in the last five minutes of this great debate. As Ludovic Kennedy told you at the beginning of the programme, Sir Anthony said this: 'If Egypt breaks the 1888 Convention again in dealing with its new Users' Association, we will take them to the Security Council of the United Nations,' and at this there was prolonged and triumphant cheering from the Labour Opposition.

The second thing the Prime Minister said was – and this was in reply to repeated demands from Mr Gaitskell for a statement on the use of force – the second thing was that we would only use force in accordance with our obligations under the United Nations, 'except', and here Sir Anthony said with great firmness, thumping the despatch box, 'and no government would say anything more than this – except in an emergency'.

There were moments – moving moments – of great drama

during Sir Anthony Eden's speech. He said ever since one had been young in uniform, war had been a background to one's life. . . . 'War is not what we want.' He picked up a bound copy of Hansard and quoted from his famous resignation speech of 1938 against appeasement. He said: 'Then the majority of the country was against me, but the Right Honourable gentleman, the Member for Woodford' – Sir Winston Churchill, and he pointed at him – 'was in agreement with me, and he agrees with me today.' Sir Winston nodded several times.

Although the Opposition divided the House, the difference between the two parties seems to be less than it was yesterday. Mr Gaitskell made a conciliatory winding-up speech and he begged the Prime Minister, as he put it, to seize his big chance. He asked him to say two things to the House, that (like Mr Dulles had said today in Washington) he would not shoot his way through the Suez Canal. And secondly, that he would only use force in accordance with the United Nations Charter. What the Prime Minister answered to that I have told you. . . .

The beginning of the afternoon was not particularly edifying. The Foreign Secretary and Mr Robens made speeches which could have been worthier of the occasion. There were moments when it seemed this great debate was going to degenerate into a personal slamming match between the two front benches. . . .

It was the back-benchers on both sides of the House who raised the level of the argument. . . . And the man who started the ball of moderation rolling was Sir Lionel Heald, QC, a Conservative, speaking with the authority of an ex-Attorney-General who had represented Britain in many international disputes. He said that we were bound to refer the matter to the Security Council before resorting to force. He said the government had never suggested otherwise, but if they were to say this, a very great deal – as Sir Lionel put it – 'a very great deal of the steam would disappear'. Up jumped Mr Gaitskell who asked the government if they agreed with Sir Lionel. The Foreign Secretary asked Mr

Gaitskell to await the Prime Minister's speech. The Prime
Minister said what you have already heard.

Although the backbenchers' part of the debate was calm
and courteous, it did have its moments of interest. There
was one member who . . . referred to the 'click-clack of the
Manchester Guardian's knocking knees which could be
heard all over the world'. A Labour Member amused the
House by suggesting that Burgess and Maclean were behind
the whole business.

Once again it brought a full house and many celebrity
onlookers. I noticed Lord Montgomery and the Archbishop
of Canterbury in the gallery. Lady Eden came to hear the
Prime Minister at the end of the debate, and Sir Hartley
Shawcross put in one of his rare appearances on the floor of
the House. . . .

The duty of reporting these momentous Suez debates was yet
another experience which convinced me that parliamentary
debates should be televised.

In mid-November 1956, I flew into Port Said from Cyprus.
This was my first foreign assignment with an ITN film crew.
British forces, and ITN star cameraman Cyril Page, had already
landed. Cyril was a masterly operator, not only with the camera.
He was even said to have got his ulcers wholesale. In Port Said
he was on nickname terms with the top Army brass. He knew
how to fix everything, and everyone, everywhere. So, in my
experience, do most TV cameramen, but Cyril Page was in a
class by himself. He was a great comfort to a green reporter.

I had landed in Port Said thinking of myself as a war correspondent, but the war, if it was a war, was over before I arrived.
The military action had ceased. A ceasefire had been ordered.
Our advance troops had been halted half-way down the Canal
at El Cap. But there was much to be filmed in that extraordinary
situation. I drove around the battle-scarred streets of Port Said
in a British Army jeep. I was shadowed by a twenty-one-year-old
national service officer who had PR duties, Second-Lieutenant
Michael Parkinson. About sixteen years later on his television
chat-show, Parkinson told me that his job in Port Said had been
'to keep an eye' on me because I was on some War Office list

of 'radicals'. I did not have the slightest recollection of him, so he cannot have given me any trouble.

The British attack on Port Said had not improved the town's sewage system. The invaders therefore put in experts to mend the system and prevent disease. Among the many Army officers who had been recalled from the reserve was a captain in the Royal Engineers, who was the Borough Surveyor of Chelsea. I found him down an evil-smelling manhole in a Port Said street. With his head and shoulders just above road level, he gave me an interview. When it ended after a couple of minutes, I turned to the camera and said solemnly, in a spontaneous adaptation of a typical commentator's hand-over: 'I return you now from the sewers of Port Said to the studios of ITN.' I understand this was much enjoyed, even by my esteemed colleague Ludovic Kennedy, who was newscasting that night.

It is odd how one's recollection of historic world events may be less of the great event itself than of some incidental remark which encapsulates the drama or absurdity of what happened. The only words I can remember of all the words I heard in Port Said about the Anglo-French action were spoken to me by a senior British Army officer. After our troops had been halted, they handed over to a blue-helmeted Danish contingent of UN troops. I spoke to the red-tabbed British officer, his eyes just able to see below his cheese-cutter. Neither camera nor microphone was with me. I asked him in a confidential voice what he thought about Eden's Suez venture. The senior British officer looked to right and left in case we could be overheard. He replied in an equally confidential voice: 'What I always say is, if you're going to be a shit, be a fucking shit.'

Colonel Nasser Drops In

Seven months later I was in Egypt again, this time in Cairo to interview President Gamal Abdel Nasser. This was the first interview Nasser had given to any British or American reporter since Suez. It was also my first major interview. The Nasser interview was an ITN scoop which made headlines not only in the British press but around the world.

The atmosphere was tense. Two British businessmen had been convicted of espionage. Britain and Egypt were not in diplomatic relations. The Foreign Office was not informed until we were on our way to Cairo. The interview had been arranged in a roundabout way, through the Indian High Commission in London, and with the help of an unofficial go-between, a maverick pro-Nasser Tory MP, Colonel Banks.

Few of my interviews have been so thoroughly prepared. Geoffrey Cox and George Ffitch took it in turns to be Nasser, fencing with me as I put questions and supplementary questions. As soon as I reached Cairo, the responsibility passed to me. I had no contact with ITN. It was for me to deal with the Egyptian officials who tried to limit my questions. The interview had been arranged on the basis that no questions were excluded and that I was to be free to raise the questions which were uppermost in the minds of the British public. I would submit areas to be covered, but not specific questions.

To strengthen my hand, I had with me the written authority of my Editor to withdraw if there was any attempt to limit my right of questions.

Nasser kept us waiting for a long week in the Semiramis Hotel, Cairo. His officials warned me against raising questions in some of the areas I had indicated. My dilemma was acute and was to be repeated in other forms, in other circumstances, many times in subsequent years. If I agreed not to put the 'banned' questions, the interview would be a sham. If I persisted and Nasser cut short the interview, the film might be confiscated and there would be nothing to show at all.

The Editor of ITN had sent me to Cairo only after it had been agreed in negotiations for the interview that I would have complete freedom to question President Nasser. In return, his answers were to be shown in full. If there was a last-minute attempt to limit my right to ask questions, I was fully entitled to pull out. On the other hand, I was not to jeopardize the whole operation by making a fuss over an inessential point or by raising delicate issues tactlessly. The responsibility lay on my shoulders. There was no producer except me. The Editor was two thousand miles away at home with his fingers crossed. I decided to speak plainly but politely to President Nasser as soon as I was able to get a word with him alone.

The Egyptian President came walking out into the sunshine with one of his little children. I was immediately struck by his size. Gamal Abdel Nasser was a big man – six feet two, with broad shoulders. He was very friendly. He autographed my copy of his book, *Egypt's Liberation*, the bible of Arab Nationalism. He asked me how much it had cost to buy in England and joked: 'I don't seem to have made much money from it despite everybody's interest in it.' I strolled with him in the garden, and explained that I felt it essential to raise certain points in the interview. Before I could go into any details he brushed the matter aside and said he didn't mind what I asked. It was a moment of great relief after the long week of waiting in Cairo, a week of wondering when the interview would be fixed, whether it would ever be fixed at all, and whether I would be prevented, when the time came, from asking vital questions.

The interview lasted nearly twenty minutes. The news agencies clamoured for the full transcript and circulated much of it around the world. Nasser had made a simple point directly to the British people: he hoped Egypt and Britain could be friendly again. It was the twig of an olive branch. Foreign newspapers made more of this than did our own. For Nasser to have given such an interview on television to the country which had recently invaded his was a remarkable event.

A sure sign that ITN had arrived on the international stage was the column devoted to the interview in *Time* magazine:

Sitting before the cameras of Britain's Independent Television News – as Russia's Khrushchev did for CBS in the US – Nasser sent an amiable grimace into several million British living rooms. . . . Confronted with a direct question of Egyptian policy toward Israel – whether he really wanted to see its destruction as a state – Nasser tried desperately to fight his way between the Charybdis of a yes that would please Arabs and the Scylla of a no that would mollify the West.

'There is a difference,' he said, squirming visibly, 'between

the rights of Palestine Arabs and the destruction of Israel.
We cannot gamble a big war.'

'Then,' said Day, 'is it right that you now accept the
permanent existence of Israel as an independent sovereign
state?'

'Well, you know,' said Nasser, 'you are jumping to
conclusions.'

'No,' said Day, 'I am asking a question.'*

In the *News Chronicle* the major significance of the interview
was appreciated by the veteran reporter James Cameron, who
saw that it was more than just a scoop. Cameron's report was
on the front page, under the banner headline 'COLONEL NASSER
DROPS IN':

Sitting in the garden of his Cairo home, President Nasser
leaned forward last night into British television screens.
And he asked that we reunite in friendly relations. He thus
did something that had never been done before in the
history of international diplomacy.

For the first time on record, a national leader submitting
a major point of national policy, by-passed all protocol and
sent his message into the homes of another state *at a time
when the two were not in diplomatic relations*.†

The Nasser interview was transmitted at the infuriatingly late
hour of five past eleven. This, Geoffrey Cox acidly observed,
'was the best time the ITV programme companies were prepared
to allocate'.‡ But though it was seen by only a minority audience, the interview impressed the professionals. Later that year
(1957) the Guild of Television Producers and Directors elected
me 'TV Personality of the Year', which was what they then called
the award given for TV journalism.

There was an interview in ITN's first year which I mention
because others regard it as memorable. It was an interview I
did with former President Harry S. Truman when he came to

Time, 1957.
†*News Chronicle*, 2 July 1957.
‡Cox, *See It Happen*, p. 111.

England in 1956 to publicize his memoirs and to receive an honorary degree at Oxford. Though the interview was lively and brisk, I was not conscious of it being anything special. But Sir Geoffrey Cox in his book about ITN devotes two pages to a flattering account, from which (with his permission) I will quote because I have no clear recollection of the details. Sir Geoffrey may be too generous, but who am I to challenge his judgment?

Ex-President Truman was making his first visit to Europe since he had left office. A don at Somerville College was campaigning against his getting the honorary degree. She argued that the man who authorized the dropping of the atomic bombs on Hiroshima and Nagasaki was no man for Oxford to honour.

I had the greatest admiration for Harry Truman and did not think he would have the slightest difficulty in coping with an opening question arising from the Oxford protest. Sir Geoffrey Cox writes, 'in the broadcasting climate of the time this might be thought discourteous to Truman and to the office he had held'.* Tradition demanded, says Sir Geoffrey, that if a question about the degree and the dropping of the bombs were to be put, if at all, it should come later. But Sir Geoffrey saw why I wanted to open with it. It was a question concerning a decision on which we had not been able to question Truman before – the gravest decision any world leader had ever taken. So when I sat down with Mr Truman in Claridge's ballroom, I went (according to Sir Geoffrey) swiftly to the point, although my first question was actually quite innocuous:

Q: Mr President, I understand one reason for your visit is to receive an Honorary Degree at Oxford?
A: That is so.

Mr Truman looked pleased.

Q: Are you aware, Mr President, that a lady at Oxford University is campaigning against your receiving that degree because you authorized the dropping of the atomic bomb?

*Cox, *See It Happen*, p. 53.

Mr Truman seemed (according to Sir Geoffrey's account) disconcerted for a brief moment.

A: No, I am not aware of that.
Q: Mr President, do you regret having authorized the dropping of the atomic bomb?

Mr Truman's concentration tightened:

A: No. I do not. I made the decision on the information available to me at the time, and I would make the same decision on the same information again. But you can read all about it in my memoirs.
Q: Mr President, this programme is going out to people who cannot afford thirty shillings even for the memoirs of a former President of the United States. Won't you explain your reasons a bit further?

Mr Truman did just that, clearly and forcefully. Sir Geoffrey Cox writes it was 'marvellous television', and confirmed his 'faith in the probing TV interview not only as a revolution in political journalism but as excellent viewing'. He even used to show it to recruits as a model!*

That such a short and simple interview, done for the news bulletin, should have then seemed remarkable or noteworthy is a measure not of the interviewer's talent, but of the dullness and stiffness and insipidity which had been so common in broadcast journalism.

My first interview series was ITN's *Tell the People*. This was the Sunday evening interview programme in which Macmillan was interviewed in February 1958.† This was the first regular series of interviews on TV with politicians and other public figures. There had been programmes like the BBC's *Press Conference* with three or four questioners, and magazine programmes like *Panorama* or *This Week* which might include a political interview. But there had not been a series consisting solely of

---

*Cox, *See It Happen*, pp. 52–4.
†See above, pp. 1–9.

interviews by one interviewer, with political balance maintained not within each programme but over the series.

Tell the People lasted only six months, from January to June 1958. The ITV programme companies were not happy about ITN thus branching out. They preferred to make their own interviews with top people. But *Tell the People*, though short-lived, was a success. It made big news, often front-page news, almost every week. Apart from the interview with Harold Macmillan, I had other memorable encounters in this series, which included interviews with Rab Butler, Hugh Gaitskell, Vice-President Nixon, Aneurin Bevan, the Governor of the Bank of England (an historic first for a holder of that office), the Soviet Ambassador, General Moshe Dayan, the Metropolitan Police Commissioner, Moira Shearer, Wernher von Braun, Pietro Annigoni, Bob Boothby, Ingrid Bergman and the great Sugar Ray Robinson, 'the finest fighter pound for pound of all time'. Not an uninteresting bunch, it may be thought. Quite a little feather in ITN's cap.

Ingrid Bergman had been a screen goddess for my generation. I nervously presented her with a huge bunch of flowers in her suite at the Connaught Hotel when I went to arrange the interview. Ingrid was of a bigger build, and much taller than I expected from her movies. Her beauty was enchanting. She boasted charmingly that she was the only actress in the world who could act in five languages.

The interview in that same series with Aneurin Bevan produced an interesting footnote to history. At the end of my interview, I asked him: 'Do you still regard Mr Gaitskell as a "desiccated calculating machine"?' This phrase has passed into the political language. It was in Bevan's speech at the 1954 *Tribune* meeting, which I had myself heard in Scarborough. It was generally taken as referring to Hugh Gaitskell. But Bevan replied: 'I never called him that. I was applying my words to a synthetic leader, but the press took it up, and it's never possible to catch up with a canard like that, as you know.' The interview was live, and at that point time ran out.

By 'synthetic' Bevan had meant that he had no individual target in mind. But in the hospitality room afterwards I tackled him again: 'Surely you must have had Hugh Gaitskell in mind when you used those words?' Gaitskell had succeeded Attlee as Leader in the year following Scarborough. Again Bevan replied: 'Of course I wasn't referring to Hugh Gaitskell. For one thing Hugh is not desiccated – he's highly emotional. And' – with a twinkle – 'you could hardly call him a calculating machine – because he was three hundred million pounds *out*!' This was a dig at a misjudgment by Gaitskell when Chancellor.

In its very early days, long before the half-hour news in *News at Ten*, ITN lacked the screen time needed to add depth and detail to its daily news programmes. Aidan Crawley had originally expected that ITN would be responsible not only for reporting the daily news, but for interpreting and analysing it in a weekly news feature. Thus would be ended the separation of 'news' from 'current affairs'. This separation, which was of BBC origin, had no parallel in newspapers, nor in American television. In Fleet Street, the editor of a newspaper was in overall control of both news pages and feature pages. In the major US networks, such as CBS or NBC, documentary and features were under the news department.

This separation of 'news' from so-called 'current affairs' was wholly artificial, with its origins in BBC doctrine, and in personality clashes. But it was a separation which in 1955 happened to suit the new ITV programme companies. They were anxious to show that they could put out programmes other than light entertainment. Accordingly, the first ITV weekly news feature (*This Week*) went not to ITN but to Associated Rediffusion.

It was nearly eighteen months before ITN was first given its own weekly feature. This was *Roving Report*, a film programme on foreign affairs. It began in March 1957 on a shoestring budget with me as the roving reporter. I was sent to the United States – the topical peg being the first Anglo-American summit since the Suez fiasco. That first *Roving Report* was more an entertaining ragbag of film clips than a documentary. Senator Hubert Humphrey was interviewed on the little underground railway on Capitol Hill. I had an enjoyable clash with Mike Wallace, then reputedly the rudest man on American television, and did some 'vox pops' on top of the Empire State building. In three days I was back in London with enough film to be cut into a watchable twenty-five minutes.

From then until I left ITN in 1959, I did *Roving Report* in many parts of the world – not every week but frequently. Other ITN reporters took their turn, notably George Ffitch. He had worked with Professor Robert McKenzie on his classic work *British Political Parties*. Ffitch became ITN's most incisive interviewer.*

The most moving film footage which I have ever brought back to London was for my last *Roving Report*. We had been in Poland, in 1959. There I had the most sickening and heart-rending experience of my life. This was a visit to Auschwitz. The concentration camp was still preserved as a monument to Nazi atrocity. The ruined gas-chambers and crematoria were there to be seen by thousands of visitors. We had a woman guide, who had been an inmate of Auschwitz. She conducted us round the camp without any trace of emotion. In calm, matter-of-fact tones she pointed out the crematoria, the gas-chambers, the railway that brought four million people to their deaths, and the execution yard where twenty-five thousand political prisoners had been shot. She took us through the museum with the rooms piled full of human hair and, most horrible of all, little children's shoes. She showed us the rows of wooden huts where the forced-labour squads had lived. Some have been cleaned out and are on exhibition for visitors to see. I asked her where she had lived. We drove with her to another part of the camp, which is so huge that some of the huts are left in much the same condition as they were when the camp was liberated. They were not part of the normal visitor's tour.

She led us to her own hut. It was still (this was in 1959) a filthy shambles with rusty soup bowls and tin cans lying about the floor. 'Where did you sleep?' I asked. As the cameraman filmed, she pointed to the wooden shelf ten feet wide where she and five other women had slept side by side for four years. I asked if she would allow me to interview her there and then. She willingly agreed. In a few minutes the cameraman and recordist had set up their sound equipment outside the hut and were filming through a window. The woman told how she had

*Later a trenchant editorial writer for *The Economist* and the *Daily Express*, and Managing Director of LBC 1979–85.

been arrested at the age of seventeen in 1940 and spent the next five years in concentration camps. As she spoke, she ceased to be an Auschwitz guide. She became an Auschwitz inmate standing on the very spot where she had lived through hell. 'Why,' and I could scarcely bear to put the question, 'why do you stay here working as a guide fifteen years after the end of it all?' Until then she had kept control of herself. Now her voice faltered and tears came into her eyes. 'So that people can see that these things will never happen again.' Our young Polish interpreter translated her answer softly, his voice trembling. But somehow we knew what she had said. In that single moment was all the agony of a broken life.

There in that hideous death camp, in the presence of that woman, the problems of our own lives seemed shamefully trivial. It was profoundly moving to us, not least for the cameraman, George Richardson, a tough old professional who had seen much anguish in his time. The emotion caught him even as he handled the camera. He closed in instinctively, following the woman's words, till at the end that face which told a terrible story filled the picture. No sooner had we finished than I wondered if we had done wrong in filming her in that state of emotion. I asked her whether she objected to our using film of her being so upset. No, she did not object. My mind was eased by the words she had used: 'So that people can see that these things will never happen again.'

A few days later in the ITN newsroom at Television House, I watched the reactions of those who saw this interview transmitted. We showed every foot of the film. Girls who had been babies when that woman was an Auschwitz prisoner stopped their chattering and typing. They were visibly affected. Yet this was not a good piece of television 'production'. It was unpremeditated, unplanned, unrehearsed, undirected. I had done nothing except to ask what I felt moved to ask. The woman had done nothing except to say what she felt moved to say. The cameraman had done nothing except to focus his lens on her face. No technique, no art – nothing – came between that woman and the viewers who watched her. It was not a piece of television, it was a piece of humanity. Television simply happened to be there, not as an art or a technique, but as a means of seeing.

This Is Treachery

My four years with ITN from 1955 to 1959 were the happiest of my television career. I have never worked so hard, nor have I ever enjoyed working so much. The excitement was never-ending. This was not merely because our business was news, or because we were in television with its studio tension and stop-watch timing. The excitement was because we were creating a new branch of journalism. We were inventing and practising new techniques every day. We were experimenting and exploring. We were doing things which had never before been done in broadcast journalism in Britain. These included: the newscaster system, the probing unrehearsed interview, the more challenging coverage of politics, the use of hand-held 16 mm sound cameras to bring events alive, and to make news on television less stuffy, less solemn and, in a word, watchable.

The newscaster system was a breakthrough because it made the presentation of news on television more human, thus communicating more effectively to the viewing public, and more authoritative, because the newscaster would be a journalist seen to be part of a news-gathering team, not a mere announcer or producer's puppet.

The BBC was spurred to bring its TV news presentation to life. But the BBC never adopted the newscaster system. It merely employed less unattractive announcers to read the news. ITN persisted with the newscaster system, as developed by Geoffrey Cox out of Aidan Crawley's original concept. The essence of that system was to build the news programme around strong central personalities who were part of the editorial team. This was later to achieve its first great popular success on *News at Ten*, with Alastair Burnet and Andrew Gardner as ITN's first twosome.

An even bigger popular success was later achieved by that glamorous couple – Reginald Bosanquet and Anna Ford. This was a new swinging model of the newscaster system. It pulled in the viewers, and proved to be a brilliant publicity gimmick. But did it enhance the authority of ITN? Did that celebrated duo (or its successors) distract attention from the news itself? These questions suggest that the newscaster concept contained a built-in self-defeating contradiction – namely, that if the newscasting personalities are too appealing, the programme may lose authority and credibility. What then should be the verdict on the newscaster system? In my opinion, the newscaster system only works as it should under two conditions. The first condition is that newscasters must have journalistic ability. The second condition is that the newscaster should be the participating presenter of a *programme*, not merely the reader of links in a bulletin.

Peter Sissons, as anchorman of ITN's *Channel 4 News*, has shown us the newscaster system in its highest form. But Sissons' success demonstrates that the system works best when there is one central personality, rather than Tweedledum and Tweedledee. I have never quite understood why there had to be two presenters for *News at Ten*. This was no doubt inspired by the success of NBC's Huntley and Brinkley, but that duo arose simply because there were two major centres of news, Washington and New York.

The ideal newscaster-anchorman is very hard to find. There are few, very few, who have the personality, the skill, the experience, the authority and the presence to hold a news and current affairs programme together, to share in the editorial planning, to interpret the news, to conduct interviews, to chair discussions and to be the viewer's guide, philosopher and friend. If Sissons is one of the few, Sir Alastair Burnet is, of course, another. Sissons should give freer rein to his sense of humour. Sir Alastair's forte is not interviewing. But Sissons and Burnet are the nearest we've had to a Walter Cronkite in Britain.

In news *bulletins*, as distinct from news *programmes*, there is now not much real difference between an ITN newscaster and a BBC newsreader. In 1955, however, they came from different planets.

Another of the hallmarks of ITN in its early days was the probing interview. I do not suggest that ITN alone made television interviewing the force it was to become in politics and public affairs. There were other pioneers in the fifties of the searching provocative question in some of the BBC's topical programmes, such as Malcolm Muggeridge, Woodrow Wyatt, Christopher Mayhew and Aidan Crawley himself.

But it was ITN, on its nightly news programmes, which first unlocked the doors, opened the windows and let in the gust of fresh air which blew through the whole of British broadcasting in the mid-fifties. Before 1955, broadcast interviews were not only much rarer, but they tended to be conducted on terms dictated by the politician or public figure interviewed. Ministers or their officials would demand to know in advance what questions would be put to them.

The deferential pat-ball interview of the pre-ITN days was beautifully parodied by George Scott in the *Manchester Guardian*:

> Q: Sir, would you say that your visit to Timbuktu had been worth while?
>
> A: Oh, yes, I would definitely say my visit had been worth while. Yes, certainly.
>
> Q: Ah, good, well, could you say what topics you discussed, sir?
>
> A: No, I'm afraid I couldn't do that. These talks were of a highly confidential nature, you understand, and you wouldn't expect me to reveal anything that might prejudice our future relations.
>
> Q: No, of course not, sir. Well, sir, you must be very tired after your talks and your journey – may I ask, sir, are you going to take it easy for a while now – a holiday, perhaps?
>
> A: Ah, if only one could. But you know a minister in Her Majesty's Government can never take it easy, never rest, not really, you know. They're waiting for me now.
>
> Q: Well, thank you very much, sir.

That was a caricature, but like all good caricatures it conveyed an essential truth, that broadcast interviews, before ITN, had too often been unworthy of a mature democracy. In ITN from the very start we followed certain clear rules about interviewing. Questions must not be submitted in advance, though it was right to indicate the areas to be covered. This preserved the interviewer's right to put supplementaries or to press a point. Likewise the interview should not be rehearsed. These rules meant that the interview was being done on the broadcaster's terms, not on the terms of the politicians.

Thus was the principle established that the broadcasters had a right and a duty to put awkward questions on behalf of the public. That principle may seem self-evident now, but in 1955 it had to be fought for interview by interview. This was not easy for an infant news company trying to make its way in the world. Politicians, and of course their public relations officers, strongly disapproved. Gradually however politicians became more confident. The shrewder ones perceived that their TV appearances were much more effective if they were stimulated by straightforward interrogation with supplementaries in parliamentary style. Harold Macmillan realized this after his interview with me on ITN was so well received.

By 1957, the television interview was developing as a new form of journalism, and as a force in public affairs. Prime Ministers, and other national leaders, by answering questions put to them on television, were speaking directly to millions, sometimes to millions in other countries, by-passing ordinary diplomacy. In British politics, ministers and shadow ministers were now willing to be cross-examined on television in a style which would have been inconceivable two or three years before.

Television interviewing had become less superficial and more searching. These healthy developments, pioneered to a great extent by ITN, put a heavy responsibility on the new breed of journalist, the television interviewer. This responsibility was heaviest when a foreign dictator was being interviewed. It was important not to permit him an uninterrupted harangue. There had to be challenging questions, firmly put and followed up. Three times President Nasser was asked in the ITN interview whether he accepted the existence of Israel as an independent state. Three times he parried the question. Viewers could draw their own conclusions.

Senior parliamentarians were now more confident at answering questions on TV. There was less ministerial jealousy of TV stars on the back benches. A couple of years earlier, Rab Butler ruefully observed that an MP who had been a 'twinkling star of television' had 'relapsed into the comparative obscurity of a Minister of the Crown'. By 1957 such a comment would have been out of date. The greatest back-bench TV star of the fifties, Sir Robert (later Lord) Boothby, was able to point out: 'As all these eminent gentlemen in the Cabinet are coming into television and doing quite well at it, jealousy is fading.'

The television interview was becoming an important source of news and a part of the political process. It was becoming both interrogative and adversarial, with the interviewer's questions reflecting an opposing point of view. This new method of interviewing combined vigorous, incisive television with fair play. Politicians who were granted access to the powerful platform of TV were not allowed to turn an interview which should be a dialogue, into a monologue. Politicians could have their monologues if they wished in their party political broadcasts, which were provided for that purpose.

Inevitably this approach was a minefield of professional hazards for the interviewer. When was a probing and incisive question a rude question? The answer, of course, largely depended on whether you were a supporter of the politician being interviewed. And take an interview which put Tory arguments to a Socialist (or vice versa) – when did this amount to bias? The answer, of course, was that bias, like beauty, is in the eye of the beholder. The 'devil's advocate' style of questioning inevitably brought charges of bias against the interviewer. Over the years, I have been branded as a Socialist by Conservative viewers, and a Tory by Socialist viewers. I have been accused of bullying, badgering, hectoring and grilling. Yet all I have done is to seek truth or clarity from a public figure on behalf of the viewer.

We had to be able to justify the wording of a question – that it was relevant, fair and courteous. This meant that, whenever possible, the wording of questions had to be carefully prepared. When this was not possible, it was essential that the interviewer should be capable, from his experience and knowledge, of putting unprepared, spontaneous questions which did not slip into bias, inaccuracy or rudeness.

Some politicians are still unwilling to accept that an interviewer has a duty to the public. I have sometimes felt obliged politely to remind Mrs Thatcher that a TV interviewer's question is not an accusation by him. This was necessary more than once in my *Panorama* interview with her during the 1987 general election.*

So long as I or my Editor could defend and justify my questioning, I have never lost sleep about being the target of criticism or abuse. Despite the heat, I have stayed in the kitchen, though the kitchen has often been too hot for comfort.

In 1961, after my first five years of TV interviewing, I drafted a code for TV interviewers. The idea was to set down the principles which could help to achieve that balance between satisfying a critical public interest and enabling people interviewed, be they statesmen or strikers, to make their case.

I have tried to follow this code myself. My use of the pronoun 'he' should not be taken as indicating disregard for women interviewers. In the prehistoric time of 1961, one was forgiven for adopting the old legal, if sexist, maxim that 'masculine embraces feminine'. That apart I would not alter a word of my code. It is reproduced here exactly as it was first published nearly thirty years ago. The reader may judge whether it has stood the test of time, and whether on television it is more honoured in the breach than the observance:

1. The television interviewer must do his duty as a journalist, probing for facts and opinions.
2. He should set his own prejudices aside and put questions which reflect various opinions, disregarding probable accusations of bias.
3. He should not allow himself to be overawed in the presence of a powerful person.
4. He should not compromise the honesty of the interview, by omitting awkward topics or by rigging questions in advance.
5. He should resist any inclination in those employing him to soften or rig an interview so as to secure a 'prestige' appearance, or to please Authority; if after making his

*See below, pp. 285–96.

    protest the interviewer feels he cannot honestly accept the arrangements, he should withdraw.

6. He should not submit his questions in advance, but it is reasonable to state the main areas of questioning. If he submits specific questions beforehand he is powerless to put any supplementary questions which may be vitally needed to clarify or challenge an answer.

7. He should give fair opportunity to answer questions, subject to the time-limits imposed by television.

8. He should never take advantage of his professional experience to trap or embarrass someone unused to television appearances.

9. He should press his questions firmly and persistently, but not tediously, offensively, or merely in order to sound tough.

10. He should remember that a television interviewer is not employed as a debater, prosecutor, inquisitor, psychiatrist or third-degree expert, but as a journalist seeking information on behalf of the viewer.

I added that if interviewers were guided by these principles the power of television would not be abused; the power of television as an instrument of democratic scrutiny would be strengthened.

There are conflicting opinions about TV interviewers. One is that they tend to be offensive, even subversive, in their approach to public figures. A different opinion is expressed by the former *Spectator* critic Richard Ingrams (late of *Private Eye*):*

There is nothing at all subversive about these men. They may, like Day, the most successful interviewer of his time, give a convincing impression as abrasive inquisitors but their fundamental attitude is one of deference. It was perfectly natural that Day should end up as Sir Robin even though Mrs Thatcher ostentatiously referred to him as Mr Day throughout a lengthy interview in 1983.†

Heigh ho! So the wheel has turned full circle! Having started

*Spectator, 22 September 1988.
†See below pp. 229–32.

out as Torquemada, did I really finish up as Uriah Heep? If my 1983 interview with Mrs Thatcher was actually ever seen by Richard Ingrams (who frequently boasted of not having watched TV programmes which he was criticizing) he will know that whatever faults it had, deference was not one.

I can only say that my interviewing has not softened or weakened with the years. Vigorous, incisive interviewing is now, thank heaven, commonplace. Thirty years ago it was a novelty. Hence I may now *seem* less fierce, less provocative. But my motto as interviewer is still the same as it always was, in the words of Montaigne: 'Sit he on never so high a throne, a man still sits on his own bottom.'

The fresh and challenging approach which ITN introduced into news coverage was continually bringing us into conflict with government departments. In September 1957 the Foreign Office tried to stop an interview of mine from going out. The circumstances were typical of the way we operated. There was no planned 'incident', no intention to insult. What happened was that ITN's news editor, Arthur Clifford, was short of reporters one morning. I was busy at my desk on some other project. Would I help him out by interviewing the Japanese Foreign Minister? Arthur Clifford was the dynamic genius behind ITN's news coverage. He was imaginative, original and very persuasive. He was well over six foot and an ex-boxer. You did not refuse a request from Arthur, even if you had good reason.

I was not in the least enthusiastic about interviewing the Japanese Foreign Minister. Why was he here? Was there anything to ask him? Clifford threw me the latest press cuttings. And please, would I be at the Dorchester Hotel for the Foreign Minister's press conference in an hour and a half?

When I looked at the cuttings, I noticed that there had been recent British protests about Japanese pirating of British designs. I made one or two telephone calls and arranged to collect an example of a Japanese product called 'Bollard' Ball Bearings, which were contained in a package remarkably similar to a British product called 'Pollard' Ball-Bearings.

At the Dorchester Hotel press conference, the Japanese Foreign Minister, Mr Fujiyama, was questioned about the pirating issue by newspaper reporters. When Mr Fujiyama gave TV interviews after his press conference, it seemed reasonable for a TV reporter to present visual evidence of pirating. I had no thought of creating a rumpus.

I produced the two ball-bearing packets (the Japanese Bollard and the British Pollard) and asked what the Japanese government was going to do about it. The Japanese interpreter was furious. 'This is out of order,' he snapped. 'If you had this in mind, you should have given the Minister notice.' I replied that the Minister had readily dealt with the subject at his press conference and had not asked for notice of questions. Poor Mr Fujiyama sat puzzled and silent. The ITN film camera continued to roll. Meanwhile the bizarre scene was fully recorded by Fleet Street photographers and reporters. I had suggested to them that it might be worth their while to see what happened in my interview with Mr Fujiyama, but I had not anticipated what happened next.

The Japanese interpreter exploded: 'This is treachery.' I could scarcely believe my ears, but thought it right to control myself. I held up the two ball-bearing packets so that the interpreter could see them and the camera could film them, and retorted, 'But British manufacturers regard *this* as treachery.' At this point another Japanese official realized the whole incident was being recorded on film, and marched in to halt the interview and to remove Mr Fujiyama.

Before leaving the Dorchester, I rang the Editor of ITN to warn him that there might be trouble. Geoffrey Cox replied, 'I've already had a call from the Foreign Office. They say that if we transmit this interview we will gravely damage Anglo-Japanese relations. I've promised to look at the film.' I told Geoffrey that at least three Fleet Street populars had taken their own pictures of the interview, ball-bearing packets included, and had their own notes of what had been said, 'treachery' included. Even if ITN decided not to transmit the interview, the incident would be all over the papers tomorrow. The Editor of ITN replied, 'Oh good. That's that.'

This little interview, arranged only as a 'filler', took up less than two minutes in the evening bulletin. It was given sensational press coverage. But its significance was more than that of a newsworthy happening.

The interview was one of the first which widened the bounds of what was acceptable. It was a striking example of how an interview, which would have been regardéd as rude or improper two years previously, was now generally accepted as fair and relevant. Generally, but not universally. The Foreign Office was most annoyed. A former British Ambassador to Tokyo wrote to the press accusing me of 'gross discourtesy to a visiting states-man'. In Japan a newspaper columnist complained that Mr Fuji-yama had been treated 'spitefully', but he admitted: 'The British have something to complain about. It is shameful to report that Japanese manufacturers have been pirating British designs.'

Another consequence of this 'discourteous' interview was that the Managing Director of Pollard Ball-Bearings, Mr John King (now Lord King of Wartnaby), heard from Singapore that Bol-lard Ball Bearings (the Japanese copies) were to be withdrawn in that area. Among the viewers who wrote to say that the interview with Mr Fujiyama was not discourteous were some of those who had suffered in Japanese hands as prisoners of war.

The comment which I most enjoyed was made to me by Aneurin Bevan in the bar of the Grand Hotel, Brighton, at the Labour Party Conference, a day or two later. Nye had seen my interview with Mr Fujiyama: 'I see you had a bit of trouble with the Japs, boy.' 'Yes,' I said. 'They accused you of treachery! D'you know what *you* should have said?' 'What should I have said?' I asked. 'You should have said "Pearl Harbor to you, boy, Pearl Harbor to you." That's what you should have said.'

Another bright idea of someone in ITN (whether Cox or Clif-ford I don't remember) was that I, the parliamentary correspon-dent, should go and interview Marilyn Monroe at the Savoy Hotel. She had come to England with her husband Arthur Miller in 1956 to make *The Prince and the Showgirl* with Olivier. I was warned that the interview with Miss Monroe would be filmed with no sound recording. My function therefore would be only to sit in, as if in conversation with her, while the ITN cameramen shot 'silent' film.

I felt an acute sense of redundancy. An interview without sound? What next? What was the point of showing the back of my right ear in shot, if there was no interview and no reason for my presence? Apparently the idea was that if I was seen, if not heard, chatting to Marilyn Monroe, the pictures would be identifiable as ITN's own. This charade did not seem very sensible. What would we talk about? The assignment was not one for which a political interviewer was suited.

My romantic and imaginative nature found a brilliant solution. I bought a lovely red rose from the florist in the Savoy Hotel foyer. I sat down in front of Marilyn. The cameras began to roll. I removed the rose from my button-hole and presented it to her in a courtly manner.

She was wearing a severely cut black dress, which was diaphanous above her breasts and over her stomach – cool, elegant and stunningly alluring. My rose was graciously accepted by her. But there was a difficulty. 'Where shall I put it?' said Marilyn. I was about to make a helpful suggestion, when I heard a familiar voice ring out, articulated for all to hear. 'What, might I ask,' said Sir Laurence Olivier, who was standing behind her with Arthur Miller, 'what is the meaning of that red rose?'

Now if one presents a red rose to a pretty girl, even if she is the world's most famous screen goddess, one does not expect to be cross-examined as to why, least of all by the world's most famous actor. I was somewhat embarrassed by his question. 'Just a gesture,' I spluttered. 'But a gesture of *what*?' persisted Sir Laurence with mock solemnity. The word 'adoration' immediately came to mind, but emerged from my lips as 'ad-ad-admiration'. Olivier smiled indulgently. Doubtless he was remembering what he was to confess later in his autobiography, that after his first meeting with her, one thing was clear, he 'was going to fall most shatteringly in love with Marilyn'.*

Feeling a little out of my depth, I rose to leave the presence. But then from the assembled mob of cameramen, whom I had totally forgotten, came a great yell: 'Give it to 'er again, Robin. The rose – give it to 'er again, will you?' The momentary magic was rudely shattered. I presented that red rose to Marilyn Monroe at least three more times. She never did know where to put it. But it gave me something to do with my hands.

---

*Laurence Olivier, *Confessions of an Actor* (Weidenfeld & Nicolson, 1982), p. 169.

The Gentleman Versus the Chap

Almost every week in ITN there was some new challenge, some breaking away from old traditions. In the autumn of 1958 I was assigned to the most difficult task I had yet tackled. This was to give the live commentary for ITV on the State Opening of Parliament by HM the Queen. This was the first time the historic ceremony had been televised. It was also the first time that there was a rival commentary on such an event as an alternative to that provided by Richard Dimbleby on the BBC. This was an assignment in which all the odds were against me. I was a novice competing with the master craftsman. Richard Dimbleby was a man who knew every jewel in the Imperial Crown, and every stitch in a Herald's tabard.

My commentary was expected to be different from the traditional BBC style exemplified and personified by Dimbleby. No one, however, explained to me how this difference was to be achieved. How *could* I be completely different in tone from Dimbleby when describing a solemn royal occasion? The problem baffled me, until I suddenly realized that there was no need either to copy Dimbleby or to aim at a different style. We were different people with a different attitude to the occasion. My simple strategy should be to look at the ceremony in my own way.

My own way of looking at the ceremony was not mocking or derogatory. I had always loved the ceremonial aspects of parliamentary government. I knew that the State Opening of Parliament was a ceremony second only in splendour to the Coronation. But it was not just an ancient royal ceremony. It was a profoundly significant expression of modern constitutional and political realities. My job was to convey the contemporary political meaning. As the cameras showed the peers assembled around the throne:

This morning's ceremony . . . dramatizes the working principles of our parliamentary system: who has the pageantry and who has the power – principles won in the struggles of the past.

Over a shot of the golden throne:

> Though the Throne is still the seat of Majesty, it is no longer the seat of power.

As the cameras surveyed the ornate chamber:

> The story of the British Parliament is simply the story of how power has been taken away from the Throne, which you saw, and from this room – taken to the other room down the corridor, through that archway in the centre, from which the House of Commons will come.

As the glittering assembly awaited the Sovereign's arrival:

> That's how we have done it in Britain. The Monarch has the pomp without the power, the Commons have the power and no pomp. The Lords, as you see, have their pomp, but very little power.

I knew that this ancient ceremony was being seen for the first time by a vast audience far outside the privileged few who had attended it in the past. My aim was to put the traditional pageantry into modern perspective. I mentioned this to the Queen's Private Secretary, Sir Michael Adeane. He at once drew my attention to a point which would help me, 'Notice,' said Sir Michael, 'that the Queen, though she is the Sovereign, must wait for the Commons, the people's representatives, to arrive. Under a less democratic type of monarchy it would be the other way round.'

The passages which caused particular irritation were at the very end of the commentary, at the moment when Her Majesty left the chamber:

> A new session of Parliament has been opened. The Queen will go back to Buckingham Palace. The crown will go back to the Tower of London. All the scarlet and ermine robes will go back to wherever they came from. And Parliament will go back to work; to pensions, education, unemployment,

strikes, Cyprus, disarmament and the rest of it. The few
moments of pageantry in the working life of Parliament are
over.

That was thought by some to be much too down-to-earth and
brusque at a moment calling for a purple peroration. Finally, as
the cameras cut to an end-shot of the empty throne:

> Everyone is wondering at Westminster what government will
> write the next speech from this throne. Before Her Majesty
> sits on it again there may be a general election. That is when
> we have our say. And what Her Majesty reads from this
> throne depends on what we put in the ballot box.

I was determined not to let either the pageantry or the politics
make the commentary too solemn. This was not a funeral or
any kind of religious ceremony. It was a parliamentary occasion,
so there was no reason why a little humour, provided it came
naturally, should not be introduced. This was striking a new
note. It was risky. I plucked up more courage when, much to
my surprise, the Earl Marshal and Garter King of Arms laughed
uproariously at one or two mildly humorous touches which were
slipped into my commentary for the rehearsal.

On the day itself, several such remarks were included. They
were all very gentle and the commentary was 95 per cent serious,
but they were picked up in the press as a sharp break with
broadcasting tradition. Over a shot of Monty, who had recently
been making frequent headlines with provocative speeches:
'. . . Field Marshal Montgomery, who has a silent role on this
occasion'. A little harmless irony over the Beefeaters' symbolic
inspection of the vaults: 'Now that we know that such an obviously thorough search has been carried out and that Parliament
will not be blown up . . .'

A remark which some thought decidedly lacking in taste was
the reference to the scarlet and ermine robes going back to
'wherever they came from'. I had at least refrained from quoting
the Duke of Windsor's account of a State Opening. He tells us
in *A King's Story* that as he looked at the brilliant scene his
senses were 'suddenly assailed by an almost suffocating smell of

mothballs given off by the colourful robes removed from storage for this formal airing'.*

In general, the touches of humour were welcomed by the press, though one newspaper rapped me sharply over the knuckles. No, not *The Times*, which referred to 'a few agreeably dry asides',† but the *Daily Express*. Its TV critic, James Thomas, sternly admonished: 'This kind of function is no place to display even a quiet wit'!‡

This was ITV's first share in a big ceremonial occasion. For me it went off better than I had dared to hope. The ITV audience was generally less than the BBC's, but it held up well considering Dimbleby's reputation. To have my name coupled, even unflatteringly, with that of the great Dimbleby was, of course, a step forward and upward for me professionally. 'Dimbleby v. Day' was the theme of press comments, or, as the *Daily Express* put it, 'The Gentleman Versus the Chap'.

As this was the first time that the State Opening had been televised, the 'authorities' were frightened that the Queen's role would be misunderstood. Accordingly, Dimbleby and I were issued by the Home Office (via the BBC and the ITA) a long and verbose explanation of the constitutional position. This explanation, drafted by a senior Home Office official, was in long-winded Whitehallese, utterly unsuitable for a broadcast commentary over pictures. I protested to the ITA that there was no point in having a separate ITV commentary if the ITV commentator (namely myself) was forced to read out the same boring government words as Dimbleby. I was told that the Home Office wording was mandatory. I was further warned that it would be 'imprudent, perhaps even discourteous, to ask for any variation from the authorized words'.

I had to read out the long official explanation, but I took the liberty of pointing out that I had been ordered to read it. Then I added with some relish: 'Now, if I may sum up in other words: if a Conservative government is in power, the Queen reads a Conservative speech. If there's a Labour government, the

---

*The Duke of Windsor, *A King's Story* (Cassell, 1957), p. 325.
†*The Times*, 29 October 1958.
‡*Daily Express*, 29 October 1958.

Queen will read a Labour speech, just as her father did from 1945 to 1950.'

The constitution survived. The Throne did not totter. But though that State Opening was a triumph for TV, it seemed wrong to me that the cameras should be allowed to show only the pageantry of Westminster, while being excluded from the chamber of the House of Commons, the central forum of our democracy. In 1958 I was virtually alone in holding that opinion.

Incidentally it was as an ITN newscaster that I first used the teleprompter or autocue. This was a novel device (which is now commonplace) to enable a newscaster, or politician addressing the nation, to look straight into the lens at the viewer and at the same time to read scripted words unrolling before his eyes. This avoids the necessity of looking down at papers or of memorizing by heart. I always detested the teleprompter, unlike all my colleagues. I have always refused one in the thirty years since I ceased to be an ITN newscaster.

I detested the teleprompter for several good reasons. First, it tended to freeze the speakers' facial expression, and to give them a glazed look. Instead of looking at the viewer, they were looking at and following a script, their eyes moving with the words. Second, I felt the device was phoney and a fraud on the viewer. Most professionals would say it was simply a legitimate and well-established convenience, both for the performer (who did not need to look down at papers) and for the viewer, who did not have the distraction of looking at the top of a head as the performer looked down. But my view was that a speech, or address, or even a presenter's link, lacked conviction and warmth and spontaneity when delivered from an autocue. Moreover, I always liked to change words or re-emphasize phrases on transmission. Autocue made this spontaneity difficult or impossible after last-minute changes had been made.

However, I am in an obstinate minority of about one. I would accept that newscasters need autocue for their bulletins, but then they are simply reporting factual information. But for someone trying to persuade, or amuse, or inspire their audience, as a politician or public figure may wish to do, then the use of autocue is liable to kill personality, sincerity and spontaneity.

Actors, or politicians who through practice have acquired

acting skills, may be able to use autocue convincingly. But though it has made talking to camera smoother and more fluent, autocue has made it less convincing and less compelling. Similarly that other contrivance of TV production, the performer's 'ear-piece', by which the producer, like an unseen puppeteer, can turn an interviewer into a mere mouthpiece. Thus even 'live' TV may not be the reality it seems. The same applies to the autocues which have now come into use for platform speakers at public meetings. These are glass panels on either side of the podium, placed so that the orator can see the eloquent words scripted for him (or her) if he turns to left and to right. The trick works – up to a point. Once again you get smoothness and fluency. But it is an unnatural fluency. A speech to an audience on a great issue should naturally have hesitations, repetitions, spontaneous touches. No autocue orator manages to have any fire or feeling, except one: Ronald Reagan. He has been the supreme master of the autocue. But most politicians are not professional actors. I have never seen or heard a rip-roaring, passionate, witty or inspiring platform speech delivered from autocue. Margaret Thatcher has switched to autocue for her platform speeches. As a result she is less eloquent than she might be.

Autocue has killed personality in the best sense on TV. On the political platform it is destroying the oratory and eloquence which once gave inspiration, wit and passion to our political life.

9

Hereford

It's Not Libel, You Fool, It's Slander

In the spring of 1959, just when I had achieved a strong position in ITN, I took a gigantic gamble. In all my earlier gambles, such as quitting the Bar, going to America, returning from America, leaving the BBC for ITN, I had, with luck, a lot to gain by doing what I did. But the gamble I took in April 1959 was reckless and ridiculous. It meant putting at risk the professional standing I had achieved during three and a half years in television, without any prospect of compensating advantage.

What I did in April 1959 was to decide to stand for Parliament as a Liberal in the general election which was expected that year. I became prospective Liberal candidate for the Hereford constituency. I had at once to cease my work as an ITN newscaster, which had been such an uphill struggle at the beginning. This was reasonable enough, because a news bulletin presented by an openly committed political activist would not be regarded as impartial.

There was no guarantee that I could return to ITN if I was not elected. As the likelihood of winning Hereford for the Liberals was extremely remote, my decision to stand for Parliament threw my professional prospects into confusion and jeopardy.

Unlike citizens with other occupations, for example schoolteachers, stockbrokers, coalminers or barristers, a TV news reporter could not just stand for Parliament and go back to his

133

occupation afterwards if not elected. Even if he gave up politics, it might take him some time (as happened in due course to me) before he was regarded as disinfected. I make no complaint about this. So long as there is an impartiality rule for news on television, obviously the presenters of that news, newscasters and news reporters, must not be currently and publicly active as political partisans. I understood this perfectly well. Why then was I so foolhardy as to interrupt and jeopardize my professional career in television for the momentary thrill of fighting a parliamentary election?

I have asked myself that question many times during the last thirty years. I really do not know the answer. It was an impulsive act of the kind you can indulge in only when you are young and without family responsibilities.

It is true that to be a Member of Parliament had been one of my ambitions. But that was not the reason for my decision to stand in 1959. Realistically my chances of winning the seat were negligible. Had my sole motivation been to enter Parliament, I would not have stood as a Liberal. I would have looked coolly and cynically at the two main parties and asked myself in which of them I could be reasonably happy.

Throughout the fifties I often considered the question in conversation or in my own private thoughts. Politics at that time were not as polarized as they have since become. There was not then the choice between a left-wing Labour Party and a Thatcherite Tory Party. Those were the years when the word 'Butskellism' came to be coined. This was an 'ism' whose name was coined by *The Economist* in 1954, by merging the name of Butler, the progressive Tory, with that of Gaitskell, the moderate Socialist. 'Butskellism' came to mean consensus between the moderates (right-wingers) of the Labour Party and the progressives (left-wingers) of the Tory Party. 'Butskellism' is a word which has not crossed many political lips for years. I mention it only as a reminder that party politics looked very different in the fifties.

Although I knew politicians in both the big parties who were of independent and rebellious minds, I did not feel like joining a party unless I could fight for it with total conviction and enthusiasm. In any event, I thought, why join either the Labour

Party or the Conservative Party if I was neither a doctrinaire Socialist nor a true-blue Tory? Perhaps I was not sufficiently cynical or ambitious. It seemed better to remain a Liberal than to become a half-hearted Socialist or a wet Tory.

But of course these ideological musings were supremely irrelevant. Even if I joined one of the two big parties, and applied to be a parliamentary candidate, the brutal reality was that I would never be adopted for a seat unless I could show the conviction, enthusiasm and partisanship which I did not feel.

The Liberal Party was led by Jo Grimond, who was one of the most attractive political personalities of the time. He articulated brilliantly and eloquently the case for non-Socialist reform. He had a first-class mind. Long before anyone else, Jo Grimond expressed the case for that realignment of British politics which was to be attempted a generation later with the founding of the SDP and the formation of the ill-fated Alliance. What Jo Grimond was saying in 1959 appealed to me at that time. When I went before the Hereford Constituency Committee, I spoke with vigour about the need for a progressive, non-Socialist alternative to Toryism.

I came to stand in Hereford because a friend, Emlyn Hooson QC (later a Liberal MP, now a peer), drew my attention to the lack of a candidate in that constituency. The Liberals were looking for a well-known or 'strong' candidate. There was even talk of Hereford being winnable. It had, thirty years earlier in 1929, returned a Liberal MP, the twenty-four-year-old journalist Frank Owen, who later became editor of Beaverbrook's *Evening Standard*, and was a biographer of David Lloyd George. Moreover, in 1956, only three years previously, Frank Owen, who was a native of Hereford, had come within 2,150 votes of winning back his old seat at a by-election. So Hereford was a seat with Liberal memories and some Liberal history. It was certainly a seat where the battle would be between Tory and Liberal, not between Tory and Labour.

What impelled me to stand for Parliament in 1959 was a mixture of feelings. There was the feeling that, having been so long a student and an observer of politics, it was time I got off my backside and joined in. There was the feeling that if I didn't do it now (I was nearly thirty-six) I would probably never do it.

I knew it might be a setback to my television career. That career had only just begun. I was in no sense a TV star. My instincts told me that the experience of the hustings, and of politics at the grassroots, would be good for me. And so it was.

I let my name go forward for Hereford. I was duly adopted, and ceased to be an ITN newscaster forthwith. My salary in that capacity ceased also, but I was able to work occasionally for ITN's *Roving Report* on foreign film stories. ITN's Editor, Geoffrey Cox, put me in touch with the Editor of his old paper, the *News Chronicle*. I was commissioned to write a weekly column for fifty guineas a time. This not only prevented my political gamble from bankrupting me, but gave me a useful platform in the pre-election period. How far my column benefited the *News Chronicle* is doubtful. It closed the very next year.

Having here written my retrospective thoughts about why I became a Liberal candidate, it is appropriate to reproduce what I wrote at the time on that very subject. Here is some of my first *News Chronicle* column, advertised with a great fanfare of publicity on the hoardings and the sides of double-decker buses. It was headed 'INTO THE FIGHT':

'You need your head examined!' That was one of the more polite things said to me when people heard that I was going to become a prospective candidate for Parliament and thus could no longer be an ITN newscaster . . .

With ITN camera teams I went wherever the news was being made – Moscow, Washington, Cairo, Port Said, Nicosia. I reported the big debates at Westminster . . .

Why, people ask me, why, why should I want to give up this ringside seat to 'mess about in party politics?' That's what they say.

The alternatives before me were each exciting and worthwhile in different ways.

Should I stay on the staff of ITN, interviewing people in the news, and reporting big events to a vast audience?

Or should I go out and do something off my own bat and speak up for my own political convictions?

Should I continue to ask questions on topics of the moment or have a try at giving the answers myself?

With the General Election due at any time, should I stay and report it, or should I go out and fight in it? There was no doubt in my mind as to the answer . . .

Maybe an individual can't do much, but it is better than shrugging your shoulders . . .*

Six months passed before Macmillan called the general election for 8 October 1959. I enjoyed neither nursing nor fighting the Hereford constituency. Before I was adopted as prospective Liberal candidate, I was asked some testing questions by local Liberals who mostly disappeared as the campaign drew near. There was a handful of devoted enthusiasts on whose help I depended. The Hereford Liberals had been divided by local feuds. It may well be that I was not the right candidate to bring them together and arouse their enthusiasm, though this seems to have happened at the end.

It was depressing that so few of the local Liberals seemed to be interested in contemporary Liberalism as preached by Jo Grimond and myself. As far as I could tell, they were usually Liberals not out of any positive conviction but from some negative feelings, like class resentment of local Tories, or because to have joined Labour would be socially inconvenient.

My constituency Chairman, aged eighty or thereabouts, was reputedly a self-made millionaire. He never uttered in my hearing a Liberal sentiment. The story was that he had become a Liberal when he was a boy, simply out of hatred, because some local Tory landowner objected to his turnips being stolen. Another leading Hereford Liberal came up to me and said, 'My boy, everything has gone wrong with this country since we gave away India.'

I found myself proclaiming a political philosophy which had no meaning to the people who supported me, let alone to those whose votes I was seeking to win. I rapidly changed gear. I dropped Liberal philosophy and picked up local non-party issues. (Many years later this was called 'community politics'.) A lot of local schools had no electricity. Accordingly my slogan became 'Turn out the Tories and Turn on the Lights'. (Anyone

*News Chronicle, 16 April 1959.

who loftily thinks that was not politics on the highest level
should be reminded that my Tory opponent, a Mr Gibson-Watt,
ran on the edifying slogan 'Watt's my line'.) Rural transport?
This was so poor, I thundered, that people could not get to a
chemist soon enough to have their doctor's prescription made
up. By the time they could catch a bus, they were either better
or dead. I can only assume I had good evidence of this disgraceful state of affairs.

A local paper, edited by a Mr Peacock, was sympathetic to
the Tories, whose agent was a Mr Alcock. After the newspaper
had published a silly anti-Liberal news item, I magisterially
declared to a cheering mass rally: 'Alcock plus Peacock equals
poppycock' – an equation which even the Tory Tuscans could
scarce forbear to cheer.

On Saturdays there were scenes to describe in my *News
Chronicle* column:

Has TV killed the hustings? No, not a bit of it. Anyone who
says straightforward, man-to-man, street-corner
electioneering is dead, is talking through his hat, and I invite
him to come to Hereford on a Saturday night at election
time.

In the city's centre, High Town, there is a fine old tradition
that lives on in the TV age.

The three candidates speak one after the other on the
same spot to large crowds, which swell as the public-houses
and cinemas empty:

I was at it till nearly midnight last Saturday, with a howling
mob of several hundred, and violent heckling from young
Conservatives and drunken Irishmen.

The candidates hand over punctually to their opponents.
Another lorry and loudspeaker van move in.

You get first-class, full-blooded knockabout argy-bargy.

Maybe you can't deal with points at length or in detail –
but at least it brings politics to life and makes people more
interested to read and judge the candidates' election
addresses.

The variety of questions put to candidates is fantastic. One
of the first flung at me was: 'What is Liberal policy on the

blasphemy laws?' Not having given this issue a great deal of thought, I only just restrained myself from breaking the blasphemy laws in reply.

High Town at ten o'clock on Saturday night was not an occasion for calm, sober discourse. Provoked by young Tory hecklers, I described Macmillan as 'an Edwardian mountebank'. A rather too clever young Tory yelled, 'That's libel! That's libel!' I ignored him and continued. So did he: 'That's libel! That's libel!' He went on yelling. At last I lost my cool and yelled back: 'It's not libel, you fool, it's slander.' This horrified my highly experienced agent, the admirable Edward Wheeler. The incident later became one of his favourite election stories.

The cut and thrust of the hustings was an exhilarating experience. It was chastening, however, to be told by a contemptuous inmate of an old persons' home: 'Why do you come here? *You're* not interested in *us*. You're only after our votes.' I could have replied smoothly, 'I have come for the same reason as the other candidates – so that you can judge us personally before you decide how to vote.' But the words died in my throat because the old man had made me feel ashamed. I was an inexperienced campaigner. I mumbled that I was sorry to have disturbed him, and walked away.

From the start of the 1959 campaign, everything was in the government's favour. The weather was good, there was full employment, there was peace. Macmillan had been to Moscow. Ike had come to London and had appeared on TV with his old friend the Prime Minister. Gaitskell had unwisely promised not to increase income tax.

Macmillan's overall majority of 100 on 9 October should not have surprised anyone. In July I had forecast in my *News Chronicle* column:

Everything now points to a Tory victory at the General Election. Unless some unforeseeable disaster comes to Mr Gaitskell's help, Mr Macmillan will be returned to power for another five years. In private, Labour politicians admit that they have had it.

At the time when the country needs a spell of reforming

government, the main Opposition party is in disarray, still deeply divided on fundamental issues on the H-bomb, on nationalization. In such a state the Labour Party is unable to rally progressive opinion, and must bear the responsibility for a Tory victory . . .

It is not surprising that some people in the Labour Party are beginning to realize that this country will be denied progressive government until there is an Opposition party which does not confuse reform with Socialism.

The campaign in Hereford was not without its moments. My microphone was smashed. I demanded police action. The Labour candidate's agent resigned in mid-campaign. Jo Grimond descended from the skies by helicopter. The *Guardian* headline was 'Deus ex machina', which slightly over-egged the pudding. I issued regular statements about being 'poised for victory'. Lady Violet Bonham Carter came to speak in my support. She eloquently likened me to 'a battleship ready to go into action, set to blow the Tory target to smithereens. What a target it is! He can hardly miss!'

But miss it I did – by 7,578 votes. At least I managed to come second in the poll with over 10,000 votes.

After the 1959 election, I promptly severed all connexion with the Liberal Party. I came to the clear and firm conclusion that the Liberal Party would never become an effective vehicle for Liberal principles and values, and that it did not have a cat in hell's chance of achieving national power.

As an organization, the Liberal Party was a shambles. As a collection of personalities, it had more than its fair share of eccentrics, crackpots and nutcases. As a party, it was likely to be hopelessly divided between the old traditionalists and young radicals. To many of its supporters it was a party of the reasonable centre. To many of its activists it was a party of the militant left. A political party could be either of these, but not both.

That was how I saw the Liberal Party as we entered the sixties. Events have not proved me wrong. Though the Liberal Party seemed to be reviving in the sixties, there was no Orpington on a national scale. And another Liberal 'revival' in the seventies ended with the Lib-Lab pact which propped up the ill-fated Callaghan government.

Then in the eighties, after the Social Democrats defected from Labour, the SDP-Liberal Alliance was hailed as the new third force which would 'break the mould' of British politics, and (echoes of dear old Jo in 1959) would 'replace Labour as the radical alternative to Thatcherism'.

That same stale slogan is now being hopefully trumpeted as we approach the nineties. But another and more revolutionary realignment of British politics has already taken place. British politics has been realigned by ten years of Thatcherism which, whether you like it or not, has transformed the Tory party, the Labour Party and the trade unions, and revolutionized the political, industrial and social scene. That realignment, the Thatcher revolution, which is still in progress, was not foreseen by Jo Grimond, nor by myself when I tramped the fields of Herefordshire thirty years ago.

The 1959 election was significant for British political history in more ways than one. It was the year that Margaret Thatcher was elected to Parliament. And it was the year that I failed to be elected to Parliament. By such quirks of the popular will is the destiny of great nations decided.

However, I took defeat philosophically. I was brought up on the maxim 'Trust the People', and in the circumstances I had little option but so to do. I took that 1959 result like a man, and so (one might say) did Margaret Thatcher.

10

Panorama

Your Window on the World

In November 1959 after the general election, I accepted an offer from *Panorama*, then the prestige current affairs programme of BBC Television. That was the start of thirty years' association, on and off, with the programme – longer, in all, than any other performer or producer. My first job was to chair a short debate on corporal punishment. Assisting me was a red-haired young man just down from Oxford, by the name of Dennis Potter. With his already keen sense of the dramatic, he efficiently arranged a fearsome birch to have before us on the table. But Potter moved on soon to higher things, like becoming the most brilliant of all TV playwrights.

I did over twelve years as a full-time regular member of the team, first as one of the reporters, then as anchorman for five years. Then, from 1972 onwards, I have continued to appear in *Panorama* for major political interviews from time to time, especially during general election campaigns.

The offer to join *Panorama* came in a personal telephone call from Leonard Miall, head of current affairs programmes in the BBC. Four years earlier he had referred me to radio. Now he needed replacements for Christopher Chataway and Woodrow Wyatt, two *Panorama* reporters who had (unlike me) been elected to Parliament in the recent election.

Miall offered me a *Panorama* contract for one year as a

freelance contributor at £4,500. This was somewhat less than I was likely to earn from staying with ITV, but there would be more professional opportunity. So off I went to Lime Grove, the dingy back street in West London, to begin thirty years, some happy, some miserable, with BBC Television.

During those thirty years, my BBC contracts have normally been for only one year at a time, never for more than two years. I have never had security of employment or of income. Now, at sixty-six, I have no pension from the BBC. What I have for pension is only that for which I have saved out of my own earnings. My BBC earnings have gradually risen over the years, and have been higher than if I had been a salaried member of the BBC staff with all the staff benefits. I have of course earned a good professional income from the BBC but very much less than, say, stars of showbusiness, tycoons of industry, stock-brokers or top barristers and solicitors. Because I have continually, for thirty years, remained under contract with the BBC, I have made no pot of gold. I have never acquired a valuable 'slice of the action' in some commercial television company or enterprise.

Nowadays, when there is such proliferation of current affairs programmes on all TV channels, it is almost impossible to convey the importance and significance of *Panorama* in the late fifties and early sixties. Those were primitive days. There were only two TV channels, BBC and ITV. Both were still black-and-white. BBC2 came in 1965. Colour TV began in 1967. Many of the now familiar technical advances (satellites, videotape recordings, electronic news cameras and so on) were in the future. The multiplicity of channels, celestial and terrestrial, which we are to have in the nineties was not even contemplated.

Panorama was a major event of the week, keenly awaited by press, politicians and people alike. Public meetings and social functions would tend not to be arranged for Monday nights. To appear on *Panorama* was regarded as a significant boost to a politician's prestige. Fifty minutes long, it was *the* platform (rivalled only by ITV's thirty-minute *This Week*) for Prime Ministers and other major public figures. It was the TV forum where national issues, political, economic, moral, were debated.*Panorama* was also, as its subtitle 'Your window on the world' proclaimed, the programme whose celebrated reporters brought dramatic film of foreign happenings, revolutions, crises and upheavals into the living-rooms of Britain. *Panorama* was the flagship of BBC Television's journalistic fleet.

Already by 1959, in its first few years as a weekly programme, *Panorama* was not only explaining the news but making the news. Notable examples were the brilliant interviews by John Freeman and by Woodrow Wyatt which led to the exposure of ballot-rigging in a major trade union, the ETU.

I was a television reporter of only four years' experience, who had made his name in the brash new commercial network. Now I was joining a professional élite. I had been recruited by the dear old BBC for its prestige programme. This gave me a quiet satisfaction. I recalled my long, frustrating failure to find a way into BBC Television. Only the fresh wind of competition from the creation of ITV had blown open the doors.

I had wanted to go back to ITN when the 1959 election was over. Though I was no longer a candidate and had given up party politics, my political partisanship was too recent for me to resume my work as an ITN newscaster and political reporter. I had hoped to get contracts for other work with ITN, coupled with work for the ITV programme companies. But there was a problem.

ITN was the only ITV company whose output was automatically networked. The programme companies such as Associated Rediffusion or Granada were regional companies whose programmes were only networked by agreement. The most I could expect from ITV was some foreign reporting for ITN's *Roving Report*, with only occasional opportunities from one of the ITV programme companies. I could be offered no regular programme work on ITV comparable to *Panorama*.

Why was it that *Panorama* in those days was a programme of such prestige and popularity? How did each edition on Monday evenings manage to present events and personalities and issues of the day with such a dramatic sense of occasion?

Ten million people would settle down on Monday evenings to watch what was then the nation's most famous topical television programme. It was a solemn moment in the British television week. The opening title music, from Rachmaninov's Symphony

No. 1 in D Minor, was imposing, almost majestic. Then the familiar voice of the nation's most famous and best-loved broadcaster intoned, 'Your window on the world.' And the camera gave us Richard Dimbleby in vision.

Panorama was not then a one-subject programme, except on special occasions. It was a 'magazine' programme with up to five items, but usually with three or four. Richard would sound the keynote with a grave reference to the major topic of the moment, to a personality in the news or to some colonial crisis. As the programme proceeded, *Panorama*'s reporters would be introduced in turn by Dimbleby: Kee to cross-examine Gaitskell, Kennedy to investigate cremation, Day in Castro's Cuba, Mossman from the Middle East.

The first and most important of many reasons for the powerful impact of *Panorama* in those days was without doubt the personality and professionalism of Richard Dimbleby, the anchorman, the host, the father-figure, the master of ceremonies.

It later became fashionable to decry Richard Dimbleby, and to belittle his importance to *Panorama*. But it was Richard's solid presence and personality which won the viewers, kept the viewers, guided the viewers and held the programme together. This big, bulky man, with his calm voice and courteous manner, pervaded the programme even when, to his annoyance, he was given little more to do than 'link' the items done by the reporters such as myself. Richard once complained to me, 'They're trying to turn me into a bloody announcer.'

In the *Panorama* chair, Richard Dimbleby personified the ordinary reasonable viewer, sharing his bewilderment or shock at what they were about to see. No presenter or anchorman has ever achieved this combination of qualities, his rapport with the viewer, his professional aplomb, his mellifluous speech, his sense of occasion, be it glad or gloomy, or his easy, natural authority.

Dimbleby was *Panorama*'s greatest asset. As a broadcaster, he had built a four-fold reputation. First on radio during the war as a courageous reporter in the battle zones and flying on bombing missions over Germany. Second, as the commentator at the Coronation (which was television's breakthrough to mass popularity and influence) and countless royal or state occasions. Thirdly, as the nation's presiding host during the all-night election results of 1955, 1959 and 1964. Fourthly, and finally, as the respected presenter of *Panorama*.

For nearly thirty years, on radio and on television, in war and peace, Richard Dimbleby had done the state some service. The highest honour he received was the CBE in 1958. That he was never awarded, even as his death drew near, the knighthood he so richly deserved, is an inexplicable mystery. Perhaps the BBC never put his name forward because he was not on the BBC staff. But did no one at No. 10 or at the Palace appreciate the services he had performed as a broadcaster for the monarch and her peoples?

That he was thus overlooked distressed his friends and colleagues much more than Richard himself, who had no arrogance. But what Richard Dimbleby really would have appreciated more than any other honour was a KCVO, a Knighthood in the Royal Victorian Order, which is in the personal gift of the Queen. What Richard said to me was this: 'A KCVO would mean more to me than anything. More than a viscountcy!'

Richard was not a great investigator or interrogator. He preferred to describe, to explain, to set a scene. He was not a political animal. Politics, which he tended to find rather distasteful, were not in his blood. He was happy to leave the probing and muckraking and cross-examining to the reporters over whom he presided.

When I joined the *Panorama* reporting team in November 1959, my colleagues were to include Robert Kee, James Mossman, Ludovic Kennedy and John Morgan. This was said to be the strongest reporting team ever gathered together for one television programme.*

Panorama was then in its prime. It had the magisterial presence of Dimbleby, with the debonair brilliance of Mossman, the romantic intensity of Kee, the passionate integrity of Kennedy, the eloquent Welshness of Morgan, not to mention the 'scowling, frowning, glowering Robin Day', with, in Frankie Howerd's legendary words, 'those cruel glasses'.†

That portrait of *Panorama*'s celebrated team may now seem

---

*Said by Michael Peacock, to whom flattery was foreign, when Editor of *Panorama*.
†Spoken on *That Was The Week That Was*.

somewhat overcoloured. Like the great Dimbleby, all the reporters (unlike those of later generations) were men of some maturity and experience, men who had seen war service, men who had worked in professions outside television, men who (again unlike their successors of later TV generations) loved words and ideas even more than pictures.

Robert Kee, that most romantic figure, had been an RAF bomber pilot, a prisoner of war and a *Picture Post* reporter. Jim Mossman had a brief spell with MI6 after Cambridge. He did not take to spying, so he went into Fleet Street. The *Daily Telegraph* sent him to be their correspondent in Cairo. It was the time of Suez. The British had bombed the airfield. Suddenly (so Mossman told us) he was summoned to a room in the British Embassy and asked for his help. He was to take a large amount of cash (£20,000 in notes) and be ready to hand it over to an Egyptian gentleman when so instructed.

Jim Mossman would tell this hilarious story with much fascinating detail. How he, a newspaper correspondent, was persuaded to co-operate because of his former service in MI6, about bizarre briefings in blacked-out rooms in the British Embassy, about putting the £20,000 in the boot of his Morris Minor. Mossman believed that the money was intended for someone, perhaps a doctor, who was going to assassinate Nasser. Be that as it may, Mossman said that his instructions were to telephone an Egyptian gentleman and say, 'Have you read the book?' If the answer was 'No,' Mossman was to do nothing. If the answer was 'Yes, I have read the book,' Mossman was to deliver the £20,000 at a prearranged place. Unfortunately when the moment came and Mossman telephoned with the question 'Have you read the book?', the disconcerting answer was 'What book?'

Mossman was marvellous company. Although I did not know him well, it was a ghastly shock in 1971 when he committed suicide.

The glamorous Ludo Kennedy, author, playwright, Old Etonian, campaigner against capital punishment, and Scottish patriot, had been a celebrity long before his *Panorama* days. The first of his many books, *Sub-lieutenant*, was written in 1942 when he was twenty-three. It was one of a famous trio of morale-boosting wartime books each written by a young officer. It was much admired by two very different experts in the use of words, Stanley Baldwin and Noël Coward. After the war, Ludo had married the glorious ballet-dancer Moira Shearer, star of *The Red Shoes*. John Morgan was proudly Welsh, with a love of whispered and malicious gossip. He was a cultivated man who brought a welcome literacy to film commentary writing. Politically he was on the left in those days, a Socialist of the *New Statesman* kind.

My own background was quite different from that of the others: four years in the new TV journalism of ITN, and before that a stint in Washington, and pupillage at the Bar, plus my painful experience as an unsuccessful parliamentary candidate.

In 1963 the *Panorama* team was reinforced by Michael Charlton. Born in Sydney of New Zealand parents, he spoke with a most un-Australian accent. He had been Editor and presenter of *Four Corners*, Australia's *Panorama*, and had earlier been a cricket commentator, covering Test matches in Australia, England, India and Pakistan. Charlton is an accomplished broadcaster with a pleasing voice and a fine gift of phrase. He became fed up with the new Lime Grove establishment, who eventually lost him to radio, where his 'oral histories' have won a high reputation.

The *Panorama* reporters were encouraged to take a critical, probing approach to their subjects, whether the subject was a politician being interviewed, or a country in crisis, or an issue being debated. We were not pundits, we were not experts, and were not presented as such. We were the viewers' enquiring representatives, their persistent fact-finders in confused situations, their interpreters in foreign parts.

There was much diversity of opinions and interests among the *Panorama* reporters. We were a colourful group, each with his own style and technique. But we were all aware of our heavy responsibility. We were working for what was then, incredibly, the BBC's only regular serious current affairs programme. This was before there were any nightly news magazines, like *24 Hours*, *Midweek* or *Newsnight*. There was no nine o'clock news-in-depth for half an hour. There was, of course, the early-evening *Tonight* programme which combined light-touch topicality with entertainment. There were many documentaries and special programmes.

So as we entered the sixties the BBC's one regular platform, forum and sounding-board was the weekly *Panorama*. It was run by a handful of young producers with the four or five famous reporters. This, as Professor Robert McKenzie would heatedly inveigh, was an unhealthy state of affairs in a mature democracy. *Panorama*, he would argue, was establishment television with a vengeance, with far too much influence concentrated in too few unrepresentative hands. Bob McKenzie was right, and before long competition was provided. But during the few years of its ascendancy, *Panorama*'s influence and position was never abused. This was due to the standards of impartiality and integrity which then prevailed in BBC Television under the watchful supervision of the editorial executives, notably Grace Wyndham Goldie and Paul Fox.

Panorama's magazine format had great advantages: flexibility permitting a quick response to sudden events, and variety with contrasting pace and style – a political interview in the studio, a colourful film report from abroad, action-film from a reporting team in a trouble spot or battle zone. The magazine format enabled *Panorama* to cover more than one major topic. This was essential for a programme which was transmitted once a week. Moreover, the multi-item magazine format was an ideal vehicle for the presentational gifts of Richard Dimbleby.

Behind the scenes at Lime Grove, however, bitter arguments raged among the *Panorama* people about the programme format. Why not scrap the magazine format, asked the whizz-kids, and get rid of the anchorman who had to link the various items? Was not the very idea of an anchorman, especially an establishment figure like Dimbleby, a boring 'fifties' television concept?

When one thinks of his great memorial service held in Westminster Abbey, of the awards established in his name to honour excellence in television, it is scarcely credible that Richard Dimbleby was regarded as expendable by some producers in the BBC. He told me how nauseated he had felt when a BBC executive who had wanted to sack him from *Panorama* was later smoothly eloquent in his honour on some anniversary of his BBC service.

Those in the BBC who argued against a Dimbleby-dominated *Panorama* were not successful. Richard's supporters were much stronger and more influential than his detractors. So he remained, securely enthroned, until his death in 1965 after a five-year fight with cancer. He was only fifty-two, a giant cut down in his prime.

The in-house argument about *Panorama*'s magazine format ran deeper than the merits of Richard Dimbleby or the idea of an anchorman. The magazine format was attacked by producers as being primarily a vehicle for reporters (which it was, and rightly so). The dispute about *Panorama*'s format reached its height in the mid-sixties, when Jeremy Isaacs was brought in to edit *Panorama* from ITV. *Panorama* under him was changed to a single-subject programme, usually on film, lasting forty minutes. I and others strongly opposed this change, believing that it would diminish the programme's topicality and variety, and therefore its appeal. But I was merely a contributing reporter, outside the BBC staff hierarchy.

Isaacs had his way. I did not expect that events would prove me right so soon. One weekend in 1966, Dr Verwoerd, Prime Minister of South Africa, was assassinated in the Parliament at Cape Town. Manifestly this sensational event and its implications demanded the fullest possible coverage in that Monday's *Panorama*. But there was already billed for *Panorama* one of Isaacs' single-subject documentaries. This was an admirable piece of work, the reporter being John Morgan. The subject was, I think, Welsh culture and the Eisteddfod. The problem was that a carefully crafted documentary of that length could not be cut by, say, fifteen or twenty minutes to make room for an item on the Verwoerd assassination. Nor could the Welsh film be postponed in its entirety. In those pre-satellite days there was no possibility of getting, at a few hours notice, enough South African material for the full programme.

Single-subject dogmatism had landed us in a mess, as some of us had clearly foreseen it would. I was incensed. I therefore ignored BBC protocol. This required a contract reporter who wished to communicate with a top Corporation executive to do so via his programme editor. Since the object of my protest was my programme editor, namely Jeremy Isaacs, I wrote direct to Huw Wheldon, who was the Controller of Programmes. I explained what had happened and why it was deplorable, just as I have related it here. My letter was short and severe. It was not acknowledged. Whether my memo to Huw Wheldon hastened Isaacs' departure from *Panorama* I do not know. He shortly afterwards resumed his upward career on ITV.

I had nothing against Isaacs personally. He was an able young man, a Granada-trained star of the sixties. I had first met him in 1955 when as an undergraduate he had invited me to speak at his end-of-term 'Farewell' debate when he was President of the Oxford Union. In 1987 Jeremy Isaacs was a front-runner for the Director-Generalship of the BBC, but the BBC's Board of Governors did not appoint him.*

That Isaacs incident in 1966 was a rare instance of my becoming involved in the internal politics of Lime Grove – rare because throughout the decade I was continually reporting abroad, or away from London. Sometimes I was abroad for several weeks at a time, in Africa, in the United States, in the Far East. I would send back, for each edition of *Panorama*, film with recorded commentary to which the film would be cut. This was a useful innovation and gave the reporter more control. Normally it would be the other way round, with the reporter's commentary recorded in Lime Grove to fit the edited film.

Life in a suitcase for long periods can be exciting and professionally rewarding, but it had not made for continuity or fulfilment in my personal life. Despite the professional preoccupation, and the globe-trotting existence, I was often romantically involved. These things cannot now be analysed or explained. But I recall my girlfriends with affection and admiration. If they really were as beautiful and enchanting as they seem in retrospect, I was very lucky to have known them, and they were sensible to have discarded or escaped me. They have all lived happily ever after, and are now, mostly, gorgeous grandmothers. So I refrain from paying them any compliments which might disturb their privacy.

*He is now General Director of the Royal Opera House, Covent Garden.

I did not marry till I was forty-one. That was due to the years of seeking a career, followed by the years of total immersion in television and its opportunities. That may be an over-simplification but it is basically true.

When I passed my fortieth birthday in 1963, I was still a bachelor. But I had fallen in love. In April 1965 I married Katherine Ainslie, a beautiful and gifted Australian, at her home in Perth, Western Australia. I had met her when she was a law tutor at St Anne's College, Oxford. She had a legal brain of superlative quality – alpha double plus. She gave up legal work when the first of our two children was born.

That my wife and I separated in 1983 and were divorced by mutual consent two years later is a matter of public record. For us and our children it was also a matter of private distress which will not be discussed or described in this book. In telling the story of his own life, a man should be allowed to respect the privacy and the feelings of others who have been part of it.

Old Sweats and Young Whippersnappers

If I had a continuous video recording of those *Panorama* years, how often would I wish to press the stop button and play it again? Old film reports for TV don't go yellow with age like newspaper cuttings but they are equally apt to look like products of another time and of a different way of thinking. What was urgent and critical the day before yesterday seems unimportant and trivial today. Giants are dwarfs in the perspective of history. The vivid immediacy of television journalism magnifies and distorts events. Today's horrific tragedy, this morning's violent death – they dominate television tonight, but they dwindle into next month's statistics.

None the less, my playback of *Panorama* in the sixties would contain many moments, historic or sensational or bizarre, which I would be tempted to see again: Fidel Castro in Havana, Cuba, boasting why the Bay of Pigs had been a fiasco; Winnie Mandela in the corner of a Johannesburg garden the day her husband Nelson had been sentenced to life imprisonment on a charge of treason. He was no Communist, she told me, but if he made common cause with Communists, so had Churchill when Hitler invaded Russia. John Fitzgerald Kennedy, the Roman Catholic Senator from Massachusetts, aged only forty-one, audaciously seeking the Democratic nomination; Jomo Kenyatta, Prime Minister of a newly independent Kenya, interpreting for me the weird answers of an unbalanced Mau-Mau general just out of the forest; Julius Nyerere, Prime Minister of a newly independent Tanganyika, showing me the sights of Dar es Salaam.

JFK making his inaugural speech in Washington on a freezing, snow-bound January morning, with the sun shining. 'The torch has been passed to a new generation of Americans born in this twentieth century . . . Ask not what your country can do for you, ask what you can do for your country.' 'Bull' Connor, police chief of Birmingham, Alabama, showing the *Panorama* audience why he had become notorious during the civil rights struggle. Those extraordinary television circuses, the American conventions: JKF's at Los Angeles in 1960, Goldwater's at San Francisco in 1964: 'Extremism in the defence of liberty is no vice. Moderation in the pursuit of justice is no virtue.' Humphrey's at Chicago in 1968 when the anti-war radicals were beaten up by Mayor Daley's cops. Chaos in the Congo, which the Belgians had quit precipitately, with a strange new cast of African characters for *Panorama* – Lumumba, Kasavubu, Tshombe. Such images and happenings and sayings crowd confusingly into my recollection of reporting in those *Panorama* years.

There were mainly two kinds of work for me in *Panorama*: film reports (mainly from abroad) and studio interviews (mainly with the leading politicians). I made dozens of films varying in length and weight from ten-minute 'shorts' to mini-documentaries of twenty or thirty minutes. Many of these films were made with me as the reporter-producer (on Castro's Cuba, on South Africa, on Kenya, on the Belgian Congo, on the frontier war with Indonesia in Borneo).

Panorama editors preferred to send out a producer (a member of the BBC staff) with the reporter and film crew. What was the aim of this cumbersome arrangement? Was it to keep the reporter on the editorial rails? Was it merely to free the reporter from the administrative chores (transport, hotels, appointments, bookings, etc., etc.) of a long and complex filming assignment? Was it the BBC's theory that the end product would benefit from the combined input of the reporter's journalistic experience and the skills of a BBC producer trained in camera direction and technical know-how? Whatever the aim, the relationship between reporter and producer was friction-fraught. The crucial question was never answered: who was in charge in the field?

All the *Panorama* reporters I have mentioned (Kee, for instance, or Charlton) were men of strong mind and much experience. Their judgment, their instinct, told them what ought to be done in a given situation. They were not the sort of men to welcome continual argy-bargy, often in conditions of difficulty and danger, with the producer.

The report, after all, was going out in the reporter's name. Richard Dimbleby would say '. . . and Robert Kee reports from Algiers,' or 'From Iraq James Mossman reports.' (Richard refused to call him 'Jim' Mossman as everyone else did because it 'sounded like a Manchester second-hand clothes dealer'.) The producer's name was in the end-credits but, for the viewer, the report was the reporter's work. It is fair to say that *Panorama* films, when made jointly by producer and reporter, were often of outstanding quality. But far too much time and energy was wasted in disputes between reporter and producer. The tension was destructive, not creative.

One producer during my years with *Panorama* was absolutely first-class at the difficult job of advising, assisting and guiding (without dictating to) the strong-minded and sometimes temperamental men who were the *Panorama* reporters. That producer was David Wheeler, who did ten years with *Panorama* from 1955 and 1965. He was Editor from 1963 to 1965. David Wheeler was an expert film director, an expert organizer, an expert at dealing with strong personalities like Woodrow Wyatt, James Mossman and Robert Kee. He had a quiet mischievous sense of humour which enabled him to keep everything in proportion, and to stop the reporter becoming too big-headed. He would never panic.

I worked often with David Wheeler. Our joint operations included a seventy-five-minute round-the-world-documentary about the effect on the Commonwealth if Britain entered the

Common Market. We never had a heated argument. He had a patient understanding of a performing reporter's psychology. His critical comments were invariably justified. David Wheeler is now a writer of novels, radio documentaries and TV criticism.

Unfortunately some of the other producers were less astute. An old sweat, like myself or Michael Charlton, had his own way of doing things. To find oneself working in tandem with a young whippersnapper who had *his* way of doing things was liable to be disastrous.

When I was first reporting for BBC television, even if the reporter was not in charge it was accepted that the producer was there to help him, not to treat him as a puppet. Mossman, Kee, Ludo Kennedy, who all made their own reports, worked on that principle. But as things developed, younger producers were not content with the 'midwife' role. They wanted to give birth themselves. The trouble with this was that you can't have things run by committee. If you recruit strong-minded, experienced television reporters, you have got to let them get on with it.

It may be suspected that these problems in the reporter-producer relationship were due to arrogant and abrasive behaviour on my part. But it was not only I who experienced the difficulties. All my reporter colleagues suffered in the same way. I suffered particularly because at ITN I had been inculcated by Geoffrey Cox with the principle that in the field the reporter is in charge, with editorial responsibility for the words spoken and the pictures taken.

After an exasperating month-long assignment with a *Panorama* producer in the early seventies, I vowed never to make a television film again. Nor have I done so. My cabled objections to the Editor were the subject of open ridicule in Lime Grove. The Young Turks enjoyed seeing me goaded into furious protest.

The experience had been intolerable. The details are too tedious to merit space here. There were endless arguments about what should be done, when it should be done, how it should be done. For the first time as a reporter, I was told what telephone calls I should or should not make. Incredibly, I was ticked off for making early contact with the British High Commissioner in the country where we were filming. This was a normal thing to do, especially in a country where a visiting TV crew may find itself, as we did, in difficulty. The High Commissioner's advice was invaluable.

I was even told off for not having dinner with the producer and the filmcrew! Objection was raised to my eating alone or eating with other people. I preferred useful talk to BBC gossip. Worst of all, there were frequent clashes of editorial judgment which were tiring and time-wasting. Life was too short to go through all that ever again.

Fifteen years ago, Polly Toynbee wrote in the *Observer* magazine: 'As Robin Day has got older, BBC producers have got younger and clashes were inevitable.'* As each new generation of producers came into programme-making, the gap between their age-group and mine became bigger. This was because the reporters had remained in the same position, though with increasing experience, ever since entering television when they were younger, perhaps twenty years previously. Meanwhile the BBC producer moves up the executive ladder. He (or she) starts as a trainee (or a secretary), becomes a production assistant, then an assistant producer, then a producer, then an assistant editor, then an editor, and so on up. So there was a continual upward exodus of producers and a continual intake of young people to become producers at programme level.

I am not the only TV journalist who had experienced these difficulties. I was one of the original generation of TV journalists. We were an entirely new breed of broadcasters who began our work on the screen in the fifties. Because of the war, and because there was no TV journalism until the fifties, we did not start in television until we were about ten or fifteen years older than the age at which today's entrants begin. We had become experienced professionals by the end of the sixties. That was the period when television expanded, bringing in a whole new generation of young producers, many straight from universities and from the revolutionary student atmosphere which was then trendy, and with no experience of anything but television.

There is an old BBC maxim that the history of good broadcast-

*Observer. 14 July 1974.

ing is the history of conflict between strong-minded people with the ability and the desire to fight for the best result. But the separation of powers between producer and reporter was an artificial and unnecessary source of friction. Whether in the BBC or ITV, this system was partly due to out-of-date assumptions inherited from the cinema, that the reporter was a mere 'performer' like an actor, who needed 'production', and that the cameraman needed 'direction' as to where to point his lens, and how to frame his shots.

As television journalism developed, these assumptions became nonsensical. Reporters were experienced journalists with political judgment who had swiftly mastered the necessary technicalities of television. Cameramen could be self-directing operators, whose skills had been forged in the coverage of wars and riots and disasters.

There is a further historical explanation for the separation which exists in television between the editorial executive and the journalist-contributor, between the producer and the performer (this being a contemptuous description appropriate to a circus animal or an actor). It goes back to an earlier era, when current affairs broadcasters were very few. They were regarded as gifted amateurs who were privileged to enjoy the patronage of the BBC monopoly power. They were 'produced' by the 'professionals' on the BBC staff.

This apartheid between producers and reporters, between the bureaucrats and the broadcasters, has been an absurd and wasteful doctrine in the BBC . Take my own case: I have contributed to the TV coverage of eight general election campaigns. Yet I have never once been invited to attend any BBC conference or committee or planning group to contribute ideas about future election coverage. I have been covering the annual party conferences for over thirty years. I have never been invited to any meeting to plan future conference coverage. During thirty years' continuous work in BBC Television, I have never been invited to any of the regular meetings at which current affairs programmes are reviewed. I was barred from attending the regular meeting at which the work of the Current Affairs Group was discussed. Whenever I asked if I could attend, the conversation would proceed on the following lines:

'No, because the meeting is for BBC permanent staff.'

'But many of the producers are *not* permanent staff. They are on temporary contract like I am.'

'But they are contract *producers*, you are a contract *contributor*.'

'Why should a contributor, especially a senior contributor, be excluded, and a producer, however new, be admitted?'

'It would be embarrassing if contributors were to attend.'

'Why?'

'Because the producers may wish to criticize certain contributors.'

'But I might wish to criticize certain producers. Anyway I am used to criticism – from the press, from MPs, from the public.'

'The meeting is not intended to be a slanging match.'

'Why should contributors not be present to hear their critics?'

'Because that would inhibit free comment by producers.'

'What if a producer at the meeting wishes to criticize a fellow producer who is present? Does not that cause embarrassment?'

'Uninhibited criticism of each other's work is part of the professional life of BBC producers.'

'But if the reporter-contributor were assimilated into these professional gatherings, his presence would be normal and not embarrassing.'

'You can't assimilate those who have editorial control (BBC producers) with those who have *no* editorial control (the contributors).'

'But I am simply asking to have my say when my work and that of the department is discussed. What would be wrong with that?'

I forget what further footling point would then be put forward in reply. Such were the fly-blown phylacteries of the BBC.

But let me not be unfair. As a reporter-contributor, I have been free to send my views or proposals on any subject to a BBC executive, even at the very top. I have from time to time done this. But it is one thing to make suggestions or to put up ideas.

It is quite another to contribute intelligently to ideas and plans on which others are working, and of which the outsider knows nothing.

My most serious objection to this apartheid between bureaucrats and broadcasters is that it expresses a fundamental BBC attitude that editorial wisdom is the monopoly of the producer-bureaucrat, and that the journalist-broadcaster is merely a front-man. Only a handful of broadcasters in television or radio have had the strength and the spirit to resist this doctrine.

Does the Word 'Shame' Mean Anything to You?

The patient reader who may recall that I mentioned the two different aspects of my work on *Panorama*, film reporting and studio interviews, will not be surprised that I preferred the latter. But I had many enjoyable film assignments, despite the problems with producers. Sometimes I was not accompanied by a producer – to save airfares or because no one was available. Throughout the sixties I was filming abroad for weeks at a time. The *Panorama* archives include many films made by me as a reporter-producer all over the world – in America, Europe, Africa, Russia, Cuba, South-east Asia, Australia, and here in the UK.

There were several reasons why I came to prefer the live studio interview to filming. The first was that responsibility for a film was liable to be divided between several people (cameraman, film editor, producer – if the film team included one – and programme editor) in addition to the reporter. A film was therefore a committee product.

In a studio interview or discussion, especially if it is live or unedited, the reporter as interviewer or chairman is briefed by his editor and then is charged with conducting the programme. He has the responsibility of dealing with any problem which that may involve. Though an interview or any studio programme requires a team, the reporter is effectively in charge during transmission. The editor of the programme, of course, retains cut-off power in the event of emergency, but this has never in my experience been exercised. The editor may, on certain types of programme, be able to give instructions, or suggestions to the reporter through his concealed ear-piece or 'deaf-aid'. Whether these are instructions or suggestions depends on how the programme is run and on the relationship of the Editor and the reporter.

I have been appalled to learn that in some topical programmes the reporter-interviewer is told through his ear-piece by the producer what questions to ask. This explains why some TV interviews are so incompetent. You have an interviewer so dim that he (or she) needs prompting, or your prompting may be by a producer whose knowledge of the subject or understanding of the argument is, to say the least, superficial. Of course, where an interview is one part of a larger event, like the general election results, the programme producer will tell me to move on to another interviewee or to mention such and such a result. That is perfectly acceptable.

My preference for studio to film was because in the studio I had the greater responsibility. But there was another and deeper reason why during the sixties and seventies I became particularly interested in the live interview or discussion. I came to feel strongly that television, which has such an enormous power to project violence and unreason, should do more to present reasoned and civilized argument. The electronic journalism of television, I felt, must do more than transmit 'bloody good pictures'. The television interview seemed to be one way in which important issues could be intelligently explored, and in which a politician or other public figure could be put to fair scrutiny.

In a democracy, TV should not be turned into an instrument of propaganda. The TV interview is one way in which this can be prevented. When politicians or powerful public figures have access to the platform of television, they should be open to questions of a critical, informed and challenging nature. This means programmes in which the questioning is by, or presided over by, an experienced political journalist. To allow politicians and other controversial public figures the soft option of being interviewed by disc-jockeys, or showbiz chat-show hosts, is nothing less than abdication of responsibility to the public.

There is another advantage of the TV interview (and this only gradually became evident). When a TV interviewer questions a politician, this is one of the rare occasions, perhaps the only occasion, outside Parliament when a politician's performance cannot be completely manipulated or packaged or artificially hyped. *Some* TV answers can, of course, be prepared by script-writers, and committed to memory, but not all. The answers cannot be on autocue as for an address to camera.

The image-maker can advise on how to sit, or what hairstyle to have, or on voice quality. But once the interview has started, the politician is on his (or her) own. The questions are chosen by the interviewer, not by a party strategist or a pollster or a public relations expert, any of whom can greatly influence the content of a speech.

Unlike a politician's platform speech, or a politician's article, or a politician's TV address, an interview on television is one public act which is not in the hands of the advertising men, the pollsters, the propagandists, the image-makers, the public relations experts, or the marketing men.

Of course, all these technicians of modern political communication would try to make their contribution, exert their influence, proffer their advice and scheme their schemes. But in a TV interview, provided there is time for probing cross-examination, the politician cannot be wholly shielded against the unexpected. The politician's own brain is seen to operate. His (or her) real personality tends to burst out. Truth is liable to rear its lovely head.

When a politician is in a difficult situation, or has said some stupid thing, or is proving an embarrassment to his cause or party, what do his advisers always seek to do above all? They try to make sure that he (or she) *does not have to answer questions on* TV. In a newspaper interview, the politician may flannel or fudge, but in a TV interview the flannelling and the fudging can be seen, and judged by the viewing public, just as the jury in a court can form their opinion of the candour and credibility of a witness.

At least *some* of the answers in a TV interview will be spontaneous, unrehearsed, impromptu. To that extent, the answers may show how the brain is working, and where the politician is weak or strong. The viewer is watching a reasoned dialogue, not a series of staged or pre-packaged responses.

The sixties was the period when the television interview became established as a new branch of journalism, as part of the political process, and increasingly as a political event in its own right. Some of us, particularly on *Panorama*, became more and more aware of the importance of the TV interview in our modern democracy. It seemed to me that if politicians or other public figures were to have access, as they should, to the powerful platform of television, they should pay a reasonable price for that access. That price should be the obligation to answer fair and challenging questions in a TV interview or debate. In other words, they should be accountable on TV.

In 1964, the political correspondent of *The Times* noted:

> Single-handed a week ago Mr Robin Day had more scope and time to call the Prime Minister to account on a range of current issues than the leader of Her Majesty's Opposition, not to say all the rest of his front-bench colleagues.*

When Sir William (now Lord) Rees-Mogg made his retirement speech as Vice-Chairman of the BBC Governors at a Broadcasting House dinner in 1986, he paid a tribute to me which was coldly received by his audience of senior BBC executives. He said that 'Robin Day had done more than any other person during the last thirty years to make politicians accountable on television'. He did not mean that I had in some mysterious way altered the constitution or had acquired some sinister power of subpoena. All he meant (I hope) was that I had worked in the conviction that those who use television to gain power, and to hold power, have the obligation to explain their policies, to justify their actions, on that same medium. Provided the questions were fair and relevant, this obligation was now generally accepted by the politicians. That was not formal accountability but it seemed to me, as a reasonable man, good sense.

*The Times, 24 February 1964.

The development of the TV interview in the sixties was an increasingly controversial feature of the political scene:

> It may be a topsy-turvy development of representative democracy, but there is no blinking the fact that the supreme test for a party leader these days has become the ordeal by television . . . Opposition back-benchers would have given years of their life to have had the Prime Minister full in their sights for twenty minutes as Mr Day did.*

Concern was expressed that the TV interview with its mass audience, its probing questions put by unelected questioners who were better-known personalities to the public than some of the politicians being interviewed, was a danger to parliamentary democracy. Was not the TV interview usurping the function of Parliament as the prime forum of democratic enquiry? Were not our political leaders being subjected to improper inquisitions, impertinent grillings and 'trial by television'?

One response to the denunciation of the TV interviewer was to point out that parliamentarians of ten or twenty years' experience were well accustomed to putting up with questions much rougher, and interruptions more brutal, than anything they experienced at the hands of a TV interviewer. The sympathy of the viewer should not be with the hard-boiled politician, but rather with the humble interviewer (such as myself) trying to elicit some clarity or truth for the public benefit. The interviewer is invariably at a disadvantage.

I recall having to interview Ted Heath when he was Prime Minister for *Panorama* live in No. 10. The subject was his new Counter-Inflation Bill published half an hour before transmission. I had that half-hour to read the Bill, and to jot down some notes for questions. Who had the advantage, the interviewer or the Prime Minister, who had spent many hours of that week, preparing his case for the Bill and arming himself with every conceivable answer to every conceivable question?

By the mid-sixties television was seen as having become a power in the land. It was becoming more than a medium of

*The Times, 18 February 1964.

'I thought they weren't allowing no more political satire until after the election.' Trog on the 1966 election campaign.

news and opinion. Television's questions, television's debates, television's confrontations between public figures, were not merely a new form of journalism. These were political events in themselves, which the other media, press and radio, felt obliged to report. Television's coverage of politics became part of the political process. A politician's performance in a TV interview, especially that of a Prime Minister, was seen as one measure of his political strength or popularity. Hence those of us who conducted TV interviews were denounced. Were we not 'self-appointed inquisitors' who cross-examined our elected leaders without ever having been elected ourselves? Were not these 'jumped up' TV interviewers getting too big for their boots?

Why, the critics still persisted, should the Prime Minister or anyone else be answerable or accountable to Robin Day or any other interviewer? This was a nonsense question because top politicians gave TV interviews only when they chose to do so. Only then did a television interviewer have an opportunity to put questions on behalf of the public. Moreover, the TV interviewer could not compel the politician to answer the question. He could only repeat his question with polite persistence. There was no presiding judge to order the politician not to prevaricate. The politician here is not on oath, unlike McCarthy in those Senate hearings.

Thus the often-made comparison between a TV interview and a courtroom cross-examination is false and misleading. A TV interview will last at the most an hour (usually a few minutes). Counsel in court may continue questioning for hour after hour, subjecting the witness to a cross-examination infinitely more penetrating and painful than anything seen on television.

I myself have often been criticized by barristers and judges for excessive gentleness to politicians, and for 'letting them off the hook'. I would explain that I had no power to do otherwise, but I listened to the reproaches and would often seek advice. I was once preparing an interview with a Prime Minister who shall be nameless. At lunch in the Garrick Club I asked a famous High Court judge, the late Sir Melford Stevenson, veteran of many forensic triumphs, what should be my first question. I knew what policy questions to raise, but how should I open the interview? I should add that the Prime Minister in question was not then (how shall I put it?) at the height of his reputation. Melford thought for a moment or two, recalling, no doubt, devastating cross-examinations by Norman Birkett or Patrick Hastings. 'You should start', he said, 'by asking the Prime Minister this: Does the word "shame" mean anything to you?'

I am ashamed to relate that, after the most careful consideration, I chickened out.

When 'non-elected' interviewers were accused of usurping the power of Members of Parliament, my professional conscience was clear. I had long urged the admission of the TV cameras to Parliament, so that the public could see their leaders questioned and challenged by those elected for that purpose. I was brought up to believe in the House of Commons, and to revere our parliamentary system. My father, though not a politician by profession, had a deep and lifelong interest in politics. He passed on to me his keen understanding of the place of Parliament in British life. I went to a school where the headmaster was a former MP who explained to generations of boys the traditions of Westminster. I have never shared the contempt of many clever people for Parliament, no matter how dull or trivial it may be, no matter how easy a target it is for the attacks of sophisticated critics.

Parliament is not a show staged for the benefit of the press gallery. It is a legislative assembly and forum of debate. Like other human beings, MPs sometimes bicker and squabble about petty things. But there are clashes of principle and moments of drama. Parliament is 10 per cent of the time a theatre and 90 per cent a workshop.

I have differed sharply from Bernard Levin about parliamentary behaviour, particular when he has treated readers of *The Times* to one of his tirades. Reaching for his adjectival automatic, Levin wrote on one parliamentary occasion of a 'mob of roaring, boring, jabbering, gibbering, bawling, squawling, perfectly appalling hooligans . . .'

Levin referred to the proceedings as a 'riot'.* I had seen nothing of the kind. There was certainly a lot of noise, and there was undignified confusion of a procedural kind. This can happen in any democratic assembly. Points of procedure, trivial though they may seem, often involve points of principle which matter to free men. Such vulgar manifestations of the democratic process do not, of course, occur in totalitarian countries with sham parliaments. Bernard Levin, for whom I have the greatest affection, has always saddened me by his sniping at Parliament. He has done this since the days when he made his reputation at it as 'Taper' on the *Spectator* in the fifties. I have also had to rebuke another good friend of mine, Frank Johnson, whose brilliant parliamentary sketch-writing in the *Telegraph* and later in *The Times* brought laughter to his readers' breakfast tables in the seventies and eighties. Frank's genius was too special to be misused in mocking the mother of parliaments. I was glad when he gave this up for higher things.

The free vote of the Commons on 9 February 1988 gave me great satisfaction. The House had at last voted in favour of TV. It passed the motion 'That this House approved in principle

The Times, July 1974.

the holding of an experiment in the public broadcasting of its proceedings by television; and believes that a Select Committee should be appointed to consider the implementation of such an experiment and to make recommendations.'

The motion was moved by a Tory back-bencher, Anthony Nelson (Chichester). His speech was a model of lucidity, eloquence and parliamentary skill. Nelson defeated with courtesy and patience the tactics of the antis who mounted a series of interruptions designed to wreck his arguments. He won the admiration of the House in a speech which presented the case for television better than I had heard in any of the previous debates.

Despite the argument for television having been launched so well, many people, including myself, who had heard the debate were astonished when the result was announced – Ayes 318, Noes 264. The opponents of TV had been powerful. The Prime Minister was against, and so was the Leader of the House, John Wakeham. From below the gangway there were caustic objections to television from Norman Tebbit, the former Tory Chairman. Those who feared that the cameras would encourage stunts and demos were able to point to what had happened the previous week in the (already televised) Lords. Three lesbians had abseiled down from the public gallery. This was in protest at the introduction of a law against the promotion of homosexuality in schools. So all the signs were unfavourable to television when the vote was taken. But this was a new House of Commons, elected only eight months previously. The old anti-television arguments had again been trotted out but many MPs who had grown up in the television age were unimpressed. They poured into the Aye lobby that night.

The Commons has now been televised since November 1989 with widely acclaimed success. On July 19 1990 the House voted to make the experimental TV coverage permanent. The Leader of the House, Sir Geoffrey Howe, made generous mention of my part, three decades ago, in pioneering the case for TV.

I was the first person to deploy the detailed arguments for televising Parliament. My pamphlet, *The Case for Televising Parliament*, was published by the Hansard Society. A copy was sent to every MP. Rab Butler wrote a foreword for me. This was a minor miscalculation on my part. In July 1963 I thought, like most political observers, that the man most likely to succeed Macmillan as Prime Minister was Rab. In the event it was the 14th Earl of Home. But though the foreword to my pamphlet did not turn out to be by the Prime Minister, it was by a distinguished parliamentarian and added weight to my case. Though of course Rab was careful not to commit himself!

I began by describing an incident which had a powerful effect on those who saw it:

> One wet and windy night this year a small group of men were huddled together under neat dripping umbrellas in Parliament Square, a few feet from Abraham Lincoln's statue. The time was 10.15 p.m. and the date Monday, June 17th 1963. Across the Square, the House of Commons had just voted in the most critical division for many years, after the debate on the Profumo scandal.
>
> The men who sheltered under the umbrellas were Members of Parliament and reporters. They were taking part in a BBC television report on the division, in which 27 Conservatives abstained. The MPs had rushed out from the lobbies to join the *Panorama* outside broadcast team waiting across the road in Parliament Square.
>
> The news, the occasion, and the weather made it a dramatic broadcast. But it was a lamentably awkward and secondhand way of using television. Many people, including MPs, suddenly realized how television is hamstrung in its efforts to communicate important parliamentary proceedings to the public.

The pamphlet stressed that I was not concerned with the interests of television. My purpose was to enable the democratic process to be served by television more adequately. The admission of the TV cameras would be in Parliament's own interests. Parliament, however, has not always been able to see where its true interests lie. Modern parliamentary government could not have developed without that reporting which Parliament fought so long to stop in its eighteenth-century struggles with the press. Let me quote from the great Erskine May – from his *Consti-*

tutional History of England. Describing in 1861 how parliamentary reporting had come to be fully accepted, Erskine May wrote:

> and what a revolution has it accomplished . . . Publicity has become one of the most important instruments of parliamentary government. Press reporting, instead of being *resented* by parliament, is now *encouraged* as one of the main sources of its influence.

And this great Victorian constitutionalist concluded: 'No circumstance in the history of our country, not even parliamentary reform, has done more for freedom and good government than the unfettered liberty of press reporting.'

In the last quarter of the twentieth century, television is even more important than the press was in the nineteenth century when those words were written. I ended my 1963 pamphlet with a flourish that was too optimistic:

> It is to be hoped that Parliament will not be so slow and stubborn about television as it was about the press. How long will it be before television takes its inevitable and rightful place in the Press Gallery? It cannot be long now. The case for televising Parliament is overwhelming. Future generations, accustomed to seeing Parliament on their television screens, will wonder what all the fuss was about.

In April 1978, the sound-only broadcasting of the Commons began. This has probably been the biggest influence in favour of television. The radio broadcasts, especially of Prime Minister's Question Time, are generally held to have lowered the reputation of the Commons. This is because all the rowdy beargarden noise somehow sounds much worse when you cannot see what is happening! The radio broadcasts have convinced many people that television would be much more favourable to the House – and incidentally to Margaret Thatcher. Radio makes her sound to many listeners like a screeching virago, battling against the disembodied barracking.

When television coverage of the Commons is at last allowed,

its value to our democracy will be even greater than when I first advocated it. Since then, television has become part of life, part of politics. Its technology has been revolutionized. Its power should be at the service of our ancient parliamentary system. The fundamental argument is the same as it has always been – that the nation's prime forum of debate should not continue to shut itself off from the nation's prime medium of mass communication. Parliament must work with the tools of the age or it will sculpt no monuments for the future.

In the early sixties, *Panorama* was the principal platform for major political interviews on British television. There were, of course, other programmes which featured interviews, such as ITV's *This Week*, and *Gallery*; the BBC's late-night political weekly. But it was *Panorama* which had the prestige, the peak hour (8 p.m.) and the length (fifty minutes). By the end of the decade I had taken part in interviews with all the Prime Ministers of the time, and with other leading world statesmen.

There was one memorable *Panorama* in which four Prime Ministers and a President sat together round a table for a discussion under my chairmanship. This was unprecedented. The occasion was the Commonwealth Conference in July 1964. The five heads of government were our own Prime Minister, Sir Alec Douglas-Home, Field Marshal Ayub Khan (President of Pakistan), Dr Eric Williams (Prime Minister of Trinidad), Jomo Kenyatta (Prime Minister – and soon to be President – of Kenya) and Keith Holyoake (Prime Minister of New Zealand).

We in *Panorama* were proud of the impressive cast we had succeeded in assembling for a round-table live discussion in the TV studio. Our distinguished group included leaders from the five continents, from both the old and the new Commonwealth, from Asia, from the Caribbean, from the Pacific, from Africa. It was a group which aptly exemplified the multi-coloured, multi-racial character of the new Commonwealth.

The televised discussion between these five heads of government was inevitably polite and platitudinous, except when Trinidad's Dr Williams, wearing dark glasses, lived up to his nickname of 'Dr No'. When asked what the Commonwealth meant, he said, 'In our part of the world it has not meant very much so far. It does not mean anything.' But the pre-programme conversation, over drinks in the oak-panelled hospitality room at Lime Grove, was more relaxed. The Conference itself had not yet begun. The heads of government had flown in only that day. Some of them had never attended such an event before and had never met any of their colleagues.

I found myself introducing them to each other. 'Mr President, do you know the Prime Minister of Trinidad?' The small talk was fascinating. The immaculate and imposing President Ayub Khan, fingering his military moustache, took Prime Minister Jomo Kenyatta aside and suavely invited him to lunch: 'Would you care to have a meal with me one day this week? At my club?' Jomo Kenyatta, fly-whisk in hand, made a genial grunt in response. Whereupon Field Marshal Ayub Khan said, 'Then I'll get my people to liaise with yours. I look forward.'

Keith Holyoake of New Zealand was a veteran of these Commonwealth summits. He clearly enjoyed the role of statesman on the world stage. He put his arm round the shoulders of Dr Eric Williams, a man of small stature and laconic utterance, as they went up to the studio. 'And how,' boomed the Prime Minister of New Zealand to the Prime Minister of Trinidad, 'And how is your economy these days?' It was like an enquiry after someone's rheumatism by a relative at a family reunion. But that, of course, is what these Commonwealth Summits were supposed to be.

As other BBC programmes started up in competition, *Panorama* had to change. It had become only one of your windows on the world. By the end of the sixties, *Panorama* was very different from the programme which I had joined in 1959. Competition from other BBC programmes was not, however, the only reason for this transformation.

When Richard Dimbleby died in December 1965, the BBC did not appoint anyone immediately in his place as anchorman of *Panorama*. There was a deeply felt emotion that no one could replace him. There was also a strong feeling that, though someone would eventually have to replace him, there was no obvious choice. Both these feelings were understandable, but regrettably they led to a two-year delay before anyone was appointed as *Panorama's* regular anchorman (or 'introducer', to use the term which had come into fashion). The delay was caused also by the growing doubt and disagreement in the TV service as to whether *Panorama* in the second half of the sixties would need a 'fifties-style' anchorman.

All this did unnecessary damage to the programme's image, which had already suffered by the tragic loss of Richard Dimbleby. Moreover, every month's delay made it more difficult for the successor to establish himself.

Sir Ian Trethowan was (like me) a political commentator on BBC programmes such as *Panorama* and *Gallery*. He later (unlike me) rose from the humble position on the shop floor to the rarefied heights of the BBC's Boardroom. He became Director-General in 1977. Sir Ian relates that in 1966 evasive treatment from the senior people at Lime Grove had irritated him: 'When Richard Dimbleby died, I was told I would replace him on *Panorama*. Then suddenly Robin Day did so.' Trethowan understandably felt that the BBC had not treated him fairly. He appealed to Huw Wheldon, the Managing Director of BBC TV, and asked to be told where he stood. Wheldon apologized to Trethowan. It was unpardonable that the BBC's promise had not been kept. Wheldon added: 'But let me say that if I had been Editor of *Panorama* I would have wanted Robin as my anchorman. Robin Day has star quality, you do not.'*

I was astounded to read this revelation in Trethowan's memoirs. That blunt message, delivered by Wheldon to him over lunch, was what led Trethowan to quit the screen and to move up into BBC management when the invitation came the following year.

To read, in 1984, that any BBC high-up had regarded me, in 1967, as having 'star quality' came as a total surprise to me. Wheldon had never indicated anything of the kind. Nor had the Editor of *Panorama* who, according to Wheldon, then wanted me as the anchorman. Not that I would ever expect BBC executives to go around telling a contributor that he has star quality. There is enough egotism in television without that. And for me to have known Huw Wheldon's true opinion would have strengthened my hand against the BBC in contractual negotiations. Nothing in my dealings with the BBC TV service had ever

*Sir Ian Trethowan, *Split Screen* (Hamish Hamilton, 1984), pp. 121 and 122.

given me to think that I was regarded as having star quality. In fact the opposite was the case.

Another reason for my surprise in reading Trethowan's account was that I had always thought that *he* would inevitably succeed Richard Dimbleby. He had already established himself as a successful presenter on *Gallery*, the BBC's political weekly. On the screen, Ian had a quiet but impressive authority. His manner was more emollient than mine. His features were clean-cut, and his words were fluent and finely articulated. As an old lobby correspondent, his political antennae were finely tuned and highly sensitive. Ian looked younger than I did, though he was in fact older.

Ian and I had been newscasters together at ITN. Our first joint appearance was on the night of 6 January 1958. That was the day that Macmillan described the resignation of his three Treasury ministers as a 'little local difficulty'. So we were old friends, well aware of each other's virtues, and tolerant of each other's shortcomings, if any.

The *Yorkshire Post* had given these descriptions of us as ITN newscasters in 1958:

> Mr Day, his head set deep in his powerful forward-thrusting shoulders, his chin jutting like a cliff over his polka-dotted bow-tie, the bridge of his nose puckered in a frown, is the searching, pointed questioner. . . . Mr Trethowan sits erect . . . but not severely, his handsome head waving well above his shoulders. He has a remarkably young face, lean but not hungry. . . . He makes a man feel his equal. . . . *

I became *Panorama*'s presenter for five years, from 1967 to 1972. But the job was being downgraded. I was told not to see myself in Dimbleby's role. Clearly they did not want another anchorman who personified the programme. When a *Panorama* report on the City by Mossman had caused the stock market to tumble, the headline was 'Dimbleby's Dip'.

I was warned that I would sometimes have nothing to say except 'good evening' and 'good night'. Within two years I was

Yorkshire Post, 8 July 1958.

merely the 'main' presenter, who would not do any presenting unless the Editor wished. Julian Critchley MP asked in *The Times*:

> What is happening to Robin Day? He has been less in evidence on *Panorama* recently. Of late the programmes seem to have consisted entirely of film; reports, contentious, bland or chummy by Pettifer, Charlton and MacNeil.*
> There has been little for Day to do except introduce the acts.†

These were unhappy years for me. I became increasingly fed up with BBC television. To many in Lime Grove I was 'old hat', difficult to work with, always trying to tell the producer how to run the programme. Robin Day, went one savage swipe, is interested only in 'talking heads' to keep his own talking head on the screen. My professional interests were too narrow, too political. What did they expect from one whose profession was reporting politics?

I was a symbol of what they called 'institutional politics'. There was even an article in the BBC's own *Radio Times* (February 1970) which referred to 'allegations' that I had 'an old-fashioned attachment to government by debate'. Note the loaded word 'allegations', implying that what I was attached to was something reprehensible. Whoever had made these 'allegations' was not asked what sort of government I should have been attached to. Government by mob? Government by petrol bomb, by Armalite, by computer? Government by jackboot?

I was not in good odour with a new generation of BBC producers. I knew that some of the younger executives wanted to be rid of me. The editorship of *Panorama* had become a training-ground for future top management. It was a job in which young men could show what they were made of, and whether they had balls – in other words (as it was said in Lime Grove) whether they could deal with Robin Day.

For much of the seventies I had to fight very hard to keep a

*Robert MacNeil, a Canadian reporter, now a star of the nightly MacNeil – Lehrer news on US TV.
†*The Times*, April 1969.

regular position on the screen. In fact, I lost any such position for several years. My contracts in the seventies were for an unsatisfying assortment of now forgotten series – *Sunday Debate* (me in the 'God-slot'!), *Talk-in* and *Newsday* (a ten-minute interview spot at the start of BBC 2's evening transmission when virtually no one was watching). There were also items in *Midweek*. Occasionally I did a political interview for *Panorama* when its editor was prevailed upon so to use me. In January 1972 I ceased to be a member of the *Panorama* team after twelve years on the programme.

My departure was reported to have been my 'resignation' from *Panorama*. In fact I had been notified in writing that my position as the *Panorama* anchorman was to be discontinued. I had wanted to continue with a further contract, but was offered only an unsatisfactory ten-week extension. So rather than accept that lame-duck position, I left when my contract expired in January 1972. That was the reason I left *Panorama* and it was not of my own volition.

Far from ever wanting to leave *Panorama*, I had always regarded it as the finest outlet for TV journalism. I have continued to appear on it from time to time, not merely at general elections, but right up to the end of the eighties.

After *Panorama*, one of the short-lived BBC series which I worked on was called *Talk-in to Day*. This had a variable format, sometimes a single interview, sometimes a discussion, sometimes a participating audience. At first this involved me in some abysmal work. The most fatuous and asinine programme I have ever endured was that in which I had to chair a discussion with an American woman who advocated 'child-free marriage'.

But there were more interesting assignments. Some of my *Talk-in to Day* programmes were produced by Christopher Capron. He incidentally was the only Lime Grove producer known to me who owned a country estate with mansion – where he would generously entertain.

Capron and I arranged at a few hours' notice the most sensational interview I had ever done. This was an interview with Lord Lambton, the disgraced Air Force Minister, who figured in the first front-page government sex-scandal since Profumo ten years earlier.

Lord Lambton MP, elder son of the 5th Earl of Durham, sat in the Commons for Berwick-on-Tweed, having renounced the succession to the earldom. The *News of the World* had obtained compromising photographs of Lord Lambton with prostitutes. Lambton resigned from the government and from Parliament.

I had met Tony Lambton several times as a journalist. Before joining the government he had written on politics for the *Evening Standard*. He was more elegant and sophisticated than most of one's fellow reporters. With his aristocratic manner, good looks and dark glasses, he was a glamorous personality.

The scandal of Lambton and the prostitutes was at its height when Chris Capron and I were arranging *Talk-in* for Thursday, 25 May 1973. No one had yet interviewed Lambton about the affair. He was the political personality of the moment. He was the obvious choice for my programme next day. But would Lambton agree to be interviewed? It was just possible that the length of *Talk-in* (forty minutes) would be an attraction for him, because this would better enable him to explain himself than in a short 'news' interview of, say, two or three minutes. I telephoned him at his stately home, Biddick Hall near Durham. Within five minutes Lambton had accepted my invitation.

We were on Christian-name terms. We talked as one journalist to another. He made only one condition: that he should not be asked any 'prurient questions'. He said he meant by that questions about the sexual details of his intercourse with the two prostitutes. Since I had no intention of asking such questions (which the BBC would not, in any case, have broadcast) I agreed. But I also put a condition of mine to him. I told him, 'I will have to ask you the kind of painful questions you would have to ask if you were a reporter in my position.' Lambton understood perfectly and immediately agreed.

Chris Capron and I were in Durham by that evening. We arrived at Biddick Hall and set up our camera and equipment. Lambton was amazingly relaxed. His son, Ned, aged about eleven or twelve, on holiday from the Dragon School, was sitting in the corner of the room as we got ready for the interview. As the camera was about to roll for the first question, Chris Capron asked Lord Lambton if he wanted his son to remain in the room. We thought he might not wish his son to hear his father answer questions about his sexual activities with whores. Lord Lambton said it was perfectly all right for his son to stay and listen as long as he kept quiet. We had underestimated an ancient family's historical sense. Obviously the boy (the future Earl of Durham) would not be allowed to miss a fascinating, if painful, moment in the family history.

While I am quite certain that this was not arranged intentionally to inhibit me, the presence of his son, who was sitting only a few feet from me, added to the strain of conducting the interview. I had never in my interviewing work asked people questions about private matters, such as their sexual activities. But, in this interview, sex had become a public matter because of Lambton's ministerial position. Even so to ask a father, in his own home, with his young son present, about the prostitutes he had been with was distressing in the extreme.

I was criticized for being excessively sympathetic in tone, 'almost apologetic', 'even more agonized than Lord Lambton', and 'anguished to the point of tears'. One government minister was reported as thinking 'Robin Day was going to break under the strain'.

Lord Lambton, on the other hand, was praised for his 'courage and candour', and for appearing to be 'completely relaxed'. But there was some criticism that Lambton was too 'bland' and 'too glib'. The *Daily Telegraph* recorded in its front-page account:

> Occasionally sipping a drink from a tall glass, he showed no embarrassment when questioned about his visits to the Maida Vale flat where he was secretly photographed in compromising circumstances with prostitutes.*

Some of Lord Lambton's answers qualified for 'sayings of the week', and won him marks for style and nerve. The forty-minute interview was reported verbatim or at great length in the press. One of my first questions concerned the security angle:

Q: There may be some people watching who find it

Daily Telegraph, 26 May 1973.

inconceivable that someone who holds a ministerial position in the department of Defence should not foresee the obvious risks involved in consorting with call-girls.

A: But the risk is really what?

Q: The risk is, I would assume, as you yourself pointed out in the case of Profumo, of a man being exposed to blackmail: not a question of a leak but a risk that security might be endangered by a man putting himself in a vulnerable position.

A: Well, I think there is this to say about this side of it, that perhaps one of my failings over this matter has been my absolute knowledge that in no circumstances whatever would I have ever consented to blackmail, and that had these films or things been shown to me instead of shown to the *News of the World* and a demand for money had followed, I would inevitably have gone to the Police instead of the Police coming to me. Therefore, in my own mind, though I admit that this was quite wrong, I knew that I would never give in to blackmail and therefore there was no, in that sense, security risk.

Then I turned to the question always discussed during political sex-scandals:

Q: Do you take the view that the private life of a public man with particular responsibilities need not be more strict than that which is expected of ordinary people?

A: I don't think there's any doubt that it has to be today, but I think that this does bring one to a really rather interesting point: I wonder how long this can go on being so much the case in the relaxed society in which we all live, because I don't think that people can be expected to be one type of person for the first thirty-five or forty-five years of their life and suddenly become a totally different type, a plaster saint . . . I should think a great number of the men watching this programme would know that they have done themselves at some time or other what I have done without endangering their jobs or anything. And I think the question which will have to be met fairly soon is whether this sort of thing should be considered, as it were, a blackmailable offence. Now I'm not for one moment arguing that it isn't. It is.

I returned to the security-risk aspect:

Q: You still say that when you were doing this, it never struck you at all that this could have put you, as a minister in a sensitive department dealing with secret and important matters, in a position of risk?

A: As I said, I regarded this as a private matter. A lot has been made of the fact that call-girls are a security risk, in the sense that they might get knowledge. I think that this is extremely doubtful. People don't go to call-girls to talk about business affairs or secret affairs. If the call-girl had said to me suddenly, 'Please, darling, tell me about the laser ray,' or 'What do you think of the new Rolls-Royce engine for the MRCA?' I would have known that something was up, that this was a deliberate plant.

Then I came to the question which elicited some of Lambton's smoothest replies.

Q: May I come to another point . . . in the way in which it was put by one of your parliamentary colleagues, Maurice Edelman, Labour Member of Parliament: 'Why Lambton, a highly personable and attractive figure, should have *bought* his sexual entertainment is more mysterious.'

A: Well, I must pay attention to that because he is a great expert on these things.

Q: You mean he writes about them in novels?

A: Yes.

Q: Why should a man of your social position and charm and personality have to go to whores for sex?

A: I think that people sometimes like variety. I think it's as simple as that, and I think that impulse is probably understood by almost everybody. Don't you?

I did not think it appropriate for me to answer Lord Lambton on that point. His 'people sometimes like variety' was much quoted and headlined.

My next few questions concerned drug-taking. Lambton admitted that he had taken drugs 'upon occasions'. He explained that when you go to a country you fall in with the local customs. He had smoked opium in Singapore, and hashish in Arab countries. Lord Lambton declared in words which have been quoted long after the incident which occasioned them: 'Taking opium in China is totally different from taking it in Berwick-on-Tweed.'

Towards the end I asked Lambton why it was necessary for him not only to resign, but to quit politics altogether, recalling the many politicians who had led lives more immoral than his. Lambton's reply was cool and characteristic:

There's all the world of difference, hypocritical as it is, between doing something and not being found out and doing something and being found out, because then you make a fool of your supporters. If you had said to an ordinary man in my division, 'Your Member went to bed with two call-girls,' he'd say: 'Good for him.' But if he was put in the position of having his Member of Parliament publicly degraded for doing that, he couldn't have the respect for his Member that must be the basis of a relationship between a Member and his constituency. If an ordinary man was told another man had been to bed with two pretty girls, he'd say, 'Lucky dog,' but if it was blazoned all over the newspapers that a Minister had done that and brought his division into disrepute, he would say the man can't get away with it: it's life, it's logic, that's what happens.

Lambton was remarkably frank and forthcoming throughout. On only one question did he decline to comment. That was when he was asked about speculation that the *News of the World* photograph showed him in bed with *two* girls, one white and one black.

After the filming had been completed, at about 10 p.m., Lord Lambton kindly invited us to have supper with him and Lady Lambton. We had cold pheasant with some claret which, had I been in a state of mind to savour it seriously, would have been judged excellent.

Then Chris Capron and I were driven though the night with the film to London. On the journey in the car we listened to a sound-only recording of the interview. We were both stunned by what we heard, even though we had both heard it when the interview was being done. We had not realized how cool, how stylish, Lambton would seem to some, or how outrageous to others. But neither Chris nor myself expected the huge press coverage which followed the interview, with front-page banner headlines such as:

LAMBTON'S AMAZING CONFESSION
LAMBTON'S TV SENSATION
WHY LORD LAMBTON PAID FOR SEX

There were mixed reactions to my questioning. I was accused of 'impertinence and unwarranted intrusion', and of being excessively sympathetic in tone. But a few days afterwards, Lord Lambton declared, 'Robin Day treated me perfectly correctly'.

Despite the headlines and the excitement, this 'scandal', this so-called 'sensation', was forgotten within a month.

After I ceased working regularly for *Panorama* in 1972, I had no role in a continuing programme comparable to that on *Panorama* in the sixties. My television work was bitty and patchy. I felt that BBC Television was not treating me fairly, or using me properly. The sixties, which were a brilliant decade for me in *Panorama*, had ended in bitter dispute and discontent. My television career had reached a depressing plateau. Luckily there were to be some peaks to climb – three general elections were to come, two in 1974 and one in 1979 – when the BBC would wheel me out on to centre-stage again.

Max Hastings, author, war correspondent and now Editor of the *Daily Telegraph*, was a reporter in BBC Television at the beginning of the seventies. Writing from his inside knowledge of Lime Grove in those years, Hastings assessed that period of my career. He was writing in 1980 on my twenty-fifth anniversary in television:

Yet his survival at the top of broadcasting has been achieved in spite of many BBC executives and producers and not because of them. The struggle that began in the BBC in the 1960s to subordinate the presenter and reporter – the face on the screen – to those behind it, almost achieved the nemesis of Robin Day ten years ago.*

I had hoped that my appointment in 1967 as the presenter of *Panorama* would be a professional advance for me. Had I foreseen how badly things would go for me in Lime Grove, I would have looked for more exciting opportunities. That same year, 1967, was the year that ITN started *News at Ten*, the most important development in television journalism since the creation of ITN. Sir Geoffrey Cox writes in his memoirs that he regarded me as 'one of the two ideal candidates' (Alastair Burnet was the other) to be the joint presenters of ITN's new half-hour news. But as Cox explains, I was 'strongly established elsewhere'. BBC TV had just appointed me to what (I wrongly thought) would be the most important job on the screen, presenter of *Panorama*.

Whether I would have been an ideal candidate for *News at Ten* or not (and I would make no such claim for myself) it was launched brilliantly by Alastair Burnet and Andrew Gardner. Its success totally vindicated the view of Sir Geoffrey Cox that television news could be both responsible and popular, and that a half-hour news would top the ratings.

I rather wish that my television career had included a spell as an evening news anchorman. I was a news anchorman at lunchtime on radio with the *World at One* for eight years. I would have loved to have done it on television. I would like to have tried my hand at being a Burnet, a Sissons or a Cronkite. But no one has ever dared risk it.

The half-hour TV news was a great advance by ITN in 1967. But I was convinced that the main TV news programmes required a further dimension. There was a need to transform them into something deeper and more comprehensive.

My view, first expressed in the mid-seventies, was that 'News'

Evening Standard, 19 September 1980.

on TV could not achieve its full potential as a balanced service unless 'News' is understood to include what all good newspapers and radio programmes include, namely the additional dimension of analysis, colour, explanation and discussion – in other words, what is now labelled on television as current affairs. I called for radical improvement in the main television news programmes – the main source of news to many millions. My reasoning was that if television news lacked the time, the resources and the courage to tackle serious issues in depth, if it succumbed to television's tabloid temptations of sensationalism, distortion and trivialization, then the basic source of facts for an entire nation would be adulterated.

So my proposal was that the main TV news should be expanded to an hour in length and transformed into a newspaper of the screen, with depth, authority, variety and colour. I urged (this was in 1975) that the Hour of News should be the next big step forward in TV journalism, the biggest since ITN had launched *News at Ten* in 1967 as a half-hour programme. So I applauded when ITN's excellent *Channel 4 News* was launched in 1982. With Peter Sissons in the chair, this hour-long news programme put into practice much the same ideas as those I had outlined seven years previously. But I claim no credit for *Channel 4 News*. The idea was obvious to any intelligent TV journalist, and its time had clearly come.

Perhaps I may be forgiven for also applauding when the system of independent production companies was adopted for Channel 4 under Jeremy Isaacs in 1981. I had proposed such a system to the Pilkington Committee on Broadcasting – in 1961. It was amusing to recall that my proposal was totally ignored.

What concerned me at the beginning of the sixties was that television should move forward from the age in which topical coverage had to be impartial because TV was controlled by only a few powerful hands (whether publicly owned or commercial). I argued that if control of programmes were spread among as many different hands as possible we could move forward to an age in which TV could fulfil a truly democratic function – the diverse and independent expression of free opinion – which could not be safely left to the increasingly monopolistic press.

The object of a democratic television system should be not the impartiality of a few but the independence of many.

I envisaged a new broadcasting authority, charged with the duty of commissioning a broadly balanced selection of programmes. Its revenue would come from advertising. It would engage a wide variety of individuals or groups to produce and present programmes. The authority would thus be a publisher, not a producer. It would select but not supervise. It would originate but not control, and of course it would deselect if commissioned programmes were inadequate. A large number of small independent groups of producers and journalists (or playwrights and actors) could be commissioned to produce regular programmes, in much the same way as books or articles are commissioned by publishers.

Obviously this was too revolutionary an idea for the great and good members of the Pilkington Committee. But such a system, outlined by me in 1961, was twenty years later to become Channel 4, as the second ITV channel came to be called. The Channel 4 system has been a great success. John Gau, one of the top BBC executives who became an independent producer, has written that 'the setting up of Channel 4 as just a publishing medium, with no in-house production . . . freed everything. This was a tremendously good thing. It changed the entire landscape of television. . . .'*

There were, of course, other and more effective progenitors of the Channel 4 system, such as Anthony Smith, who argued persuasively for it to the Annan Committee. But Lord Annan himself has noted:

the palm might well be handed round to Sir Robin Day who, in 1961, advocated '. . . a Commission that would originate but not control. It would select but not supervise. It would be a publisher not a producer.'†

I never understood why this idea, which is now seen as the prevailing wisdom, took so long to surface in influential circles. Perhaps the answer is, as so often, that:

*Quoted in *The Times*, April 1989.
†Letter to *The Times Literary Supplement*, 21 November 1986.

There is a tide in the affairs of men,
Which, taken at the flood, leads on to fortune.

In 1961 my idea was floated on a tide too low and too early.

11

The Decline of the BBC

The Fault Lies at the Top

In 1976 I decided to make a bid for the topmost job in broadcasting. The position of Director-General of the BBC had to be filled following Sir Charles Curran's retirement. Why did I, a mere reporter with no executive experience, throw my hat into this particular ring? My application to be the Corporation's Chief Executive was not a publicity stunt, nor was it made out of overweening self-regard. I put my name forward for three reasons. First, I was invited to apply by the Chairman of the BBC Governors, Sir Michael Swann. Second, by applying I could demonstrate my profound belief that the BBC badly needed strong, politically aware leadership from its Editor-in-Chief. Thirdly, my application would at least show that I was ready to take on greater responsibility than that of an interviewer or commentator.

My application was bound to become public (as it duly did) and the chances were that I would merely look silly for having had ideas above my station. My bid for the post of Director-General was another gamble. In return for the slight possibility of gaining some professional kudos by being a short-listed candidate, I risked becoming a joke-figure, the troublesome TV personality whose fame had gone to his head.

It was a difficult time for the BBC (when was there a time for the BBC which was *not* difficult?) and the report of the Annan Committee on the future of broadcasting was imminent.

Curran's likely successor seemed to be Ian Trethowan, who had been plucked out of the television studios by Lord Hill, the then Chairman of the BBC Governors, and appointed to the BBC's Board of Management. By 1976, Ian was Managing Director of BBC Television, having earlier been Managing Director of Radio.

But despite Trethowan's strong claim, the Board of Governors and its Chairman, Sir Michael Swann, were reluctant to appoint the 'inside' favourite, simply because he was well known to them and was obviously *papabile*. Accordingly the post was advertised and several distinguished 'outsiders' applied or were asked to apply. As someone who had been a contributor to BBC programmes for many years but had never been on the BBC staff, I was an inside-outsider or perhaps an outside-insider. Anyway Sir Michael Swann invited me to apply and to appear before the Board of Governors. At fifty-three I was not too old.

In submitting my formal application I enclosed a memorandum to the Chairman. It was written in the circumstances of November 1976, but today the reader may think it has stood the test of time. My memorandum was as follows:

November 1976

To Sir Michael Swann, Chairman of the BBC Governors
From Robin Day

The Role and Responsibility of the Director-General

1. The Corporation faces a very serious crisis. The BBC's survival as the great national institution we have known may be in jeopardy. The verdict of Annan could be highly damaging at a time when financial difficulties may be acute.
2. It is my respectful submission that no Board of Governors, however wise and determined, can fulfil their responsibility as strong and effective Trustees of the public interest unless they are served by a strong and effective Director-General.
3. A strong and effective DG would embody the BBC's

determination to uphold its integrity, independence and standards. A prime aim of the Board should be to restore the prestige and authority of the DG as the first servant of the Corporation.

4. The DG should first and foremost be an *Editor* in chief, not a bureaucrat in chief. ('The issues that a DG has to be concerned with are fundamentally editorial' – Sir Charles Curran, *Listener*, 21.10.76.) The essential need of the BBC will be for creative editorial leadership to encourage and to stimulate no less than to control and to discipline. Such leadership would raise morale inside, and win respect outside – by firm policies clearly communicated.

5. This is not to see the Corporation solely as an organ of news and opinion. Its achievements in the arts and popular entertainment are crucial to its claim on the public's respect, the public's affection and, not least, the public's money. But across the whole spectrum of programmes, standards must be upheld and encouraged by judgments which are essentially editorial in character – what is fitting, what is fair, what is reasonable, what is responsible, what is honest, what is first-rate.

6. Lack of conventional administrative experience should not necessarily be a disqualification. Lack of executive experience within the BBC machine could be a positive merit. There is much to be said for a mind uninfluenced by the entrenched departmental attitudes which too often affect the thinking of BBC executives at the expense of what matters most – the quality of programmes.

7. Among the most urgent priorities for the new DG should be to improve the content and organization of News and Current Affairs, and to clarify the chain of editorial command.

8. In the critical post-Annan period, the public reputation and personality of the DG should be such as to command respect and restore confidence. Managerial competence will not be enough.

9. There can never be another Reith. But there can and

should be a DG whose leadership is inspired by strong convictions about the rights and duties of broadcasting, and especially of television, in our democracy.

That statement of the Director-General's position was not entirely unrelated to my own qualifications or lack of them. My chief shortcoming was lack of any administrative or executive experience. But in emphasizing editorial leadership I truly believed this to be the quality most needed in the DG. Administrators, executives, financial managers – from the world of industry, commerce or the public service, or from within the BBC – were to be had two-a-penny. Not so a strong editor-in-chief with political nous.

At first the Board of Governors gave me a gentle ride in the interview. Then in a tone of some impatience there came a blunt, loaded question from the formidable Lord Greenhill of Harrow, formerly Permanent Under-Secretary of the Foreign Office. Lord Greenhill asked: 'How much experience have you had, Mr Day, of running an organization of twenty-six thousand people and a turnover of hundreds of millions?'

My reply was swift: 'None whatsoever. That is precisely why I have applied. I do not consider the Board should be looking simply for an executive with experience in management of an organization like the BBC.'

From the audible silence before I replied, I had sensed that some of the Governors felt that Greenhill's question was unnecessary, because they all knew that my application was based on my editorial and political experience, not on any managerial qualifications. But I was prepared for such a question and dealt with it straightforwardly. I went on to argue the overriding need for strong *editorial* leadership, as set out in my memorandum to the Board.

The BBC Governors chose, of course, Ian Trethowan, my old friend and colleague from ITN days. In Ian they had both a television journalist with great editorial experience *and* an executive with management experience in the BBC. If I had been in their shoes, he would have been my choice from the available applicants.

But I think the Governors were interested to see me. I had

never met most of them before. At any rate the Chairman wrote me a nice little note in his own hand afterwards which was very pleasant to receive, if only because it made me feel that in agreeing to put my name forward I had not made a complete fool of myself.

BROADCASTING HOUSE
LONDON W1A 1AA

CHAIRMAN
SIR MICHAEL SWANN
16th December 1976

My dear Robin,

I wanted to let you know, in advance of hearing it on the air, or reading it in the Press, that the Board of Governors has appointed Ian Trethowan as DG.

This will, I fear, come as a disappointment to you, but the board wanted me to tell you various things: how grateful they were to you for coming to meet them; how much they valued some of the insights you gave them; and how they would somehow like to see your wisdom more built into the system. Perhaps we can talk some time.

Yours ever,
Michael

A grateful letter – but somehow that 'wisdom' of mine was never 'built into the system'.

My memorandum to the Chairman about the Director-General's responsibility had expressed exactly what I had long felt about the professional leadership of the BBC. In 1987 I sent to Chairman Hussey, when he was about to choose a successor to Alasdair Milne, a copy of that 1976 memorandum. I was no longer a candidate for DG, but my statement of the DG's role seemed more relevant in 1987 than ever.

My belief was and is that the decline in the BBC's reputation since the sixties had been due to inadequate leadership at the top. This decline has been one of the most depressing developments in the life of Britain. Thirty years ago, the BBC had a reputation for excellence, integrity and fairness. To belong to the BBC was something to be proud of, like belonging to an élite profession or crack regiment. It was stuffy and bureaucratic and was known as 'Auntie', but it was respected by all political parties and held in much affection by the public.

The arrival of ITV competition in 1955 had made the BBC wake itself up, especially on the news and current affairs. It withstood the challenge of ITV without losing its standards. The BBC went into the sixties with confidence. It was given a second channel, BBC 2. But thereafter the BBC began to lose the respect of one political party after another, and to make a series of major errors for which the Director-General of the day must be held responsible.

Here let me say that the BBC has continued to put out programmes of all kinds which command admiration for their excellence, integrity and fairness. The BBC *still* puts out such programmes. It remains a very fine broadcasting organization, which is particularly appreciated when you are deprived of it. That is precisely why the decline in its reputation is such a tragedy. All the goodwill and prestige accumulated by hours of quality productions on radio and TV is set at naught by incidents of shocking errors of editorial judgment – incidents which have caused bitter political reaction. So much so that one former DG, Sir Ian Trethowan, writes in his memoirs that at the beginning of the eighties:

> Distrust of the BBC was widespread among politicians of all parties. In the wake of *That Was the Week* and *Yesterday's Men*, there was strong feeling that the BBC was not so much hostile to any particular party as contemptuous of the whole Parliamentary process. Equally serious for the BBC, senior civil servants to some extent shared their masters' views.*

Writing some fifteen years ago, I declared, 'Whatever its faults, the BBC is an unrivalled example to the world of independence and excellence in broadcasting.' I urged the Annan Committee: 'Don't muck about with the BBC.' But since then, unfortunately, the BBC's reputation and standing, particularly in the political

*Trethowan, *Split Screen*, p. 162.

world, has been cumulatively and gravely damaged by lapses of judgment and taste. Those lapses have been editorial lapses. The editor-in-chief is the Director-General. Either the DG of the day took wrong decisions, or he failed to reorganize the editorial chain of command so as to ensure that editorial blunders did not occur, or he failed to fire people for gross misjudgment and so make an example of them.

In my memorandum to the Board of Governors about the Director-General's position, I emphasized the importance of the DG being a strong editor-in-chief. In the sixties the DG's authority had been weakened by the Board of Governors taking too much executive power into their hands. This was after Lord Hill had been appointed by Harold Wilson to curb the power of Sir Hugh Carleton Greene. Yet a board of twelve part-time Governors cannot hope to run the BBC, which is, as Lord Greenhill reminded me, an organization of twenty-six thousand people with a turnover of hundreds of millions. That is why I urged that a prime aim of the Governors should be to restore the prestige and authority of the Director-General. Running the BBC must be the job of the DG, assisted by his professional colleagues.

My impression so far is that this is what Michael Checkland has effectively been doing as the present DG. He has put John Birt (his Deputy DG) in charge of the BBC's journalism, and has appointed Paul Fox in charge of BBC Television. The results of this cannot yet be judged, but there seems to have been a strong and dynamic exercise of the DG's authority. Checkland's early editorial decision to give *Newsnight* a regular fixed starting time (something Milne had said could never be done) was highly encouraging. In an LWT interview in 1979, Milne warned that despite BBC journalists' demands for a fixed starting time for BBC 2's *Newsnight*, overall scheduling policy would make that impossible. Milne said, 'We could never give them a regular start point,' because plays and films shown later in the evening were of variable length.*

Having appointed a Director-General, the Governors should either back him or sack him, that is to say, leave him to exercise editorial and executive authority and, if he does not turn out to

---

*LWT's *Look Here*, 9 March 1979, in interview with Andrew Neil.

be a wise choice, get another DG. The first time a Board of Governors did just that was when Marmaduke Hussey's Board abruptly sacked Alasdair Milne in January 1987.

The reputation of the BBC has never recovered from the more serious errors of editorial judgment for which successive Directors-General must be blamed. These errors and the accompanying political storms have been often documented in blow-by-blow accounts in the writings by ex-Directors-General and others. There was the shameful incident of the INLA interview in 1979 about Airey Neave's murder (see Chapter 14). But there have been other episodes which need only be mentioned to stir the memories of those concerned with broadcasting: *Yesterday's Men* in 1971, which infuriated Harold Wilson and did the BBC great and lasting harm; the BBC's Falklands War coverage, aspects of which outraged Tory back-benchers; *Real Lives* in 1986 which rocked the BBC to its foundations; *Maggie's Militant Tendency*, the defamatory *Panorama* for which the BBC in the end had to apologize; *The Monocled Mutineer*,* a drama production, misleadingly publicized as historical truth; the series on the security services by, of all people, Duncan Campbell; the Carrickmore episode; the BBC's refusal to put on the Falklands play by Ian Curteis.

In 1977 the Annan Committee delivered some unwelcome judgments on BBC programmes. The italics are mine:

> The weaker part of the output seemed to us the current affairs programmes. Some affliction of feebleness has struck the current affairs output . . . The quality of individual programmes was patchy, sometimes dull and on occasion superficial to the point of banality. We have the impression that *the fault lies at the top*.†

In January 1984 Max Hastings made a vitriolic attack on the BBC in the London *Standard*. Hastings wrote:

> Never has the leadership of the BBC seemed more pitifully

---

*Described by Lord Annan as 'a programme compounded of malevolent falsehood' (House of Lords Debates, 27 April 1988).
†*Report on the Future of British Broadcasting*, HMSO, 1977, p. 192.

inadequate, bankrupt of ideas, lost for a cause . . . The BBC has become like a great fat man incapable of seeing over his own bulk to his toenails.

Hastings referred to the 'hapless' Alasdair Milne and the 'abrupt and graceless' Brian Wenham.* Hastings was fiercely expressing his own opinions, but those opinions found an echo in many quarters. He was invited, in August 1984, by the organizers of the Edinburgh Television Festival, an annual professional gathering attended by executives and producers, to state his case. I took the chair. It was a heated occasion. Alasdair Milne, the BBC's Director-General, listened to the debate from a seat in the gallery, and was angry at what he heard.

In his speech Hastings delivered a further denunciation of the BBC's condition:

> Even five years ago it would have been unthinkable that thoughtful, moderate people in the broadcasting industry should be asking questions about the very rationale of the Corporation's existence.

To some people, no doubt, Hastings' onslaught may have seemed exaggerated and unfair. But he could see the storm gathering. Two-and-a-half years later, the Director-General, the 'hapless' Alasdair Milne, was unceremoniously sacked.

The Board of Governors were right to sack Milne. It is curious that Milne was not only the first DG to be sacked in this way, but he was also the first DG to have risen to that position right up the BBC hierarchy. He was the first TV professional to become DG, and the first DG to have spent virtually his entire career in the BBC. Yet his BBC career ended in ruins. I felt some sympathy for him. But the truth is Milne was not the man to be DG. He was well qualified in every way except one. He had brains, energy, professional experience and technical knowledge, but (and I gave this as my opinion at the time of his appointment in 1982) he lacked the qualities required in leadership. He was not a natural communicator, he was impatient of slower minds

*Then Director of Programmes BBC TV, and a clever Corporation apparatchik.

opposed to his, and his political antennae were not sufficiently sensitive. Had I been a Governor on George Howard's Board, I would not have voted for Milne's appointment. Had I been a BBC Governor on Marmaduke Hussey's Board, I would have approved Milne's dismissal in 1987. He was one of those brilliant professionals one comes across in institutions and in many walks of life, men who are well equipped for every post except the top one.

In Broadcasting House, that building shaped like the stern of an ocean liner, the portraits of past Directors-General are displayed like those of headmasters in a school hall. They make a strange gallery of personality and experience, none of them, except Haley perhaps, comparable in stature to Reith, the founding father of the BBC.

I met Reith once, at the twenty-fifth anniversary dinner of BBC TV in 1961. We merely shook hands, without conversation. But to be briefly in his presence was to sense the grandeur of his personality. He was an immensely impressive figure, with the face of an Old Testament prophet. He was magnificently attired in full evening dress, loaded with medals, stars and across his chest the the GVCO riband, across his face the scar of his 1915 bullet wound. Looking at Reith that night, it was incredible to recall that he had retired from being Director-General at the height of his reputation and prestige when he was only forty-eight.

Since the Second World War, the Directors-General of the BBC have been an odd assortment. There was William Haley in 1944, the first newspaper executive to become DG. Long after he had left both the BBC and *The Times*, Sir William explained to me how he had seen the role of the DG: 'I would tell the Governors, that is my decision or this is my appointment. If you don't like it you can sack me.' That was Haley's robust, if retrospective, assertion of the DG's position.

After Haley, the DG was Lieutenant-General Sir Ian Jacob. He was the first professional soldier to become DG. He had been a member of Winston Churchill's wartime entourage. This experienced, able staff officer may not have been the best man to lead the BBC into the post–1955 television jungle. But he is held in high esteem. He held the fort as DG when ITV launched its attack on the BBC monopoly in 1955. The story goes that Winston Churchill when Prime Minister in 1952 sent to the Chairman of the BBC Governors, Sir Alexander Cadogan, a message on the following lines: 'I see you have to appoint a new Director-General. That is of course entirely a matter for you, not for me. But I would have no objection to your appointing my old friend Ian Jacob.' That is probably apocryphal, but has an authentic ring.

Hugh Carleton Greene, brother of the novelist Graham Greene, took over in 1960. He was the first professional broadcaster to become DG. Greene is the Director-General whose name is most often coupled with that of Reith as being a great DG. Reith built the BBC into a great but stuffy national institution. Greene, it is said, opened the windows and allowed the fresh air to blow through. Or as Nancy Banks Smith wrote: 'Reith made the BBC respectable, Greene made it exciting.'

Greene was an agnostic, a bohemian and an iconoclast. He saw the DG as having a duty to be a thorn in the side of the establishment. The prevailing and fashionable verdict on Greene as DG was that 'he carried the BBC struggling and kicking out of its Auntie image into something much more relevant to the decade'. Under Sir Hugh Greene, the same admirer claimed, the BBC began to mirror the attitudes of a new young generation 'instead of the respectable old-fashioned, middle-class values of a past that was over and done with'.*

This contempt for 'respectable middle-class values' may have seemed refreshing, but it sowed the seeds of Greene's eventual downfall, and of the decline in the BBC's reputation. These were years when the BBC began to abdicate its position as an upholder of certain values and standards, and instead began to be a reflector of the so-called 'swinging sixties'.

Sir Hugh Greene is usually accorded greatest praise for the satire boom (*That Was The Week That Was* and so on) in the early sixties. Suddenly, with Greene's benevolent encouragement, politicians could be unjustly lampooned, and religions offensively mocked. BBC standards of fairness and accuracy went out of the windows which Hugh Greene had thrown open. For

*T. C. Worsley in the *Financial Times*.

a brief period, Frost, Sherrin and the rest had a box-office triumph with undergraduate-style satire.

But one or two things went wrong with this 'fresh air' revolution under Hugh Greene. The first was that the other BBC people had to soldier on under the old rules of fairness and accuracy, and reasonable respect for those elected to office. Those other BBC people were regarded as fuddy-duddies, while Frost and company (briefly) were privileged to indulge their snide and mocking pleasure. So the BBC was seen to be applying two different standards: one for its normal current affairs output and for its light entertainment programmes, but a wholly different standard – iconoclastic, anarchic, contemptuous, smutty, biased – for the licensed Young Turks of the satire department.

Then, of course, the BBC's satire explosion was soon seen to be in flagrant breach of the BBC's Charter. The Labour Party, then in opposition and thirsting for power, at first loved the 'satirists' for their crude mockery of the Tories. But the shrewder of them realized that there could be no place for anti-government satire by the BBC under a Labour government.

In January 1963 David Frost introduced a *That Was The Week That Was* item called the Consumer's Guide to Religion. Milne, then the executive in editorial charge, frankly admits in his memoirs this was 'calculated to offend nearly everybody'.* This sketch was applauded by the Director-General. Hugh Greene's message for those involved was 'Tell them I take off my hat to them.'

The BBC's historian, Lord Briggs, writing about *That Was The Week That Was* records even-handedly: 'Many liked its vitality, wit and absence of cant. Many others were shocked by blasphemy, schoolboy sexual jokes, and lavatory humour.'† That the latter elements should have been tolerated in a BBC programme, and one in which the Director-General himself was taking a close editorial interest, was deplorable. This could not be justified as 'challenging' or 'anti-establishment'. It is not surprising that Milne records how early in 1963 the programme was 'savaged' by his own colleagues in the TV service. At a

*Alasdair Milne, *DG* (Hodder & Stoughton, 1988), p. 37.
†Asa Briggs, *Governing the BBC* (BBC, 1979), p. 218.

meeting called because of pressure from heads of departments, the Head of Light Entertainment (records Milne) declared that because of *TW3* he had never been so ashamed of the BBC in the twenty-five years he had worked for it.

That protest may help to explain why I deplore the excesses of the BBC 'satire boom' in the sixties, while proudly recalling the birth and growth of robust TV journalism in the fifties. These were not two sides of the same anti-establishment coin. We in ITN, and in *Panorama*, were not anti anything. We did not knock for the sake of knocking. We were in the business of straightforward journalism, not showbiz. We were breaking new ground in public service broadcasting. We were out to make topical television relevant, probing and professional. We were not unfair, we were not biased. We were not offensive or smutty.

Despite the regular Saturday night audience of over ten million viewers, *That Was The Week That Was* was a constant anxiety to the Board of Governors. They objected to 'adolescent smut' and 'items offensive to sincere religious feeling'. The Vice-Chairman of the Governors came near to resignation, but Hugh Greene bowed to the inevitable and took the programme off at the end of 1963. The convenient excuse was that 1964 would be an election year and that the political satire would become difficult.

For the Director-General, the programme had been both a success and a disaster. He had openly encouraged it, yet had to take it off when it got out of hand. The extraordinary aspect of the whole episode is that the BBC's Director-General (not some errant young producer) should have encouraged and permitted such an obvious breach of BBC standards. The BBC's Charter was there to be honoured, not defied.

If we had as many TV channels as we do newspapers, and a diversity of programmes independently produced, then perhaps there need be no restraints. Programmes could be as barbed and biased and personally offensive as the laws of libel and obscenity would permit. But given a BBC operating under Charter, paid for by the licence-holder, a programme like *That Was The Week That Was* was a gross error of judgment for which the Director-General, Sir Hugh Greene, was responsible.

Greene was also responsible for a dubious reinterpretation of the BBC's duty of impartiality. In the BBC *Handbook* for 1960, Greene was quoted as follows (the italics are mine):

> I do not mean to imply that such a broadcasting system should be neutral in clear issues of right and wrong – even though it should be between Right and Left. It can, for instance, encourage the right attitude on the colour bar. In my job in the BBC, I should not for a moment admit that a man who wanted to speak in favour of racial intolerance had the same rights as a man who wanted to condemn it. *There are some questions on which one should not be impartial.*

In 1965, in a remarkable address to a meeting in Rome, Sir Hugh developed his theory of impartiality. He again declared that:

> There are some respects in which the BBC is not neutral, unbiased or impartial. That is where there are clashes for and against the basic moral values – truthfulness, justice, freedom, compassion, tolerance. Nor do I believe that we should be impartial about certain things like racialism, or extreme forms of political belief.*

Many would applaud such sentiments. But who would decide, and on what principle, which issues the BBC would treat impartially, and on which issues the BBC would (*contrary to its constitutional obligations*) express its opinion? This doctrine of selective impartiality does not appear to have been thought through with rigour.

After Greene's controversial Rome speech in 1965 on impartiality and on how the BBC should see its responsibilities in society, the gulf between the DG and the Board of Governors – who reflected political and public concern – was becoming wide and deep. For example, Sir Hugh Greene had declared in 1965:

The BBC should encourage the examination of news and

---

*Speech to the International Catholic Association for Radio and TV, 9 March 1965.

opinions in an atmosphere of healthy scepticism. It follows that in its search for truth . . . a broadcasting organization must recognize an obligation towards tolerance and towards the maximum liberty of expression.*

But the Board of Governors published their own document in 1968 called *Broadcasting and the Public Mind*. They were emphatic that:

it is no part of our responsibility to appear to deride, or despise, or destroy, merely because they are traditional or conventional, the moral standards to which sections of the public are attached. There are people who are deeply hurt by the intrusion into their homes of what they believe to be the BBC's amoral or anti-moral attitude. We should take care not to offend such people needlessly.

There were other differences of outlook between the DG and the Governors to whom he was responsible. Sir Hugh Greene's view was:

I believe we have a duty to take account of the changes in society, to be ahead of public opinion rather than to wait upon it. I believe that a great broadcasting organization . . . should not neglect to cultivate young writers who may, by many, be considered 'too advanced' or 'shocking'.†

The BBC's Governors for their part were careful to stress that freedom carried with it responsibility.

We must reconcile the dramatist's need to express himself with the nature and susceptibilities of our audience . . . A fully responsible producer or editor is one who by reason or instinct recognizes and eschews anything that involves a risk of damage disproportionate to the importance of the objective.

*Rome speech, 9 March 1965.
†Rome speech, 9 March 1965.

In the same month as that document from the BBC Governors was published, July 1968, Sir Hugh Greene announced that he would be resigning as DG. In the end Greene was dealt a humiliating blow by the leader of the political party which had originally and enthusiastically welcomed his 'fresh air' policy. The Prime Minister, Harold Wilson, appointed as Chairman of the BBC Lord Hill of Luton, the old radio doctor, Charles Hill, who had talked about constipation at breakfast-time. He had later become a Tory Cabinet minister, and then Chairman of the ITA. Greene's furious resentment was a petty misjudgment. Lord Hill was not an intellectual, nor an aesthete, but he was a shrewd politician of much commonsense who knew his way around. What is more, Hill had the greatest respect for the high traditions of the BBC.

After Greene it was decided to have a DG with a lower profile and less authority. So Charles Curran was appointed in 1969. Born in Dublin, Curran was the first Roman Catholic to become DG. He was a grey BBC bureaucrat who had spent virtually his entire career climbing up the administrative side of the BBC. He had an encyclopaedic knowledge of radio technicalities, wavelengths and internal BBC staff organization. He was a competent administrator. He knew little of television. He was not a political animal. In short, Curran was an unimaginative appointment. His Chairman was Lord Hill of Luton. That was doubly unfortunate for Curran. He was thus the first DG to serve under a Chairman who was determined to run the BBC himself, and he was the first to serve under a Chairman who had more experience and knowledge of television than his DG.

The man who should have been appointed was Sir Huw Wheldon, who was then Managing Director of Television. He had his shortcomings, like talking too much and enjoying being a personality too much. And his interest had always been much more in the arts than in politics. But Wheldon was a real, red-blooded man, not a faceless bureaucrat. He was a man whose company was enjoyed by all those, especially politicians, who met him. He had presence, he had flair. He could speak in public. His eloquence was legendary, as also was his robust good sense. Here is one Wheldon dictum which was loudly applauded by me: 'No real programme was ever made by a committee.

You insure yourself against failure by having a committee, but you also insure against triumph.'*

Wheldon was a man whom people were proud to look up to and follow. He had a huge sense of humour. He had been presented with his MC by Monty on the field of battle. He could use the language to persuade, to flatter, to cajole, to inspire. He was a leader. The failure to appoint this great broadcaster to be Director-General was a major error by the Board of Governors.

The other matter to be greatly regretted was that Paul Fox was not persuaded, or could not be persuaded, to return earlier to the BBC. He would have been an excellent choice for Director-General in 1982 when the Governors appointed Alasdair Milne. It was a wise move of the present DG, Michael Checkland, to bring in Fox as Managing Director of BBC TV in 1988, when the Corporation needed a steadying hand amid the upheavals and traumas resulting from the Hussey-Checkland-Birt revolution.

Paul Fox is by far the most outstanding figure in the British television industry. He has now been thirty-seven years in the business. He is President of the Royal Television Society. He has been a successful executive in BBC TV and in ITV. He began at the sharp end as a scriptwriter in TV news.

I first met him in 1960 when he became Editor of *Panorama* after being Editor of *Sportsview*. That seemed an unpromising transition. He did not then know the first thing about politics. But he soaked it up in no time at all. I would come into his office with a suggestion. Paul would say, 'Who is Dick Crossman?' Then 'Who else would you have?' Then 'What would they talk about?' Then 'For how long?' In a few minutes an item was arranged, or shot down. Paul Fox swiftly became an editorial executive of flair and authority. He was a leader. He knew how to manage people, when to encourage, when to rebuke, when to congratulate.

He had been a paratrooper in the British Army and was wounded shortly after D-Day. He has an unerring instinct for the audience appeal, or non-appeal, or an item or a programme.

---

*Sir Huw Wheldon, Dimbleby Lecture 1976.

He is a great television showman, yet his showmanship is coupled with keen news-sense and political judgment.

As I have already related, when Curran went in 1977 the Board chose Ian Trethowan to be DG. Ian was probably the best-qualified man in terms of varied experience ever to become DG. He had been a newspaper journalist and a political correspondent. He had also been a working TV journalist, appearing on screen, and a TV executive. He had worked in ITV as well as for the BBC. Ian was a political animal to his fingertips. When he was a Westminster lobby correspondent for the *News Chronicle* back in the fifties, I had noticed his perceptive interventions at lobby meetings. He was an articulate man of considerable presence, a man, I thought, who should come into television, which he later did. He was a great asset on the screen, especially during the elections of the sixties. Eventually he moved up into top BBC management.

I did not always agree with Trethowan's judgment as DG, notably over the disgraceful INLA interview in 1979.* His period as Director-General did not inspire me. Nor, as I am sure Ian would say, was it meant to. Ian was first and foremost an 'operator'. I do not use that word in a pejorative sense. He is a man not given to confrontational relationships or to striking attitudes. He was a man who would often solve problems by letting them solve themselves, which may be a good idea. As Director-General he did not change much or shake things up. But his political diplomacy succeeded in getting the BBC's Charter extended to 1996, and secured an agreement that the licence fee would be indexed to inflation. As for the way he ran the BBC internally, his regime left untackled many of the weaknesses which Milne inherited and which were not dealt with until the shock treatment administered by the Hussey-Checkland-Birt regime from 1987 onwards.

To me personally, Sir Ian was always kind and considerate, even when he must have thought I was being an intolerable nuisance. I was much moved by his handsome gesture of giving a grand banquet for me in October 1980 to mark my twenty-fifth anniversary in television. Apart from BBC colleagues, there

*See below, pp. 299–302.

were present several parliamentarians with whom I had crossed swords on the screen: Ted Heath, Denis Healey, Enoch Powell, Jo Grimond and Shirley Williams. Also two old friends from my pre-bbc days, Mr Justice Waterhouse, who had telephoned me in 1955 about the opening in itn, and Chris Chataway.

Another esteemed guest was the venerated head of the Carvel dynasty – Robert Carvel, like his father before him and his son today, a leading lobby correspondent at Westminster. I had benefited for more than thirty years from Bob's wise advice, frank criticism and sparkling company. A long-time political editor of the *Evening Standard*, he contributed some waspish paragraphs to the next day's 'Londoner's Diary':

> There was an impressive muster of the Corporation's top brass to pay affectionate tribute to Robin Day. He was gracious enough to say he recognized many of them . . . Sir Ian Trethowan described Day as 'a national monument'. Mr Heath spoke of him as 'human, compassionate, and generous'. Mr Healey expressed gratitude that the Grand Inquisitor is good enough to treat politicians as equals.
>
> It was a distinguished and happy gathering to honour (as Heath said) 'the most distinguished television interviewer and commentator of our time'.
>
> Faced with such eulogies, the Grand Inquisitor couldn't resist his own comment: 'After careful consideration, I have decided to go,' he told the company. 'I'm sorry, my teleprompter has broken down, so I'll say that again. Ah yes! After careful consideration, I have decided to go – on.' Much laughter.*

Evening Standard, 16 October 1980.

An ingenious and original cartoon of the author drawn for the Radio
Times.

12

Eight General Elections

A Lady from SE23 Wants a Straightforward Yes or No

My busiest years as a political interviewer were the ten years
from the mid-sixties to the mid-seventies. The work came mainly
in intermittent bursts – at general elections, during the party
conference season, and from time to time on *Panorama*. There
were five general elections (four of them won by Harold Wilson)
in the ten-year period from October 1964 to October 1974. This
was the golden age of the swingometer. In the eloquent hands
of Robert McKenzie it ruled supreme until the coming of the
three-party system and the computer made it obsolete. The
swingometer gave us Harold Wilson by a whisker in 1964. Next,
in 1966, it was Wilson by a landslide. Then over to Heath in
1970, surprising everyone, not least Professor McKenzie. In
1974 the swingometer hovered in the centre. In February of that
year, Wilson scraped back to No. 10, but without an overall
majority. In October 1974, Wilson held on to power with an
overall majority of only three.

These were also the years when television's political coverage,
particularly of elections and party conferences, was developed
and invigorated. As television threw off the shackles, the politicians threw down the gauntlet. Increasingly television got
tough with the politicians. Not surprisingly, the politicians got
tough with television.

The impartiality of television was exercised less passively than in the past. Fairness had to be more than a balance of opinions or the reporting of available facts. The duty to be fair had to be carried out actively by seeking, probing and disclosing facts.

Having been a shackle, impartiality had become a sword. This change in the application of a basic principle of British broadcasting was gradual. It had not come about by virtue of any decree or conscious decision. The change was still evolving, as most changes in Britain had evolved, by experience, step by step, case by case, interview by interview, programme by programme, election by election.

This may be illustrated by reference to the programmes on which politicians could be questioned at election time. Until 1959, it should be remembered, the political parties had monopolized all broadcasting concerning politics from dissolution to polling day. This, admitted Sir Hugh Greene, Director-General of the BBC from 1960 to 1969, was 'a tremendous abdication of responsibility on the part of the BBC'. In 1959, broadcasting had made its debut in a general election campaign. Even then none of the party leaders was exposed to critical interrogation by journalists.

The 1964 election had been the first time that the party leaders appeared to answer questions in special election programmes arranged by television. The major innovation in 1964 was *Election Forum*. The three party leaders, Douglas-Home, Wilson and Grimond, appeared in separate programmes to answer questions put to them by Ian Trethowan, Kenneth Harris and myself. But (and here can be seen how restricted TV still was) the questions could not be ours. Each question had to be read out from one of the ten or fifteen thousand postcards which had been sent in by the public.

Trethowan or Harris or I would therefore say, 'Now Sir Alec (or Mr Wilson): Mrs Bloggs in Scunthorpe asks "What is your policy on immigration?" ' Our job was merely to choose the question-cards to be read out. But ingeniously we managed to improvise an interview by having a selection of cards ready to be used as supplementary questions: 'If that is your policy, Mr Wilson, then Mr Higgins of Bristol would like to ask "Where will the money come from?" ' I was particularly keen to use the cards in this way, but the supplementary questions were not always available on the cards. And supplementaries of our own were kept to a minimum because *Election Forum* was supposed to be a programme for viewers' questions, not ours.

The creator of *Election Forum* was Mrs Grace Wyndham Goldie, Head of Current Affairs in BBC TV. Her idea was to put back into electioneering what television had taken out of it -the individual's right to question. But, as it was, the viewer got poor service.

The politicians could not be probed on any point. All three party leaders got away with grossly inadequate replies. Moreover, the *Election Forums* were stiff and artificial. Though the cards had come in from the voters, the questions to be put to the politicians had to be selected by us. This was done in discussion with the programme Editor. Selection would partly depend on the number of cards sent in on a particular issue.

However fairly we chose the cards (and we chose them with scrupulous care and fairness) *Election Forum* fell between two stools. It did not have real audience participation by visible electors in the flesh (as *Question Time* was to provide during later elections). Nor did *Election Forum* offer independent probing by professional interviewers who could be relied on to ask, and to follow up, relevant and up-to-the-minute election questions.

The most serious shortcoming of *Election Forum* was that all three programmes went out *before* the dissolution, in other words before the campaign was under way. The voters' questions could not deal with the issues as they had developed during the campaign. *Election Forum* was therefore an inadequate contribution to the electoral process. But it was a small step forward.

TV coverage of the '64 election ended on an unforgettable note of high comedy. The marathon results programme was nearly over. Wilson was in with a precarious majority. I was in the TV studio interviewing George Brown, Labour Deputy Leader who was at Transport House. At that moment Labour's majority was not yet clear. I put to George Brown the suggestion of Robert McKenzie that Labour might have to make a pact with the Liberals to have a safe working majority. George Brown thereupon hit out in reply.

Q: Can you govern without a clear majority?

A: We shall govern. The country has given us power . . .
We shall proceed to govern accordingly.

Q: From the results so far, does not Mr Grimond seem to
be in an influential position?

A: I would not worry yourself about that . . . You are
interviewing a member of what looks like the new
administration. We shall govern according to the policies we
have put to the people . . . We shall govern and do our best
to put the nation back on its feet.

Q: Would you tell us whether with such a narrow Labour
majority you will be less likely to renationalize steel?

A: I have already told you. Goodness gracious, Robin,
you don't seem to listen . . .

Q: Mr Brown, may I call you brother?

A: I would be delighted.

Q: Goodbye, brother Brown.

A: Goodbye, brother Day.

The studio rang with applause and laughter from the studio
'audience' of scores of technicians, producers, researchers, cameramen and others working on the results programme.

That was in the first of the eight marathon results-night programmes in which I have taken part. These television spectacu-
lars, first with their swingometer then with their computers, not
to mention their psephologists, became great national occasions
watched until 4 a.m. by millions. Like no other TV programme,
these election-night marathons provided excitement, emotion
and humour. In the best Shakespearean tradition, high drama
was mixed with low comedy. And amid all the graphic techno-
logical wizardry, the old-fashioned interviewer still had his
humble part to play.

On election night 1966 this memorable dialogue took place
between Quintin Hogg MP (formerly Lord Hailsham, later Lord
Hailsham of St Marylebone) and myself:

Q: Mr Hogg, will you now take a back seat in the Tory Party
after this Labour victory?

A: I shall play as big a part as God allows me.

209

Q: And how big a part do you think God will allow you to play?

A: You will have to ask Him.

Q: I don't think He is on our list of people that we interview.

A: No. You would have to pay Him too big a fee.

For the 1966 campaign, *Election Forum* was repeated with the same stiff formula as in 1964, and with the same political leaders except that Edward Heath had replaced Sir Alec. And the same old interviewers struggled manfully to act out the anger or the cynicism on the viewers' cards:

A lady from SE23 wants a straightforward yes or no: 'Will Mr Wilson give a definite yes or no. After seventeen months of watered-down Socialism, can we expect the full dose if Labour gets a big majority? No prevarication please!'

That refrain ran through *Election Forum* and we had to sing it: 'Yes or no? No politician's answer please.' An understandable but rather futile request to Wilson or Heath or Grimond.

But though *Election Forum* had its limitations, the 1966 coverage gave television more scope of its own. Party leaders could be interviewed in ordinary current affairs programmes, such *24 Hours*, by independent, well-informed reporters. Slowly the BBC election coverage was growing up and finding its feet. The shackles were being cast off. The swords were being sharpened.

The 1970 election campaign opened with a *Panorama* featuring the three party leaders. My interview with Mr Heath was described (in the *Daily Mirror*!) as pugnacious, aggressive and outrageous. This was in addition to the postcard ritual of *Election Forum* again, this time with Wilson, Heath and Thorpe versus Day, Charlton and Michael Barrett. But somehow the questions were sharper, or we chose sharper ones. The veteran political columnist, Hugh Massingham wrote:

For the first time one can remember, Mr Wilson looked badly rattled. Mr Robin Day set the tone with this viewer's question: 'Since you have lied, and broken promises, do you

expect the electorate to place any reliance on your word?'
This [*Election Forum*] interrogation of Harold Wilson was
one of the most savage performances the BBC has put on –
and it was none the worse for that.*

Somehow, by experience and ingenuity and nerve, we had managed to make *Election Forum* come alive. And in other TV
programmes election coverage in 1970 was wider, deeper and
harder than ever before.

Which brings us to the year of two elections, 1974. The contrast with 1964 was tremendous. TV coverage had greatly
expanded. Even 'steam' radio, as it was then unfairly called,
rose to the occasion with *Election Call*.† This was a landmark
in the history of democracy and broadcasting.

According to David Butler's book on the February '74 campaign, 'the great success' of campaign coverage by TV and radio
was BBC's *Election Call* on Radio 4. It was a fifty-five-minute
phone-in at 9 a.m. every morning.

It attracted over a million listeners and up to nine thousand
calls. It was chaired with exemplary fairness and skill by
Robin Day. The public's questions were often penetrating
and sometimes blunter than any professional questioner
would dare to be . . . Clearly a new campaign tradition had
been born.‡

So television's *Election Forum*, with voters' questions on those
same old cards, was overshadowed in February 1974 by radio's
Election Call, with its questions to the party leaders from real
live voters, albeit in voice only. A veteran lobby correspondent.
H. B. Boyne, wrote of *Election Call*: 'To have the Prime Minister answering impromptu questions fired at him over the telephone by listeners in many parts of the country was a unique
experience'.§ According to Martin Harrison (writing in David
Butler's book on the February 1974 election) both BBC and ITV

---

*Sunday Telegraph, 31 May 1970.
†Born out of my weekly phone-in *It's Your Line*, which ran from 1970 to 1976.
‡David Butler, *British General Election February 1974* (Macmillan 1974), p. 157–8.
§*Daily Telegraph*, 1 March 1974.

'provided a fuller and more varied service than ever before . . . yet weaknesses remained . . . there were too many cursory and inadequately prepared interviews'.*

One notable exception was the interview for BBC news which elicited from Hugh Scanlon, leader of the Amalgamated Engineering Union, a denial that there was any specific agreement between Labour and the TUC on wage control. Whether there was such an understanding was a key issue underlying the election. What Scanlon said was much quoted and discussed. Television, by impartial enquiry, had thus illuminated the election debate.

But in February 1974 television still had to watch its step. There were loud protests about a pair of interviews by me. I was accused of bias in favour of Lord Chancellor Hailsham and of bias against Labour's Edward Short. The interviews were run side by side in the same programme. Unfortunately the interviews were conducted in completely different circumstances and styles. My interview with Hailsham was conducted on film in the fresh open air of the Scottish Highlands near Inverness that morning. My interview with Short was done in the tense, tired atmosphere of the TV studio late that same night at the White City Television Centre. Hailsham was in his most ebullient knockabout mood. I fell into the error of indulging in some jolly cut-and-thrust instead of serious interrogation. The interview with Edward Short was severe and humourless. He had just watched the Hailsham interview on film and accused me of having one standard of interviewing for Labour MPs and one for Tories. That's what it looked like. But if a politician makes jokey, flamboyant responses, his interviewer is tempted to come back at him in similar style.

The juxtaposition of these two interviews was an unfortunate error. Obviously it was asking for trouble to follow a waggish Hailsham by a grim Ted Short, with whom no one could be knockabout. Had the Hailsham interview been followed by an interview with, say, George Brown, we could have had a pair of colourful characters. As it was we followed the rumbustious

*In David Butler, *British General Election 1974*, p. 152.

Hailsham with the headmasterly Short. How could any interviewer have made the second interview match the first?

But the item was a blunder. It did not look fair. It made me look biased. It was an item which proved that television's expanded and more independent election coverage had to be handled with scrupulous care. We had not only to be impartial, we had to be *seen* to be impartial.

Election campaigns should, however, be fun. There were also some interviews with moments which helped to prevent the television coverage from being too boring.

There was the vintage discussion, about statutory incomes policy, between Harold Lever (the financial wizard of Labour's front bench) and Hugh Scanlon. 'I have with me,' ran my introduction, 'a millionaire and a Marxist.' Harold Lever retorted: 'Robin, my personal wealth is merely an agreeable irrelevance.'

Harold Wilson had a clash with me. I had persisted in asking him, 'Do you think the miners are justified in continuing the strike?' This was the question which Ted Heath had that day challenged Wilson to answer. So, in lieu of any TV confrontation between the two party leaders, the question had been put by me. Harold Wilson answered 'I think the nation is getting a little tired of those questions put by Mr Heath for purely political purposes, and now peddled by you.' Foolishly (it was late at night and the day had been long) I bridled. I objected to the word 'peddled'. Had I not properly invited comment on an opponent's challenge? My mistake was to sound irritated. Wilson, who was in a Norwich studio, immediately seized his advantage: 'Don't get so sensitive. You're in politics. Don't behave like a child about it. Don't get touchy about it, Robin.'

Not an exchange of great political importance, but one of the unexpected sparks which helped momentarily to illuminate the grey election screen.

The Tories' Tony Barber landed a neat jab after I'd said to him: 'I'll leave you with this final thought: that even if the Conservatives win, there might be a different Chancellor.' Barber retorted smartly: 'And I'll leave you with this final thought: there might be another interviewer.'

Certainly the election of February 1974 was the busiest I had known as a broadcaster. This was reflected in the bewildering variety of adjectives showered upon me by letter-writers and critics: rude, disgraceful, biased, redoubtable, indefatigable and battle-scarred were a few of them.

To have kept a diary during the campaign would have been beyond me. Fortunately the *Sun* newspaper kept one for me, at least for twenty-four hours or so. It was called 'A HECTIC DAY IN THE LIFE OF ROBIN'.

Who runs Britain? It could be Robin Day. The man is everywhere.

He is there on Radio 4 at 9.05 in the morning taking listeners' questions.

He is at the Labour and Tory morning press conferences. He is hurrying to lunch. He is rushing to the BBC's election studio in the afternoon.

He is writing scripts through a babble of camera technicians and political bullfighters. He is there on television every evening, shoulders hunched, brow centre-furrowed, looking intense. Sometimes he seems the only man taking this election seriously.

Robin Day is a serious man.

Not even the birth, a fortnight ago, of a son, Alexander Ainslie, can deflect him from his duty as The Communicator, to us, The People.

Take one day this week. He was up just after 8 a.m. He was in the studio with William Whitelaw and Margaret Thatcher before 9 a.m. and began taking questions from telephone callers.

A miner told Mr Whitelaw he was lying. Robin let Mr Whitelaw deal with it. It was a rough political ride.

Broadcast done, straight to London Airport. Plane to Inverness.

Interview with Lord Hailsham. Flight back to London. In studio at 8.30 p.m. More than a thousand miles covered.

Preparation for live TV Election Special. Argument with Labour spokesman Edward Short in programme.

Home at midnight.

Next morning up at 8 a.m. to read newspaper stories of Edward Short remarks . . .

Working hard?

'Yes,' he admits, 'but no more so than the hundreds of people involved in this election.

'In this studio there are lots of people working harder than me.

'I'm just the icing on the cake.'*

That 'diary' mentions the birth of my elder son. Alexander was born on 5 February 1974 just after 8 p.m. At that very moment I was on the air, at the microphone, in BH, presiding over my weekly radio phone-in, *It's Your Line*. The guest was Len Murray of the TUC. The miners were about to strike. The dissolution was to be announced two days later. Polling day would be 28 February.

The birth was not expected till late that evening. But Alexander arrived a little early. The hospital rang Broadcasting House to tell me. Unfortunately the BH switchboard refused to take a call for me. They thought it was someone pulling a fast one and trying to get into the phone-in. So the hospital was told to ring the phone-in number 580 4411 – which of course was jammed solid. So I did not know a son had been safely born till I arrived at the hospital at about 9 p.m., having raced there immediately the phone-in was over. On arrival I was shown a little blue object in a plastic box. I said (according to my wife), 'What's that?' She said, 'It's yours.' She then told me that when she had gone into labour her gynaecologist had suggested that she should listen to my programme on the radio 'to keep her relaxed'. The only trouble was that what I was saying on the radio about the crisis was not very relaxing. My opening words were something portentous like 'This is a grave and difficult moment for us all.' My wife laughed about this – retrospectively.

Some weeks after the election, I was chatting to Enoch Powell. I mentioned that I had become a father. Jabbing his finger at me gleefully, Enoch said, 'You have justified your existence at last!'

In February 1976 I became a father for the second time. Again a boy was born, whom we christened Daniel.

*Sun, 23 February 1974.

In November 1978 our family life suffered a grievous blow. Our elder son Alexander, aged four and a half, was severely injured in a fall. He had been escorted to the London Zoo with his brother while his mother and I were in Oxford for the day attending a lecture. We returned home that evening to learn that Alexander was in the intensive-care unit at University College Hospital with extensive skull fractures and a compound fracture of the right thigh. He had fallen about twenty-five feet into a concrete vehicle yard. He had got through some railings, having broken away in playful mood from his escorters.

Alexander survived, and made a miraculous recovery, in due course, thanks to the skill of the distinguished neurosurgeon Mr Bernard Harries, to the care of UCH, and not least to the devotion of his mother who was by his bedside in the hospital for several weeks.

For a week after the accident there was terrible uncertainty. The first sign of hope came when I was sitting by Alexander's bed. My wife Katherine was resting briefly. Alex lay silent, his head and one eye heavily bandaged, the other shut. The nurse-physiotherapist suggested that I should keep chatting gently to him to see how he reacted. For a long time there was no response. I mentioned that lots of people had written to wish him better. And there had been some lovely get-well cards. I said, 'There's a card from Leeza. You remember Leeza, don't you, Alex? The little girl who used to let you ride her pony in the country. Isn't it nice of Leeza to send you a card?' I babbled on. No response. I repeated myself. 'You remember Leeza, don't you, Alex?' Suddenly he opened his undamaged eye and said quietly but clearly, 'It's not Leeza, it's Liza.'

I shall never forget that wonderful moment as long as I live. From that two-second, five-word response, I knew that he could speak, that he could think, that he could remember, and that he could even tick off his stupid daddy for mispronouncing Liza's name.

One later aspect of the surgery was of particular interest. The specialists were considering how to repair the skull. They had a discussion, of which I was a very respectful chairman, as to whether they should mend the gap in the skull by a bone-graft, or whether this was necessary, or whether they should screw a

"Daddy thinks I'll
ask simpler questions"

Daily Mail *cartoon to mark the birth of Alexander Day, February 1974.*

specially moulded piece of titanium into the skull to cover the gap. The third option was suggested by Mr Crockard, the neurosurgeon who had pioneered this technique at the Royal Victoria Hospital in Belfast when dealing with terrorist bomb victims. The technique was new in London. The other two specialists and I asked questions – such as if you screw in a metal plate to the skull of a little boy of four and a half, isn't there a problem as his head grows bigger? The answer was that the skull would not change in size on that particular place and outgrow the two-inch square metal plate. The bone-graft specialist watched the titanium being screwed in and was most impressed. My layman's account has, I fear, been inadequate to explain with accuracy what was so skilfully done for my son in that operation.

The next few years were a severe strain for Alexander and for his mother. He had a series of operations on his fractured skull, on his eyes and on his ear. He endured all the surgery and the frequent hospitalization with wonderful pluck and resilience. He is now a robust and happy schoolboy of nearly sixteen and we are very proud of him. To list his gifts and qualities in the public print would embarrass him. Like his father, he is very modest.

Our younger son, Daniel, a spirited and athletic young fellow, has had some experience of boyhood injuries of the lesser kind. He had a remarkable escape on one occasion very early in his life. Daniel will not remember this, because it was shortly after his christening in 1976. Our family were that summer the tenants of Kelmscott Manor, near Lechlade in Oxfordshire. A hundred years ago, Kelmscott was the country home of William Morris, who shared it for a time with Dante Gabriel Rossetti. The sixteenth-century house is full of historic examples of the art and craftsmanship of Morris and his friends.

It is a few yards from the Thames, and has a beautiful garden. We had a party there after Daniel's christening in the village church. A more idyllic setting for a christening party could scarcely be imagined than underneath the three-hundred-year-old mulberry tree in the garden at Kelmscott, on a glorious English summer's day. But the summer of 1976 was one of the hottest and driest ever. Suddenly a large part of the ancient mulberry tree split off with a loud crack and crashed to the ground. The heavy branches landed exactly on the spot where little Daniel had slept peacefully during the party, and where one of his godparents had also been snoozing.

To conclude this chapter of accidents, grave and otherwise: in July 1975 I was the subject of various newspaper headlines which may have given their writers wry amusement:

> Robin Day's jaw broken in street mugging
> Muggers beat up Robin Day
> Why didn't you use the bow-tie, Robin?

For three weeks or so my jaw had to be wired up with steel. I was unable to speak except through my teeth which were locked together. My speech was scarcely comprehensible. Luckily some programmes of mine had been filmed or pre-recorded for transmission during the holiday period.

The time was just after midnight. I was out walking in Addison Avenue near Holland Park in west London. It was my habit (recommended by my doctor) to take a short walk round the square before going to bed.

I walked round the corner from my house, past St James's Norland church, into the tree-lined Addison Avenue, a wide and dignified street, with large houses. I thought I heard the sound of someone opening the gate I had just passed. Before I could see anyone, or say anything, blows rained on my head and body. The assault was instantaneous.

From television and the cinema, you have the illusion that if you're attacked you may have time for a swift display of vigorous resistance – a neat karate chop, or at least a sharp knee in the genitals of your attacker. But I was knocked to the ground immediately I was attacked. I remember thinking, 'What should I shout?' I remember thinking also (in a space of about half a second) that 'Help!' would sound silly, that 'I've been mugged' was too long. So I uttered at the top of my voice several four-letter obscenities. To my disappointment, none of the respectable residents of Addison Avenue came rushing to my aid from the houses where lights were on. To my relief, however, my assailants (both white) were running away in the rubber-soled shoes which had enabled them to creep up on me silently.

I picked myself up off the pavement, found that my wallet had not been stolen, but that my new suit had been badly torn in what must have been a vigorous, though brief, assault. I walked the few yards back to my house in St James's Gardens. My wife, who had been out to dinner with me, was asleep. I did not know until two days later that my jaw had been broken. I noticed a black eye in the morning.

Next day I happened to telephone my friend Ronald Waterhouse QC. I told him of my adventure and said I was feeling sore but fine. Ronald urged me to see a doctor at once, in case the blows on my head had been more serious than I thought. So I saw a doctor, and a dentist. An x-ray of my jaw showed a hair-line fracture – not a major injury but one which required mending.

To suffer such an attack in a quiet church square on a midsummer night in London was an unpleasant shock. I had become a part of the deeply disturbing criminal statistics.

My jaw was soon back to normal. There were some predictable jokes about my mishap, some sympathetic messages from politicians, and an unexpectedly large number of good wishes from viewers.

The Robin Day Problem

One way and another, I have been a broadcaster for nearly thirty-five years. All that time, except for my Liberal aberration, I have stuck to my last. My energies have been largely confined to being a political reporter on the screen or at the microphone. This is in contrast to some of my distinguished colleagues such as Robert Kee and Ludovic Kennedy, who have won glittering off-screen reputations as authors and campaigners. Television has been only one of their accomplishments. Other contemporaries, too, have moved on or moved up in their careers. Sir Ian Trethowan quit the TV studios for the topmost rank of BBC management. Sir Alastair Burnet launched *News at Ten* when he was also Editor of *The Economist*. He later ascended into the ITN boardroom and has continued as a newscaster. The late, great Robert McKenzie, king of the swingometer, was not only a brilliant popularizer of politics for the TV millions, but also a distinguished professor of politics at the London School of Economics.

Those are not the only stars of TV journalism who have displayed an enviable versatility of achievement. Brian Walden was a brilliant back-bench MP until his talents, and his parliamentary style, were transferred triumphantly to television, and in turn to a newspaper column. Peter Jay has been an award-winning TV commentator, an influential economics editor and HM Ambassador in Washington, not to mention Robert Maxwell's chief of staff.

I would dearly like to have been a man of multi-faceted talent, a gifted polymath, gliding with seemingly effortless superiority from one career to another – television, politics, literature, business, journalism, the City, academia – displaying all the while a versatile genius, creative, analytical, executive, imaginative.

Alas, fate has decreed otherwise. My work has been 'cabin'd, cribb'd, confin'd' in the single sphere of broadcast political journalism. Yet my professional life has been agreeably diverse. It has involved me in the rise of tele-journalism and in the renaissance of radio. I have been a parliamentary correspondent in the press gallery. I have attended most of the major debates and dramas at Westminster during the last thirty-four years. I have been a TV newscaster and a TV film reporter. It is difficult for me to judge the value or significance of all this broadcasting in vision and sound. If some of it has contributed to a clearer understanding of events and to the democratic process, I shall be content.

A crucial element of my work has been the asking of questions, to clarify, to illuminate, to challenge and to seek the truth from political leaders. It has been as an interviewer that I had a central role in the coverage of eight general elections,* and in the 'results' marathons which brought each campaign to its climax. This election coverage has been by far the most exciting,

---

*For those whose memories are non-political, these eight general elections were in October 1964, March 1966, June 1970, February 1974, October 1974, May 1979, June 1983 and June 1987.

the most satisfying, and the most controversial of all my broadcasting activities.

In each of these eight elections, as TV's coverage was liberated from the old restrictions of the radio age, my contributions escalated and intensified. It was during the general elections that I was fully stretched, that I felt this was how all my broadcasting experience and all my political knowledge could be put to the best possible use. Each general election was for me another mountain peak to be conquered. A general election was as important for me professionally as an Olympiad to a sports commentator. That comparison should not be taken too far, however. Your commentator at the Olympic Games, or for a Test Match series, does not participate in the action, as does your interviewer at a general election. The latter does not merely watch and describe. He raises issues, clarifies argument, elicits new facts, exposes contradictions.

An illustration of how the interviewer, by asking a perfectly legitimate question, can expose an important difference of opinion may be given from the '87 campaign. This was the campaign which was to prove disastrous for the Alliance. I was interviewing David Steel and David Owen together in *Panorama*, I asked Dr Owen this question:

Q: Do you think that a Tory government would be a greater evil than a majority Labour government. Which is the greater evil in your view?

A: In the last analysis, the one issue on which I will always judge anyone – and this is somebody who would put at jeopardy the defences and security of this country. Unless the Labour Party changes its defence and security policy, in my judgment they are not fit to govern this country.

Q: You are saying that a majority Labour government would, therefore, be a greater evil than a majority Tory government?

A: In the final analysis, I don't want either. And I'm not prepared to support either. And I don't believe it's in many ways a fair question. But the one fundamental must remain the security of our country and the security of Western

Europe. And on that big test, the Labour Party massively fails.

I then put the same question to David Steel – which majority government, Labour or Tory, would be the greater evil? I pointed out that this was not the same old question as that asked so often before.

A: Well, yes, but you invited me as a Liberal over the years to make a preferential choice between the Conservative and Labour Party. Quite frankly, if I had such a preferential choice I might as well have joined them all those years ago. I don't believe either is capable of providing a government which can unite this country again . . . and I am not going to be driven to making a choice between the two of them.

Q: I'm not asking you to make a choice.

A: You are.

Q: I'm really saying which do you think would be the greater evil?

A: Well, I don't believe either of them is going to be a successful government. I don't see why I've got to start getting out the measuring rod and saying 'Well, one would be slightly better on this one, slightly better on that one.'

Q: Dr Owen has no hesitation in bringing out the measuring rod.

A: He brought out one very good issue. There are others as well of which I would feel equally strongly. Defence is certainly one . . .

David Owen tried to repair the damage:

Owen: Sir Robin . . . listen, I am notoriously indiscreet. David [Steel] is much wiser than I am in handling –

Steel: You go too far.

Owen: – your attempt to try and get us to decide. The fact of the matter is that for the first time the people of this country are not faced with this horrible choice . . . the electorate are going to say they want neither Labour or Conservative.

Recalling this episode the following year, David Steel wrote bluntly:

> The good doctor dropped an almighty clanger on our joint
> *Panorama* interview with Sir Robin Day, by expressing a
> preference between the other two, something no
> experienced third party leader would ever do, and which I
> and Roy Jenkins had always avoided . . . David [Owen]
> realized he had put his foot in it before the discussion
> ended.*

Some months later David Steel, referring to the defeat and break-up of the Alliance in the '87 election, said this to me: 'It was you who started the rot, you know, with that question to Owen and me on *Panorama*'.† If one simple question could 'start the rot', the rot must already have set in. My question did not divide the two Davids. It merely served to reveal the division which already existed and which they wished, naturally enough, not to advertise.

My own involvement in all these general elections was sometimes said to be excessive. There were anticipatory worries about this as early as 1964. A warning was given about me by my esteemed colleague, Bob McKenzie, to readers of the *Observer* in an article concerning the TV coverage of the '64 election: 'Then there is what might be called for want of a better phrase the Robin Day problem. How does one prevent interviewers, like Robin Day, from playing too great a personal role in the campaign?'‡

As things turned out, nobody except Professor McKenzie (who himself enjoyed a reputation as a forceful and authoritative interviewer) seemed to be terribly worried about 'The Robin Day problem'. At any rate nobody did much about it. In fact, my work on the screen during elections steadily increased from campaign to campaign, whatever criticisms of me were made.

In the February 1974 election, Lord George-Brown, who was

---

*Article in the *Scotsman*, 7 June 1988.
†In private conversation, which he has kindly authorized me to quote.
‡*Observer*, 23 February 1964.

no longer in the big fight, gave a caustic commentary from the ringside, or rather the fireside:

> Seeing Mr Heath or Mr Wilson worsting or being worsted by Mr Robin Day is largely irrelevant. After all, Mr Day isn't in the election is he? Although sometimes he gives the impression that he thinks he is the only one who is.*

A more sophisticated criticism came from David Wheeler, the former Editor of *Panorama*. He wrote in the *Listener* about the 1979 election coverage:

> Today when a PM announces his intention of carrying the fight to the country, what he really means is carrying the fight to Robin Day, who has been positively omnipresent. Day began his career as counsel to the cathode-ray tube, has long since taken silk, and is now the Lord Chief Justice of the political arena. His indispensability is a tribute to his professionalism and commitment, but is an indictment of other tillers in the field. It seems faintly unhealthy both for the BBC and democracy, if that is what we have.†

In that last sentence, the 'Robin Day problem' had reared its ugly head again. I had just managed to resist imagining myself in the LCJ's robes when the imagination of another critic, Richard Last of the *Telegraph*, was even more fanciful: 'Robin Day is the nearest thing we have to the People's Tribune that Rome used to interpose between rulers and ruled before the rot set in.'‡

The press coverage of my many election programmes was massive and detailed. There were verbatim reports, and critical reactions. Each programme provoked a ripple of reaction, a wave of comment or a storm of protest, and occasionally, thank heaven, a little laughter throughout the land. I had the illusory sensation of being at the epicentre of events.

In the '83 election, the TV and radio output was bigger than

Daily Mail, February 1974.
†*Listener*, 3 May 1979.
‡*Daily Telegraph*, 4 May 1979.

ever before and the atmosphere was the most relaxed the broadcasters had known. The proliferation of TV and radio programmes made it harder for the political parties to monitor all that the broadcasters were up to.

If all these general elections are to be seen as a range of professional mountain peaks, then the general election of June 1983 was my Everest. My work in the '83 election was the culmination of my broadcasting career. This was the election in which we saw the Roy Jenkins anti-climax, the Michael Foot débâcle and the Thatcher triumph, with her landslide majority of 144 seats despite unemployment of over three million.

In that '83 election I interviewed each of the three leaders (Jenkins, Foot, Thatcher) in separate *Panoramas* for the first time in a campaign. I chaired three uninhibited editions of *Question Time*, which had not existed in the '79 election. And I presented sixteen *Election Call* programmes. These were now being simultaneously transmitted on television as well as on Radio 4. In all I did over twenty-two hours of live television during the four-week election period.

At the beginning of May 1983 when the election date (9 June) was announced, I was doubtful how my health would stand the strain of the election work to come. In March I had broken my pelvis in a ski-ing accident. I had not recovered fully from a winter of severe bronchitis. The previous year, 1982, I had been hospitalized with pneumonia, which had kept me off the screen during the Falklands War.

So in the spring of 1983 I was not at a peak of fitness. But by some miracle (or perhaps the simple remedy of hard work) I went through the campaign month with no difficulty and great enjoyment. One reason was that I had thrown off a long-standing and unhealthy addiction. I had been a heavy smoker of cigars and cigarettes for twenty-five years. I had stopped the previous year. I suffered no withdrawal agony. Rather did I feel a great sense of triumph and relief.

Though the election weeks of '83 were a peak professional period for me, that spring and summer was a time of personal distress. My wife and I separated with the intention of divorce. Though this was by mutual consent, it was painful to us both.

Divorce is all too commonplace a happening now, but it is none the less a traumatic experience when it happens to you.

It so happens that almost all my closest friends have not been divorced. They have all lived happily with the same partner since their wedding days thirty or forty years ago. I think particularly of Peter and Jennifer Blaker, George and Pam Ffitch, Keith and Susan Kyle, George and Betsy Newell, Howard and Betty Shuman, Dick and Janice Taverne, John and Sally Thompson, Ronald and Sarah Waterhouse, and their families. To have observed their happiness and to have been welcomed in their homes so warmly has been an abiding pleasure of my life.

In the three or four weeks of the 1983 campaign, all my experience as an interviewer, as a chairman, as a phone-in 'host' – all of it came to fruition. I did not make any blunder, or become involved in any major row. During the pre-campaign week there was what the press called a 'clash' or 'flare-up' with Roy Hattersley on *The World at One*. Mr Hattersley was objecting to being questioned on the 10 per cent of the Labour manifesto with which he disagreed, rather than the rest. I told him to 'chuck it', which make a headline or two.

The different types of programme in which I appeared (*Panorama, Question Time* and *Election Call*) each enabled me to perform a different service to the electorate, interrogating their leaders, chairing debates for them and (in the phone-ins) being the voters' friend.

In my three *Panorama* interviews of forty minutes each, with Jenkins, Foot and Thatcher, my function was to attempt something which had become more and more difficult as our political leaders had become more and more at ease in setpiece TV interviews. My job was to try, by probing and cross-examining, to make clear that which was unclear, to seek truth where truth was in dispute and (not least) to compensate for the lack of face-to-face debate between the party leaders. My job was to put Thatcherite questions to Foot and Footite questions to Thatcher, yet without sounding biased. The trouble is that, in the heat of an election campaign, the devil's advocate looks remarkably like the devil himself to the partisan viewer.

In the cut-and-thrust of a fast-moving interview, the interviewer cannot stick to prepared questions. The interviewer's off-the-cuff supplementary, interjected with increasing difficulty, is liable to be phrased argumentatively instead of interrogatively. For example, instead of asking 'Won't this mean higher inflation?' the interviewer might say, 'But this will mean higher inflation.' He is then liable to be charged with bias.

Even during an election campaign, lengthy setpiece interviews with political leaders on television, as will be recalled by many who have endured them, are not always compulsive viewing. But in 1983 each of the three *Election Panorama* interviews had its moments to be relished and remembered.

Roy Jenkins, leader of the SDP and 'Prime Minister Designate' of the Alliance, loftily handed down his judgment on the other two leaders: 'Mrs Thatcher is undoubtedly a more competent Prime Minister than Michael Foot could possibly be.' Someone unkindly described this interview as 'Woy and Wobin wambling on about the gwoss national pwoduct'. That *Panorama* with Roy Jenkins must have had a certain style. A critic who described us as 'Golden Oldies of the political scene' wrote: 'It was as if Donald Budge and Bunny Austin had laid on an exhibition match on the centre court.'

Michael Foot was up against not only Margaret Thatcher but also the opinion polls showing a Tory lead averaging over 15 per cent. This seemed to me an opportunity for television to strike a blow for the democratic process. What was the point in having election arguments, election debates, election interviews, if politicians on one side (that is, Labour) were asked only about the opinion polls rather than about the issues they were seeking to raise? Accordingly, when Michael Foot had his time on *Panorama*, I deliberately and explicitly ignored the polls (which seemed to be determining the outcome) and concentrated on the issues (which were what the election was really about). I therefore questioned Michael Foot as a potential Prime Minister. One of my opening questions was:

Q: Now let's . . . ignore the opinion polls. Forget about them. So let's imagine you are victorious on Thursday. And let's imagine you are Prime Minister . . . In 1988, Mr Foot, under your Prime Ministership, will we still have the British nuclear Polaris weapon?

A: No, we won't. We will have carried through the negotiations that we have promised to carry through.

Thus the interview with Mr Foot proceeded, tackling him on what he would do as Prime Minister. I was careful to refer to a Conservative victory as a possibility not as an inevitability. But no punches were pulled:

> Forty-three years ago, Mr Foot, you wrote a little book, the most famous polemic in British political history, *Guilty Men*, about the Tory appeasers and the men of Munich. I put it to you today that if there is a Tory landslide those responsible, the guilty men, will be you and your Labour party colleagues who have quarrelled and feuded and have appeased the extreme left in your own Party.

This suggestion was hotly repudiated. Later, Michael Foot wrote in his book on the 1983 election that many TV and radio programmes merely reflected the press coverage of the campaign. He went on:

> But there were some honourable exceptions. One such was the programme conducted by Robin Day. I had long regarded him as the most skilful cross-examiner in the business. And in the *Panorama* programme I had with him on that last Monday evening I had the chance, not to say everything I wished, but to put some controversies in what I thought was the right perspective.*

Michael Foot printed virtually the entire transcript of my interview with him in his book.

My *Election Panorama* with Margaret Thatcher in 1983 is one of the best remembered TV interviews with any political leader in recent years. This was not because of any historic utterance by her, still less because of any exceptional contribution by her interviewer. This *Panorama* interview with the PM on 31 May 1983 is memorable to most people for the utterly unimportant

---

*Michael Foot, *Another Heart and Other Pulses* (Collins, 1984), p. 125.

and irrelevant fact that she called me *Mr* Day throughout. This minor slip of the tongue was seized on in dozens of press reports and editorials. She was reported as having 'persisted' in 'dropping the knighthood' which she, as Prime Minister, had recommended to the Queen. She had, it was said, 'appeared to snub' me.

I even had letters from outraged viewers, including some from 'Conservative voters', who said they would not now vote for Mrs Thatcher on account of her discourtesy. Even now, more than six years later, people still refer to this interview and ask, 'Did she do it on purpose?'

The truth is very simple. First, there was not the slightest discourtesy on the Prime Minister's part. She apologized charmingly when her *lapsus linguae* was pointed out to her – not by me but by Gordon Reece,* her TV adviser. Immediately after the interview (which had been recorded in Downing Street) Gordon Reece came over to her and said, 'You seem to have stripped Sir Robin of his knighthood.' 'Oh dear!' said the PM. 'Robin, you don't mind do you? Did I call you *Mr* Day?' To which I am said to have replied, 'Eight times, Prime Minister. But never mind. It's not important. It does not matter to me, but the viewers will notice.' I spoke truthfully. It did not matter tuppence to me. I had scarcely noticed how she had addressed me, so intently was I concentrating on rather more important matters, such as mass unemployment and the nuclear deterrent. In any case, having not been knighted very long, I was very frequently addressed as 'Mr'. But there was one inaccuracy in my reply to the Prime Minister when she apologized. She had said *Mr* Day not eight times, but only five times.

The last word on this episode should come from Michael Foot. Having seen the *Sun* headline, 'MAGGIE BEATS SIR ROBIN IN BIG TELLY BATTLE', he seized the opportunity for some fun. In a speech that day he feigned shock at her calling me 'Mr Day' so often: 'You can't treat the aristocracy like that, can you?' And again he brought down whatever house he was addressing by his next question: 'Who does *she* think *he* is? A member of the Cabinet?'

*Later *Sir* Gordon.

The explanation of the incident is, of course, that the Prime Minister, with other things on her mind at that moment in the campaign, quite simply addressed me in the way she had always addressed me in the previous ten years. Her lapse of memory was all the more understandable because she had not been interviewed by me at all during the two-and-a-half years since I had been knighted. It is true that under our honours system most knighthoods are recommended to the Queen in a list of thirty or so names submitted by the Prime Minister of the day. But it may be doubted if a PM remembers, two or three years later, every name which was on every such list.

I still meet people who, incredibly, are convinced that it was all a none too subtle ploy by Mrs Thatcher to put me in my place. I hoped the incident would have been closed by what she said when she appeared with me a few days later on *Election Call*. When a caller said with emphasis, 'Good morning *Sir Robin*,' the Prime Minister briskly interrupted:

Quite right. Thank you very much. I didn't mean the other day to demote Sir Robin. I was concentrating so much on the questions that I quite forgot. Now, Sir Robin, shall we go ahead?

As to the political content of this *Panorama* interview with Mrs Thatcher, it ranged over the campaign issues – unemployment, the nuclear deterrent, the Health Service. Unfortunately we became bogged down in a not very illuminating wrangle about the true cost of unemployment. The Prime Minister insisted that the figure I had given was false, phoney and distorted. I insisted that it was neither false, phoney nor distorted: 'I wouldn't put them to you otherwise,' I said. My figure was a widely used and authoritative estimate. Her 'cost' was based on a different way of estimating it. Both figures were arguable. My mistake was to mention a particular figure for the cost of unemployment. I should have anticipated that she would challenge it.

This acrimonious exchange served only to obscure the rest of 'this bruising encounter', as the press called it. I was deeply depressed about it. My feeling was that I had let the viewing voters down. When I was telephoned by newspapermen, I told them frankly that I was very unhappy. According to a *Times* report, under the headline ' "Mr Day" takes the blame', I said:

> I handled it badly. I failed to ask important questions to which viewers were entitled to have answers. Whether the people of Bootle and cities all over the country found it useful that the Prime Minister and the interviewer were having a wrangle about statistics, I am not sure . . . It must be my responsibility and not the Prime Minister's.

I went on to say that a politician's reaction to a TV interview is like the sea to a ship's captain. Whether there is a violent storm or utter calm, the captain's job is to get through it. 'In this case there was a rough sea. If I did not negotiate it properly it is my fault.'*

Perhaps there was no need for me to have donned sackcloth and ashes. Perhaps Mrs Thatcher was in a mood to beat down any interrogator, whatever he asked. She came in for the interview carrying a huge array of papers and references – ammunition ready to be used, and she used them. I had never before seen a Prime Minister come thus armed for an interview. These tactics obviously impressed the viewing voters, or a good many of them.

In my depressed, self-critical mood, I was pleasantly astonished to read what Ian Aitken, that robust veteran of the lobby, wrote in his *Guardian* report. He generously described it as a 'devastating 40-minute interview on BBC *Panorama*, the most courageous of a long and abrasive career'.† But I still think I mishandled it. To abandon the maritime metaphor, if you are confronted by a steamroller, you don't drive head-on into it.

In her interviews with my opposite numbers (Sir Alastair Burnet and Brian Walden) the Prime Minister was again overpowering and virtually unstoppable. But if the professionals failed, a housewife from Cirencester did not. This was on *Nationwide*, edited by Roger Bolton whose programmes had infuriated Mrs Thatcher before. Mrs Diana Gould asked Mrs

---

*The Times, 2 June 1983.
†*Guardian*, 1 June 1983.

Thatcher a series of pointed, detailed questions about the sinking of the Argentine cruiser *General Belgrano*. The Prime Minister could scarcely conceal her cold fury. She had not expected anything like this. She had understood, or assumed, that she was to appear on the programme to answer questions from *ordinary voters on election issues*. Mrs Gould was an ordinary voter, though she appeared to have an extra-ordinary grasp of the nautical considerations involved. She was a former Geography teacher. She had also been a WRNS officer and had taken a First Class in both parts of the Geographical Tripos at Cambridge.

My own view is clear. The sinking of the *Belgrano* may have been mentioned or discussed during the campaign, but it was *not* an election issue, if by that is meant one of the issues which the election was about. In that opinion, I am in agreement with the publicly expressed view of the then Leader of the Labour Party. In his 1983 *Panorama* election interview with me, Michael Foot, when asked if it was fair or relevant that the *Belgrano* sinking should be an issue in the campaign, said, 'No, I don't think it's an issue in this campaign,' and repeated that view in the same answer.

So it is not surprising that Mrs Thatcher took exception to Mrs Diana Gould's questioning. But in the rough-and-tumble of an election campaign, even Prime Ministers have sometimes to cope with awkward questioners, and with TV programmes which do not turn out as expected. The PM could have said: 'This is not one of the issues on which the people are voting in this election. I have fully explained to Parliament the decision to sink the *Belgrano*, and there is nothing to add.' This would have been criticized as evasive and arrogant, but it might have earned the Prime Minister less abuse than she got for her pointless battle with Mrs Gould.

The '83 campaign may also be remembered as the campaign of 'Pym's gaffe'. This was the celebrated remark by the then Foreign Secretary, Francis Pym, warning against too large a Tory majority:

Landslides on the whole don't produce successful governments . . .'45 was the obvious example, the massive landslide to Labour . . . I think a majority of between fifty and a hundred would be better than one in three figures.

That was said in *Question Time*. Mrs Thatcher acidly retorted at her press conference:'I think I can handle a landslide majority all right.' She dismissed Pym's remarks as the 'natural caution' of a former Chief Whip. And she dismissed Pym himself from the Foreign Office three weeks later. She had a triumphant majority of 144.

Until the '83 election, no nationally networked TV programme like *Question Time* had been transmitted during the campaign period. There had been programmes with questions from an audience and answers from spokesmen put up by the parties. What happened in 1983 was that *Question Time* continued to be transmitted in the normal form except for there being only three panellists. The audiences were invited by the BBC and so were the panellists. Nothing was rigged or arranged. The four or five questioners I called by name were, as usual, selected by the Editor, Barbara Maxwell, and myself. The questioners who caught my eye were called entirely at random.

Nothing so spontaneous and uninhibited had ever been seen on television during a British election. *Campaign Question Time* revived the old hustings tradition of the people face to face with the politicians. It was all that *Election Forum* could never be. It was fast-moving, unpredictable and funny. On the eve of the general election campaign, I introduced the three eminent parliamentarians on the panel by their nicknames: the boy David, Worzel Gummidge and Tarzan. Fortunately Messrs Steel, Foot and Heseltine took it in good humour, which is just as well because the audience was delighted.

Apart from its entertainment value (which was no small achievement during a heavy election campaign), *Question Time* was a significant platform for exchanges between people and politicians. Denis Healey had accused Mrs Thatcher of 'glorying in slaughter' during the Falklands War. When he was faced with the *Question Time* audience in Birmingham, Healey was asked if he had not descended into gutter politics. He replied:

I regret using the word slaughter. I think I should have used the word conflict . . . Of course what I really meant was her appetite for conflict, which is a very dangerous thing in international affairs.

Cecil Parkinson immediately accused Healey of 'laundering his original allegation'. At the pre-programme dinner, Parkinson had refused to sit down at the same table as Healey. The bitterness came through on the screen.

There was another TV programme, new to the screen, which enabled politicians to be confronted by the public. This was *Election Call* (with its success on radio and three previous campaigns behind it), now televised as well as broadcast on radio. Breakfast television, which was over by 9 a.m., had recently been launched. From 9 a.m. there was then some vacant screen time. I suggested that TV cameras should simply come into the studio at Broadcasting House. The callers would not be seen, of course, but their effect on the politicians would be clearly visible. I never imagined that BBC management would agree to televise *Election Call*. I gather there was heated argument about it high up in Broadcasting House. But, to my amazement, a couple of cameras were wheeled into the small basement studio in BH. Some extra lighting, a make-up lady and, hey presto, we had radio-vision.

That improvised televising of *Election Call* must have been the cheapest hour of television in the BBC's output. The studio was small, cramped and hot, but the atmosphere crackled with vitality and spontaneity. The entry of the TV cameras did not, as many people feared, spoil the relaxed informality of radio which had made *Election Call* so successful in the campaigns of February 1974, October 1974 and May 1979.

The verdict, after one or two initial gripes ('Why put the wireless on the telly?'), was overwhelmingly favourable. The experts at Nuffield College noted:

The most widely praised series of all was again Sir Robin's *Election Call*, now seen on BBC1 as well as heard on Radio 4 . . . While a brisk courtesy prevailed, leading politicians had to face some raw feelings of ordinary voters.*

*Martin Harrison in Butler's *The General Election 1983*, p. 169.

Sir Geoffrey Howe was denounced to his face as the worst Chancellor since Philip Snowden. Shirley Williams had to answer a Labour caller who felt deeply betrayed by her defection to the SDP. Willie Whitelaw struggled for an answer to an unemployed woman aged fifty-three who had applied for a hundred and sixty-two jobs in the previous six months.

What pleased me more than anything was that the televised *Election Call* enabled viewers to see me as their friend, helping to pin the politicians down, to guide the callers (if need be) to the point which I knew they really wanted to put but, due to inexperience or nerves, had not been able to put. This made a change from my usual role on television. Instead of the politician's interrogator, I was the citizen's friend. I noticed too the effect on a politician of having the camera on his face continuously for a whole hour. No longer could he or she (as on radio only) grimace or yawn or scratch their face while a caller was talking. The politician had to look interested and concerned and, dare I say it, 'caring', even if the caller was an infuriating bore.

There was only one slight hitch in the series. That, as luck would have it, was when it came to the turn of Mrs Thatcher. Her media advisers had obviously failed to explain the simple mechanics of the televised *Election Call*. Answering the first caller, the Prime Minister suddenly stopped and said (on the air): 'Where is he? I can't see him. I can only hear him.' Gently I explained: 'That's right, Prime Minister, he's on the *telephone*.' I could see the production staff in hysterics on the other side of the studio control window. Mrs Thatcher had been thrown by the fact that I was peering into a monitor screen (which put up the names of callers). She must have thought it was a screen on which I could see the caller. Understandably, she too wanted to see a screen. Being quick on the uptake, the Prime Minister came only momentarily unstuck.

The 1983 election may be fairly described as the first real television election, if the volume and variety and vigour of election coverage is the test. My own contribution should be judged against that background. The various programmes in which I was involved made big headlines and provoked sharp reactions, but in relation to the multiplicity of programmes –

morning, noon and night – on the four TV channels and on radio my work was but one small part of the output. That part may have *seemed* bigger than it really was, especially to viewers who could not stand the sight or sound of me. But if there was ever a 'Robin Day problem', that problem had disappeared when television's coverage proliferated and diversified as it did in 1983.

There was, however, a different Robin Day problem a few months earlier in 1982, though this was not at election time. This was when an extraordinary incident took place which is unique in my entire television career. A Cabinet minister got up and walked out of the studio in the middle of my interview with him.

The Rt Hon. John Nott MP was then Secretary of State for Defence. He had been addressing the Conservative Party Conference that day at Brighton. The Conference was the first since the Falklands War earlier that same year. The Conference debate on defence, to which Nott had replied, had not reflected the numerous motions on the agenda urging the government to 'rethink', 're-examine' and 'reappraise' their defence policy, particularly the Royal Navy cuts, in the light of the Falklands experience.

Nott came into the BBC's Conference studio to record his interview for the early-evening *Nationwide* programme. I put it to him that the critical Conference resolutions about naval cuts had not been debated by the Conference. Nott brushed this aside. I persisted with questions which reflected the deep dissatisfaction with Nott's policy towards the Royal Navy as expressed in the Tory Conference resolutions. I referred also to public statements by the First Sea Lord, Admiral Sir Henry Leach.

Mr Nott, who was obviously irritated by these questions, said:

It really does not do the integrity of the services much good if respected people like you seek to draw divisions between ministers and chiefs of staff. This is damaging to the services.

He sharply denied that his now-cancelled decision to sell HMS *Invincible* had been an error of judgment. He dismissed the Admiral's criticisms with: 'He would say that, wouldn't he?' I

And don't flannel me — this isn't the Jimmy Young Show.

referred to the fact that Nott had recently announced his retirement from Parliament at the forthcoming election and asked:

> Why should the public on this issue believe you, a transient, here today and, if I may say so, gone tomorrow politician, rather than a senior officer of many years' experience?

Nott tore the microphone from his lapel and threw it on the table, saying:

> I'm sorry – I am fed up with this interview. It is ridiculous.

And as he walked out of the studio I am reported as having said, 'This is the first time I have ever had the microphone thrown at me.'

As happens in the convivial atmosphere of party conferences, I bumped into John Nott a few hours later in the Grand Hotel. He said, 'I hope we are still friends.' I replied, truthfully, 'Of course.' Nott explained that my quotations from Admiral Sir Henry Leach had infuriated him.

The veteran political correspondent of the Press Association, Chris Moncrieff, had been in the studio, note-taking, during the recording. He wondered if the 'walkout' would be transmitted or not. He came up to me after Nott had made his dramatic exit and asked if it was OK for him to file what Nott had said and done, on the assumption it would all be transmitted. I am told that my advice to Chris Moncrieff was: 'Bugger off quick and file it before anyone says you can't.'

The interview, which had lasted only two or three minutes, echoed through the headlines ('ANGRY NOTT STORMS OUT'), through the front pages ('NOTT IN TV STORM'), through the opinion columns and then through letters to the editors for two or three weeks.

There were conflicting reactions to the interview. Undoubtedly many people applauded Nott for his walk-out, and for giving that impertinent Robin Day his come-uppance at last. Many others (I never discovered what the balance of opinion was) congratulated me. One of Nott's Cabinet colleagues at the Brighton Conference was puzzled by the walk-out: 'Why on earth walk out? The question was not a difficult one to deal with.'

But another of Nott's Cabinet colleagues championed him in the correspondence columns of *The Times*. This was the then Secretary of State for Wales, Nicholas Edwards. He expressed sympathy for Nott in his refusal to respond to 'an offensive question, offensively delivered'. Edwards, better known now perhaps, or perhaps not, as Lord Crickhowell, declared that:

> Sir Robin was challenging our whole system of democratic responsibility and putting forward exactly the same argument used by the supporters of General MacArthur against President Truman, and the generals against Lloyd George . . .

Edwards continued:

> Democracies are dependent upon a belief in the ability of those 'here today and gone tomorrow' to listen to conflicting professional advice and form a judgment. They are equally dependent upon a belief in the ability of an electorate to use its judgment.
> Sir Robin is fully entitled to challenge a minister's judgment, but he does nobody a service by being rude or by questioning a principle so fundamental to our system of parliamentary responsibility.

Had I really been 'rude'? That must be a matter of opinion. In my defence, I would quote the judgment of the late T. E. Utley, the great Tory commentator, who wrote in the *Daily Telegraph* that John Nott:

> petulantly stormed out of an interview with Sir Robin Day who, incidentally, was cross-examining him with no more than legitimate vigour, a duty which Tories on the conference floor had almost entirely shirked.

Perhaps I would not have provoked John Nott's walk-out had I put my offending question in a blander form, but spontaneously the phrase 'here today and gone tomorrow' came out, and stung the already irritated Secretary of State for Defence.

More serious than the familiar accusation of rudeness was the charge that I was challenging our democratic system of parliamentary responsibility. That, from a Cabinet minister, called for a response. Accordingly this letter from me was published in *The Times*.

Sir,

The Secretary of State for Wales alleges (Oct. 12) that in my television interview with the Secretary of State for Defence I was 'challenging our whole system of democratic responsibility'. I was doing nothing of the sort. Nor was I arguing that 'professional expertise, rather than political judgment, should decide policy'. I am aware of the fundamental principle that policy is the responsibility of Ministers answerable to Parliament.

But that principle does not mean that the relative merits of a Minister's judgment and that of his professional advisers should not be discussed and enquired into by journalists. Conflicts between the frock coats and the brass hats have often been matters of intense public interest. Your own leading article today (Oct. 13) refers to the First Sea Lord's 'long-running argument with Mr Nott over the cuts in the Navy.'

That argument was reflected in my questions to Mr Nott. Another relevant fact was that resolutions submitted for the Tory Conference showed a strong body of Tory opinion without much faith in Mr Nott's policy for the Royal Navy. One reason for this, perhaps, was Mr Nott's now-cancelled decision to sell HMS *Invincible*.

It was in that context that I put the question which Mr Edwards describes as 'offensive'. It was not so described by the charming Tory lady at the Brighton Conference who practically embraced me after the interview. But then she came from Portsmouth and was very concerned about the Royal Navy.

Yours faithfully,

Mr Nott was knighted in the next Honours List, but not, I think, for his TV walk-out. I am happy to say that I have met or interviewed Sir John several times since the Brighton episode with much pleasure. He is always the most stimulating company.

13

Six Prime Ministers

A Question from the Wrong Man in the Wrong Place

In 1957 when Harold Macmillan became Prime Minister, the television revolution had only just begun. Yet by the end of his premiership, in 1963, television had become the prime medium of mass communication in our democracy. Almost everyone had a TV set. Politicians took television seriously. How television covered politics had become news in itself. Ministers, even the Prime Minister, and other parliamentarians were ready to appear on TV and to be questioned vigorously and without the unctuous deference of earlier years.

'Television,' declared Macmillan in an after-dinner speech, 'has introduced a new dimension into politics, and some of us don't quite know what to make of it.' But Macmillan, though affecting distaste for what he usually called 'the television', had a shrewd politician's grasp of what it could achieve. He knew it provided direct communication with the electorate. Macmillan also saw that TV was an ideal medium for his own highly developed gifts of showmanship, his wit, polish and timing. He was, after all, often referred to as 'the old actor-manager'.

His style of dress carefully reflected his personality. There was the famous white fur hat which he wore on his 1959 trip to

Moscow. It may have been an old hat, picked up years ago in Finland, but Macmillan wore it magnificently.*

His style of wearing his evening-dress bow-tie, with the ends underneath the collar tips of his shirt, immediately re-created a fashion for dandies. His attachment to what seemed to be a much-loved, moth-eaten woollen waistcoat reminded the world that an English gentleman should never be too smartly dressed.

I do not suggest that these details of style were adopted especially for television. But they were all part of Macmillan's consummate showmanship. This was displayed to even greater effect during the twenty-five years after he had retired from office. It was then that he gave his masterly reminiscent TV interviews, and later made his highly polished speeches in the Lords as Earl of Stockton. At the age of ninety, he was the matinée idol of the Upper House.

When Macmillan proclaimed ignorance or dislike or fear of television, his tongue was in his cheek. He liked to pretend that a TV interview was some sort of modern ordeal, for which he deserved the viewers' sympathy. He protested about the paraphernalia of the TV studio: 'The camera's hot, probing eye, these monstrous machines and their attendants. A kind of twentieth-century torture chamber, that's what it is.'

I interviewed Macmillan many times between 1957 and 1976. I never detected any sign of the acute nervousness from which he was reputed to suffer before a major public appearance or speech. He was even said to be sick before a really big speech in the House. I can only say that he never betrayed any sign of nervous strain before a major TV interview with me. Was the famous 'unflappability' or 'insouciance' merely a mask to hide the inner torment, or just another example of Macmillan's histrionic talent in action?

I never discovered the answer. But I know that whereas I might feel tense before an important interview with him, Macmillan would be as relaxed as could be, often referring in the pre-programme chat to some non-political matter, utterly irrelevant to the occasion, perhaps some literary or scholarly allusion – 'Do you remember that verse by Belloc . . . ?' I never knew

*See below, p. 249–50.

whether this was his own long-practised technique for taking his mind off the ordeal ahead in the twentieth-century torture chamber, or merely a subtle trick to make the interviewer feel ignorant and at a disadvantage.

Macmillan himself confirms that he suffered from extreme nervousness before some TV performances. I always found it difficult to understand how a veteran parliamentarian, who had been twenty-five years in the rough and tumble of the House of Commons, and before that had been through the mud and blood of the trenches in the First World War, could suffer from nerves before a TV interview.

When Anthony Eden resigned in 1957, the Queen sent for Macmillan rather than for R. A. Butler, to the surprise of almost everyone except Randolph Churchill. Rab was the favourite of the press, of the intelligentsia. He had been acting-Prime Minister for Churchill and for Eden. He had been the great education reformer and the architect of the new 'progressive' post-war Conservatism. But to many Tories he was the arch-appeaser, the intellectual whose name had been coupled with that of the Socialist Gaitskell to coin 'Butskellism'. Harold Macmillan, on the other hand, had served with courage in two world wars, and had been a trusted lieutenant of Churchill in the second. He was seen as the stronger man to pull things together after Eden's Suez débâcle. And his good personal relations, with Eisenhower, and later with Kennedy, did much to restore the Anglo-American alliance.

Randolph Churchill took part with me in an ITN 'special' on the night that Harold Macmillan became Prime Minister. In expansive mood, Randolph, who was somewhat the worse for drink, declared himself 'tired of being governed by babies, women and children'. But 'Harold Macmillan is a grown-up man'. This he went on repeating. When he told us for the fifth time that 'Harold Macmillan is a grown-up man,' I retorted not too gently, 'At sixty-three he ought to be.'

For thirty years, first as Prime Minister then as elder statesman, Macmillan was a great performer on the stage of British politics. Was he a great Prime Minister? A great politician, yes, whose professionalism was admired by his opponent Harold Wilson. A distinguished parliamentarian, yes, though his Commons style was somewhat formal and stiff. But I doubt if history will rank Harold Macmillan with Disraeli, Gladstone, Lloyd George or Churchill. Perhaps we are still too close to his time to make a fair judgment, but the Macmillan years can already be seen as the years when the rot set in, when not enough was done to modernize Britain, or to make us capable of competing with the nations we had defeated in the war.

At the beginning of 1989, when the 1958 Cabinet papers were released, Macmillan was much condemned for having 'funked' the first great challenge which faced him. This was whether to control inflation by curbing public expenditure as demanded by his dissenting Treasury ministers, Peter Thorneycroft, Enoch Powell and Nigel Birch. They were Thatcherites, says Powell, long before the time of Thatcher.

It must in fairness, however, be remembered that in 1958 Macmillan had been Prime Minister for only one year since the damaging Suez débâcle. Domestically and internationally Britain required a steady recovery. Hence Macmillan's unwillingness to permit disinflation, which he warned could lead to a stagnant economy and could provoke industrial unrest. Having regard to the strength of his feelings against mass unemployment, dating back to his pre-war years as MP for Stockton, Macmillan's political rejection of monetarist logic in 1958 is understandable. It is scarcely surprising that Macmillan, though he had been preferred in 1957 to the 'wet' Rab, turned out to be a high priest of consensus welfarism, of appeasement of trade unions and of policies which stoked up inflation, and became, in the eighties, a critic of the Thatcher-Lawson economic strategy.

It was at some time in the early years of Macmillan's premiership that I first learned how to address a Prime Minister correctly. At the British Embassy in Paris I was filming a short interview with Macmillan after one of his visits to General de Gaulle. My first question began: 'Mr Prime Minister . . .' This was, unconsciously, following the custom of saying, for example, Mr Chairman or Mr President. One of Macmillan's private secretaries, Philip de Zulueta, a punctilious Foreign Office diplomat, took me aside forcefully to express his distaste at what he regarded as an Americanism. 'The proper mode of address when speaking to the Prime Minister is "Prime Minister" . . .' 'But,'

I asked, 'won't that sound, to people watching, abrupt or impertinent?' 'They will soon get used to it,' said de Zulueta, 'if you stop using the American style.'

So it was 'Prime Minister' from then on. But I was right to anticipate viewers' objections. Almost immediately, and for some time afterwards, I received angry letters accusing me of brusqueness and discourtesy in so addressing the Queen's First Minister. I took considerable pleasure in writing to reply that 'Prime Minister' was correct and proper, and that I had been rebuked for not using that form of address. De Zulueta was right also: the complaints soon stopped.

In February 1959 I was fortunate to cover, for ITN, Macmillan's most memorable mission as Prime Minister – his ten-day visit to the Soviet Union. Nikita Khrushchev was in power. No western head of government had visited Russia since the end of the war. There was worldwide interest in the visit, mostly approving. But there were suspicions, especially in the United States, that the British Prime Minister would try to do more than break the ice. Macmillan described his visit as 'a perilous undertaking' and 'a voyage of discovery'.

So it proved. Surprise followed surprise. The world watched as the Russians practised their Pavlovian psychology with the British Prime Minister to be baited and demoralized. Without warning to his British guests, Khrushchev suddenly made a public speech attacking the capitalist west and its diplomacy. Then there was the bizarre insult of Khrushchev's tooth. He had to have it filled. So he could not, after all, accompany Macmillan to Kiev. The Prime Minister and his colleagues continued their tour with stiff upper lips. The press corps, especially the Americans, were reporting the visit as a 'monumental flop' and a 'snub to Macmillan'.

I followed the Prime Minister during those fantastic ten days. Snubbed by Khrushchev's toothache excuse, Macmillan went to Kiev. He plodded on with his tour, escorted by minor Russian officials. When he landed at Kiev airport, unaccompanied by Khrushchev, the scene was bleak and bizarre. The Prime Minister walked alone from his aircraft to the microphones and camera which were there to record his remarks. However furious he may have felt, he spoke as if he were opening a flower show in his constituency: 'It gives me very great pleasure,' he intoned, 'to be here among the people of Kiev . . .' The 'people of Kiev' in fact consisted of Malcolm Muggeridge, Randolph Churchill, Don Iddon, Cyril Ray, myself and about a dozen other western journalists who had flown ahead to cover Macmillan's arrival in Kiev. About fifty yards away, behind a barrier, were herded some bemused, ill-attired Ukrainians.

At the Prime Minister's final press conference, there was an incident in which I was involved. I did not come out of it very well. The press conference was a joint affair for newspapers and television. I hoped to get in one question for ITN. I telephoned London for advice. What was the main talking-point at home at the conclusion of Macmillan's visit? I was given two suggestions: the prospect for Summit talks, and the timing of the general election, which speculation had fixed for May or October that year, 1959. Questions were put about Summit prospects long before I could catch the Prime Minister's eye. So, when my turn came, I put a question about the likely date of the British general election.

The year 1959 was a time of intense pre-election speculation. Macmillan took my question as implying that his Moscow visit had been undertaken for electioneering purposes. This implication had already been made in the House of Commons when the Moscow visit was first announced. Macmillan was inclined to be sensitive whenever the forthcoming election was linked with his Moscow trip. We now know from Macmillan's memoirs how Chancellor Adenauer had angered the British Ambassador in Bonn by saying that the only useful point of Macmillan going to Moscow was as an election manoeuvre.

The purpose, however, of my question was not to imply that Macmillan had come to Moscow for electioneering reasons. The visit seemed to me an admirable British initiative, wholly justified as an exploratory diplomatic mission. At the same time, Macmillan's efforts for peace in Moscow would bring him new prestige as a statesman. This would obviously not be unhelpful to him in the forthcoming general election. The date of that election, therefore, looked like being sooner rather than later. Hence my question about when the general election was now likely to be. He took immediate offence. In front of three hundred newsmen and diplomats, Macmillan delivered a crushing reprimand: 'That is a question which, if I may make a plagiarism, is made by the wrong man in the wrong place.'*

He had well and truly slapped me down. Afterwards my newspaper colleagues twitted me mercilessly. The Prime Minister's public rebuke of one of their bumptious television rivals had delighted them. On no other occasion have I known such back-slapping *bonhomie* from newspapermen. Mr Macmillan's rebuke was painful, but if an interviewer's question misfires he must take the consequences.

In the *Spectator* Cyril Ray commented:

In that flash of asperity at the Hall of Journalists one could guess what it must be like to be subjected to alternate slaps on the wrist and pats on the back; three ceremonial visits to the ballet in three widely separated cities in four days . . . when all you really want to do is to curl up with your bullet-holed copy of Æschylus.†

Later that year Macmillan called the general election for 8 October 1959. His mission to Moscow was made much of in the Tory manifesto:

Thanks to the initiative of the Conservative Government, the diplomatic deadlock between east and west has now been broken. The Prime Minister's visit to Russia in February began a sequence of events which has led to the present easing of tension.‡

Macmillan won that election by an overall majority of a hundred seats. His Moscow trip in that famous white hat may have

---

*Macmillan's plagiarism may have been of General Omar Bradley on General MacArthur's proposal to carry the Korean war into China: 'The wrong war, at the wrong place, at the wrong time, and with the wrong enemy.'
†*Spectator*, 6 March 1959.
‡According to Macmillan's official biographer, the British Ambassador in Moscow felt, in retrospect, that the PM's 'voyage of discovery' had been projected 'for the wrong motives – with electoral advantage in view'. Alistair Horne, *Macmillan*, vol 2, p. 128.

been made for the most statesmanlike of reasons, but it was certainly not a vote-loser.

In October 1976 I had a long TV interview with him at his house, Birch Grove, about the state of the nation. It was to be Macmillan's first intervention in contemporary politics since he had been Prime Minister. He wanted Britain to have a coalition government, a government of the centre, with 'men of goodwill' of all parties. Pressed as to who would lead this 'government of national unity', Macmillan, then aged eighty-two, told me: 'Somebody will come along.' But this idea was promptly rejected by the Prime Minister, Mr Callaghan, and by the shadow Prime Minister, Mrs Margaret Thatcher.

In advance of the interview, Macmillan took me to Buck's, one of his seven London clubs, for lunch. Sipping Buck's Fizz, for here was where that delicious drink was invented, we considered what to eat. 'Would you like to start with some oysters?' Trying not to sound too eager, I replied 'That would be very nice.' Macmillan then asked, 'How many would you like?' Then, happily, before I had time to reply that half a dozen would be fine, he said 'I think six is too few, and twelve is too many. So how about nine?' At this, emboldened by the champagne, I risked a little repartee: 'Of course. How wise! *The Middle Way?*' This allusion to the title of Macmillan's famous pre-war book on economic policy made him smile.

I treasure two personal letters from Harold Macmillan. One, in 1978, was to express his sympathy to me after my elder son had been severely injured. The second, in 1981, expressed his 'great pleasure' in seeing my name in the New Year's Honours List.

He Has Eaten the King's Salt

After the great actor-manager, whose professionalism in politics even Harold Wilson greatly admired, came the 14th Earl, the 'amateur from the grouse moors'. Rab Butler had again seemed to many the obvious choice. Hailsham had been Macmillan's original preference. But from his sick-room in King Edward VII Hospital, after soundings in the Tory Party, Macmillan advised the Queen to invite Lord Home to form a government. This Home duly did, after Rab Butler, by agreeing to serve under him, had shrunk from staking his claim.

The year 1963 had been the year of the Profumo scandal. The appointment of the 14th Earl of Home to be Prime Minister was the climax of that most sensational year in British politics. Lord Home was not well known to the public. Not everyone knew that his name was pronounced Hume and not Home. He was an hereditary peer. No peer had been appointed Prime Minister in this century since Lord Salisbury in 1900. Though Lord Home had been an MP (as Lord Dunglass) for twenty years, he had been out of the Commons for twelve years.

Lord Home had been Foreign Secretary under Macmillan. He was derided by the intelligentsia. In a notorious satirical programme on BBC Television Bernard Levin actually called Home a 'cretin'. But Lord Home was highly respected in Westminster and Whitehall, whatever the clever people outside thought.

I was made aware of this long before there was any question of his becoming Prime Minister. In 1960 I was holding forth one evening at a cocktail party. I mentioned the *Daily Mirror* gibe that Macmillan's choice of Lord Home as Foreign Secretary was 'the most reckless political appointment since the Roman Emperor Caligula made his favourite horse a consul'. My reference to this old cliché of editorial invective was overheard by the octogenarian Viscount Stansgate, father of Anthony Wedgwood Benn MP, whose party I was attending.

Lord Stansgate, that fiery radical and veteran parliamentarian, rounded on me fiercely. He said he was 'not going to hear anything against Alec Home'. He spoke vigorously in praise of Lord Home's integrity and ability. 'Don't underestimate Alec Home,' was Lord Stansgate's vehement and repeated advice to me and everyone present. This made a lasting impression on me, coming as it did from a long-time political opponent.

My most memorable television encounter with Lord Home was at the 1963 Conservative Party Conference at Blackpool. This was by far the most exciting party conference which has ever been held by any British political party in my experience. It was more like an American presidential convention, with television following the 'candidates' everywhere. On the first day of the Conference Macmillan had announced his resignation. All hell broke loose. No one, certainly not the television teams, took the least interest in the Conference debates on education or local government or anything else. All the interviews were about the succession, and the 'candidates'. There was Lord Hailsham, who, with a dramatic flourish, threw his hat into the ring by renouncing his hereditary peerage to become plain Quintin Hogg again. There was Rab Butler, his crumpled face looking none too happy at the public shambles into which the Party had got itself. There was Reggie Maudling, who muffed whatever chance he had when his big Conference speech came up. And there was the 14th Earl of Home, not canvassing but being affable to everybody and obviously enjoying it. He even agreed to be interviewed by me.

In the BBC's improvised studio in the basement of the Imperial Hotel, I questioned Lord Home in a late-night live interview. Lord Home's biographer (John Dickie, diplomatic correspondent of the *Daily Mail*) records that 'Lord Home revealed a distinct shift in his position towards the leadership'. This interesting Day–Home dialogue ensued:

Day: Are you aware, Lord Home, that you are widely regarded as an increasingly strong contender?

Home: Yes, so I've heard, but then I also heard Mr Randolph Churchill say this was rot just now, so I don't know myself what to believe. But I've taken a perfectly clear view on this, that I am not going to say anything about anybody else because I don't think this is the right thing to do. And what we ought to do is – among ourselves to consider who is most likely to command the support of the party as a leader, and then we shall arrive at a decision which I hope will be supported by the whole party in the country and in Parliament.

Day: Are you discouraging people here from advocating your name?

Home: Oh, I'm neither discouraging nor encouraging them. I'm taking no part in this at all because I don't believe that people ought to go around canvassing for themselves or

canvassing for other people. We leave this ascertaining of
opinion to the various people in the National Union and in
Parliament, who know how to carry out this job.

Day: But if it is in the national interest to get this business
over quickly, are you prepared to simplify the matter by
saying now quite categorically that you intend to remain the
fourteenth Earl of Home as long as you live?

Home: Well now, this is the question which I told you just
now I wasn't going to answer.

Day: Oh, I thought it was a slightly different one – I'm
sorry.

Home: Well, it's much the same. It's the same question
in a different form, and I'm not going to comment on myself
or anybody else with regard to the leadership of the
Conservative Party. But be quite sure we shall find a leader
all right by the customary processes, which the party want.

Day: Well, leaving aside yourself and any other specific
individual, Lord Home, is it possible in the Conservative
Party, of which you have great knowledge, that, given strong
enough support, a reluctant individual could be drafted to
serve as leader of the party?

Home: It would depend on the individual and how
reluctant he was. And I don't know who you have in mind.
It might be the same way – the third way – of asking the
first question which you asked, and again I must say that
I'm not going to be trapped, or induced really, to answer
any questions on the leadership, except to say that it will
be settled by the normal, customary processes which we've
done time and again before and which we shall complete
again.

Lord Home's biographer then explains: 'In fairness to Robin
Day it should be added, in case the dialogue seems harsh in
cold print, that Lord Home made light of the "ordeal". He
ended with a smile, saying: "It doesn't matter to me, you see,
because I never answer a question which I don't want to. So it's
really all quite OK with me." '*

*John Dickie, *Uncommon Commoner* (Pall Mall Press, 1964), pp. 173–5.

The interview over, Lord Home left the studio. Reggie Maudling, who had been sitting on an upturned empty orange-box, listening at the side of the studio, came over to sit in his place. What easy-going Reggie said in his interview I don't recall, but I vividly remember what he said as soon as the programme was off the air. 'Well,' he said, 'Alec is obviously going to run.' The fact that Lord Home had come to the studio simply to refuse to declare whether or not he had any intention of running was evidence enough for Reggie that Alec would run.

Others were likewise commenting that Lord Home was going to run. One veteran Tory back-bencher, Nigel Birch, was openly campaigning for Home in the hotel and around the Winter Gardens. I had heard Birch speak in the debate on the Profumo scandal that June. He had no time for Macmillan, who had dismissed Birch's resignation from the Treasury with Thorneycroft and Powell as a 'little local difficulty'. In the Profumo debate, Birch delivered the most biting attack on a Prime Minister I had ever heard from the government benches. Birch quoted from Browning's *The Lost Leader*:

. . . Let him never come back to us!
There would be doubt, hesitation and pain,
Forced praise on our part – the glimmer of twilight,
Never glad confident morning again!

With Macmillan gone, Birch was determined that Lord Home should succeed him. I watched him buttonholing everybody assiduously. He even buttonholed me. In every ear his message was the same: 'It's got to be Alec. He has eaten the King's salt.'* Several of my colleagues in the press thought I was behaving very strangely when I took them aside and whispered knowledgeably, 'Alec has eaten the King's salt!'

The premiership of Sir Alec Douglas-Home lasted less than a year. The conventional wisdom is that Sir Alec cut a poor

---

*This glowing reference to the 14th Earl's sense of duty echoed the famous words of Wellington: 'I have eaten of the King's salt, and, therefore, I conceive it to be my duty to serve with unhesitating zeal and cheerfulness, when and wherever the King or his Government may think it proper to employ me.' Quoted in Elizabeth Longford's *Wellington: The Years of the Sword* (Panther Books, 1971), p. 161.

Election results night, June 1970. The puppets of Heath and other Tories were a Labour gimmick to launch the derisive slogan 'Yesterday's Men'. But Labour lost and the anti-Tory slogan rebounded sharply.

The King of Swing: Professor Robert McKenzie of the LSE with his beloved swingometer on election night, 1970.

An election night marathon in the seventies, before the author gave up smoking.

The zenith of the author's career – his appearance on *The Morecambe and Wise Show*, 1975.

HRH Princess Anne, President of the Society of Film and Television Arts, presenting the author with the Richard Dimbleby Award in 1975 'for his enormous contribution to political journalism on television'.

With Edward Heath at a Conservative conference in the '70s.

The author interviewing Harold Macmillan, October 1976, for his first intervention in British politics since he was Prime Minister. He called for a coalition government 'of men of goodwill'.

Interview with Prime Minister James Callaghan during the 1979 election campaign.

Chairing *Election Debate* in the 1979 campaign – with Michael Heseltine, Jo Grimond and Michael Foot.

Prime Minister Margaret Thatcher, escorted by BBC brass, visits the *World at One* office in Broadcasting House, 1980.

Bernard Levin asking me (BBC2, 1980) whether it was not rather odd that whereas he was hired to express his opinions, I was hired not to express mine.

The author with his sons Daniel (left) and Alexander (right) at Buckingham Palace after his investiture, February 1981.

The author, after receiving his knighthood at Buckingham Palace in 1981 with Lady Day and their two sons, Daniel and Alexander, then aged five and seven.

At the Variety Club Dinner, July 1982, to celebrate the sixtieth anniversary of the BBC televised live from the Dorchester Hotel. Laughing on the left, Sir Ian Trethowan.

e author interviewing Prime nister Margaret Thatcher live from . 10 Downing Street for *Panorama*, ril 1984.

Around the *Question Time* table with me (from left to right), Michael Heseltine, Dr David Owen, Susan Crosland, Dennis Skinner in March 1988.

The author with his sons Alexander (thirteen) and Daniel (eleven) by the sea in Dorset, Christmas 1987.

The author in the Chair at a public meeting (of the legal profession) 1989.

figure on TV in how he looked and in what he said. I disagree.
It is true that he had become Prime Minister with no preparation
for TV. Occasionally his choice of words was inept, as when he
referred to 'donations' for old-age pensioners. But this was not
an example of his inexperience of television. It was due to his
having been out of the House of Commons for twelve years,
and to his specialization in foreign rather than home affairs.
Again, there was his famous confession that he needed to use
matches to understand economics, though this may have won
him much sympathy and fellow feeling. Against such lapses by
the 14th Earl may be set his memorable and much-quoted retort:
'I suppose Mr Wilson, when you come to think of it, is the
fourteenth Mr Wilson.'

Sir Alec Douglas-Home did not speak with the sonorous formality of Macmillan, nor with the sharp-witted fluency of the
young Harold Wilson. But he spoke crisply, lucidly and incis-
ively. He sounded more straightforward than either Macmillan
or Wilson. If my estimate of Lord Home is thought over-gen-
erous, it should be remembered that in the 1964 election he
came within four seats of victory. Whatever may be said about
his TV image, that result was remarkable. He was fighting to
defend the record of thirteen years of 'Tory misrule'. He was
fighting a young and aggressive Labour leader. Never was 'Time
for a change' a more difficult slogan to counter. To lose by only
four seats was, in the circumstances, no small achievement.

Would Rab Butler have done better than Sir Alec in that
1964 election? Alistair Horne's masterly biography of Macmillan
reveals that in his old age Macmillan admitted that, perhaps, it
would have been better if Butler, not Home, had succeeded
him, and that Rab could have won the '64 election.*

Certainly Rab was experienced, moderate and wise, but would
he have inspired the Tory faithful? Rab would not have been
such a convenient target for Wilson's grouse-moor jibes, but
would Rab as leader have fought a vigorous campaign?

We know that Rab made an uninspiring speech at the crucial
moment of the 1963 Conference. We know also that Rab failed
to seize his chance later that year by not refusing to serve under

---

*Alistair Horne, *Macmillan*, vol. 2: 1956–1986 (Macmillan, 1989), p. 582.

Lord Home. In Enoch Powell's metaphor, Rab was handed a loaded revolver but he would not pull the trigger.

The 14th Earl of Home, formerly Lord Dunglass MP, later Sir Alec Douglas-Home MP, later still Lord Home of the Hirsel, detested television. But I am happy to say, as one of the attendants in the torture chamber, who on more than one occasion must have caused him discomfort, that I never detected the slightest animosity from him towards me then or since. I have always liked him for his friendliness, his good humour and his total lack of pomposity.

Do You Know What You Should Have Asked?

If for Sir Alec, television was torture, for his successor it was the twentieth century's key to political power. Harold Wilson was the Prime Minister whom I interviewed most often.

For twenty years, from the mid-fifties to the mid-seventies, I interviewed Wilson, when he was Shadow Chancellor, Leader of the Labour Opposition, Prime Minister, Labour Leader again, and Prime Minister again. Throughout those twenty years, especially the sixties, I watched him develop into a television 'professional', a witty platform speaker, a formidable parliamentarian, and a master politician uniquely well equipped for No. 10 in the television age.

Uniquely well equipped? He was the first PM to enter office with professional mastery of the techniques of television, as much as others had mastered the techniques of Parliament, or of platform oratory, or of writing books. He was the first trained economist to become Prime Minister. He was young and vigorous. At forty-eight, he was the youngest Prime Minister this century. He had been a Cabinet Minister when he was thirty-one.

Wilson had made many friends in television during his thirteen years in opposition. When he came to office as Prime Minister, he found that the broadcasters had an awkward tendency to maintain their independence and impartiality.

Harold Wilson clashed and quarrelled with both BBC and ITV (mainly the BBC) on a series of occasions throughout the sixties and into the seventies. The rows have been endlessly chronicled and described in autobiographies, memoirs and election histories. Wilson appeared to develop a persecution complex about the BBC. The rows concerned programme policy, arrangements for broadcasts, editorial decisions. By the end of 1969 things had got to the point of Wilson summoning Lord Hill, the Chairman of the BBC (whom he had himself appointed to put the BBC's house in order) to Downing Street for a dressing-down. Lord Hill sturdily denied there was any conspiracy or bias in the BBC against Wilson or the Labour Party.

None of my own interviews with Harold Wilson himself was the subject of any protest. But one incident which involved me personally will illustrate Harold Wilson's extraordinary state of near-paranoia about the BBC when he was Prime Minister.

The occasion was one of those large late-night parties at the American Embassy residence in Regent's Park. Ambassador David Bruce and his wife Evangeline were the hosts. Supper was taken informally at small tables. The party, for politicians, journalists and diplomats, was taking place at a time of international tension. I was chatting over my supper when one of Wilson's private secretaries came over. 'The Prime Minister wonders why you haven't come up to speak to him.' Rather surprised, I said: 'Surely there are many more important people here for him to talk with than me?' But the Prime Minister wanted me to have a word, so I went over to his table. To my utter amazement, Harold Wilson spent the next twenty minutes or so complaining to me about the BBC's film coverage of the recent Durham Miners' Gala. The Prime Minister alleged the coverage to have been biased, and gave details about camera angles and so on. I listened patiently. I told him I had not seen the coverage but that the BBC news cameramen were unbiased professionals. I pointed out that it was not a programme for which I had any responsibility. I tried to change the subject. But Wilson kept repeating his complaint.

Why should a busy Prime Minister bother talking to me at length about so trivial a matter in the midst of a diplomatic function at a time of international crisis? Why did he appear to have a persecution complex about the Corporation? Why did he pursue an apparent vendetta against the BBC even when its

Chairman was Wilson's own appointee, Lord Hill? The explanation is not psychological but political.

Wilson's war against the BBC had, in my judgment, a simple root cause. This was the fact that television, because of its obligation to be politically impartial, was, in his eyes, the most powerful ally which the Labour Party had. Hence the paramount need, as Wilson (and his kitchen cabinet) saw it, to prevent the BBC from going off the rails. Hence the continual pressure which was brought to bear on the BBC's top brass, such as Charles Hill and Hugh Greene, or on the Corporation's frontline foot-soldiers such as John Grist.

Wilson's irritation with the BBC was acentuated during the first eighteen months of his premiership. He was then on a knife-edge majority and was very nervous politically. That is when the rows occurred. The notorious midnight row with John Grist at Blackpool was in October 1965. Wilson was infuriated by an interview I had done with the left-wing trade union leader, Clive Jenkins. This was alleged to have been unfairly included in the BBC's Conference coverage. Grist, the BBC's Conference Editor, was summoned to the Prime Minister's suite in the Imperial Hotel. Wilson threatened, in effect, that if the BBC did not mend its ways the government would see that it did. Similar words were exchanged later in the week after another interview of mine, this time with George Brown. Wilson angrily attacked the BBC's Conference coverage. Grist, a tall, genial man who was the very embodiment of BBC independence, robustly reminded the PM that the Conference coverage was a matter for the BBC's editorial judgment.

Wilson knew that Labour would be ruined if the BBC developed into a free-wheeling, trouble-stirring, government-knocking outfit. There had been signs of this, notably in the satire programme, *That Was The Week That Was*.

I recall being in the TV lounge of the Royal Hotel, Scarborough, late one Saturday night during the Labour Party Conference of 1963. Several members of the Party's National Executive, who had been having their pre-Conference meeting, came in to watch *That Was The Week That Was*, then at the height of its notoriety. I sat quietly in the corner, watching the enthusiastic reaction of the NEC members. Barbara Castle was one, and Tony

Greenwood was another. They revelled in the pillorying and abuse of the Tory government. This provoked shrieks of delighted laughter. The programme's occasional swipe at non-Tory targets, such as trade unionists, did not affect the NEC members' enjoyment.

Those Labour politicians knew perfectly well that much of what they had applauded was a gross breach of the BBC's obligation to be impartial. Some of them could see the dangers for a Labour government. In a taxi from Lime Grove to Westminster, Dick Crossman, MP, in one of his enjoyable moments of appalling frankness, said to me about *That Was The Week That Was*: 'Marvellous stuff! Marvellous! But of course the BBC won't be allowed to get away with it when Labour are in power.' There is no doubt that *TW3* helped to create a strong feeling among politicians of all parties that BBC people had contempt for the parliamentary process.

As Dick Crossman foresaw, Wilson and his entourage were determined to prevent the BBC from straying from the straight and narrow path of strict impartiality. That Labour needed a strictly impartial BBC was an overwhelming imperative of the Wilson years. This was seen as Labour's only protection against the hyenas of Fleet Street, about whom Wilson was no less paranoic. But television, especially the BBC, was both more important to him, and more susceptible to government pressure.

Given this attitude, which was understandable, there grew up an absurd climate of suspicion in which every programme dispute, every editorial wrangle, every rough interview, was liable to create friction. Sometimes Wilson was annoyed, as other Prime Ministers have been, by BBC arrogance. In considering whether his resentment towards the BBC was ever justified or not, one must remember that other and very different politicians have voiced similar resentment and have made intimidating noises.

Iain Macleod, now the patron saint of 'One Nation' moderate Tories, was scathingly immoderate in his accusations of hostility by the BBC towards the Tories in 1970. The election was imminent. Macleod was Shadow Chancellor. I telephoned him privately in the hope of persuading him to appear in the BBC programme, *24 Hours*. Macleod's response was crushing. He had already declared publicly that the political programmes of the BBC were 'of such sustained hostility to the Conservative Party that it is a net loss to appear'. Macleod said the same to me only more acidly. He had a bell-like orator's voice which sounded magnificent on the platform. Even on the telephone it rang out as if he were in the pulpit, uttering a fearsome imprecation.

Sixteen years later, the Tory Chairman was Norman Tebbit. He had rather enjoyed being called by Michael Foot 'a semi house-trained polecat'. In 1987 Tebbit, who prefers political fighting with the gloves off, accused the BBC TV News of inaccuracy and imbalance in its coverage of the US bombing of Libya. With a general election coming up, Chairman Tebbit obviously felt, as Harold Wilson had felt, that a shot or two across the BBC's bows would help his cause.

Politicians seeking to win or to retain power can behave like bullies. This, however, is not to say that because the BBC has been abused and subjected to attempted intimidation from both right and left it must therefore have been impartial. But it is silly to pretend that no one in the BBC has ever been arrogant, unfair or irresponsible.

My own relations with Harold Wilson were extremely good. I was never on terms of personal friendship with him, but enjoyed our many private talks together – provided he kept off the iniquities of the BBC, which put me in an embarrassing position. Though I interviewed him again and again over a twenty-year period, he never once complained or protested about any interview by me with him. Nor did he ever ask to know the questions in advance.

Harold Wilson enjoyed the sword-play of a good TV interview, just as he enjoyed the much fiercer cut-and-thrust of the House of Commons. Often when an interview was over, he would chide me for missing a good question: 'Do you know what you should have asked?' He would add tantalizingly: 'Something I'd have found it very difficult to answer.' I then had to prepare myself for the professional humiliation of learning that I could have elicited some important news if only I had been more on the ball.

Though a famous pipe-smoker on the screen, Harold Wilson liked to smoke a Havana cigar after a TV appearance. I also in those years was a cigar smoker. After one major television interview with him on *Panorama* when he was Prime Minister, I offered him one of the special Havanas I had bought for myself to enjoy as a treat after the interview, which I knew was likely to be difficult. Wilson accepted my cigar. We both puffed away happily as we argued and gossiped over drinks (brandies for the PM) in the hospitality room.

A few weeks later, there was another interview. Without thinking about it, I offered Harold another cigar. Then several months later, after a particularly hard-hitting interview, I pulled out my cigar-case but Harold said, 'No, no. You've given *me* cigars. It's my turn tonight.' And he produced two whacking great Havanas which he had bought specially, one for himself and one for me. That he should have thought to do this, after several months, was very civilized. From then on, he or I would say after an interview, as we took out a cigar, 'Is it your turn or mine?'

Having made himself into an adept and agile parliamentarian, he was in his element when involved in some clash or kerfuffle with TV interviewers. Once in *Panorama* he faced three of us. I was in the chair, and annoyed my colleague, James Mossman, by moving to another topic. Mossman protested loudly that his supplementary had been suppressed. I insisted, even more loudly, that the chairman had a duty to the clock and to ask some questions about Rhodesia. The Prime Minister looked on in amusement. At the end he said, 'I thought I wouldn't try and mediate between you.' This, though simple enough to say, was a brilliant stroke. It made him look tolerant and sensible. He made us, his interviewers, look like squabbling kids.

In the general election of February 1974 there was an incident which the press reported: 'Wilson in clash with Robin Day'.* I cannot recall any other occasion when Harold Wilson took exception during an interview to one of my questions to him.

Wilson, by the way, was the first of the television Prime Ministers to call me by my Christian name on television. This is alleged to have been part of the deliberate informality and mateyness of his TV manner. I never gave it a moment's thought.

---

*See above, p. 213.

It was obviously natural for him to call me 'Robin' as he had done in interviews for years ever since I had become a TV interviewer. It would have seemed forced for him to have suddenly started calling me '*Mr* Day' when he became Prime Minister.

In my many conversations and contacts with Harold Wilson I never felt in the presence of greatness. I admired his intellectual agility, his parliamentary wit and his political wizardry. Even one of his political enemies, Norman Tebbit, concedes: 'Harold Wilson handled the difficult business of minority government, in the midst of an economic crisis and under the looming shadow of another election, with great skill.'*

An often-heard criticism of Wilson is that some of those whom he recommended for knighthoods and other honours were unworthy recipients. If he deserves such criticism, Harold Wilson also deserves credit, which he is never given, for including in his Honours lists some eminently deserving and long-overdue names – Sir Charles Chaplin, Sir Noël Coward, Sir P. G. Wodehouse, Dame Daphne du Maurier and, not least, Dame Vera Lynn.

Wilson's footwork was dazzling. On the Common Market his twisting and turning was worthy of the Great Houdini. In opposition he sounded anti-Market. In office he became pro-Market. In opposition again he went along with the referendum idea, infuriating Roy Jenkins and the pro-Marketeers. But in the end it was that referendum under Wilson's second premiership which clinched Britain's membership for ever.

I admired Wilson's cleverness in leading the Labour Party and in seeking to reconcile the irreconcilable. But two aspects of Wilson's record prevent me from holding him in the highest esteem as a statesman. Firstly, too often the unity of the Labour Party had too high a place in his priorities. Secondly, he seemed to lack that steeliness of principle and conviction which gives a political leader moral force.

Politics is a cruel business. For several years, Harold Wilson dominated Westminster and Whitehall. Now, except when an alleged plot by MI5 to destabilize his government has caught

---

*Norman Tebbit, *Upwardly Mobile* (Weidenfeld & Nicolson, 1988), p. 136.

media attention, he has become a largely forgotten Prime Minister. Perhaps that is due to his withdrawal in retirement, as Lord Wilson of Rievaulx, from public debate, and to poor health. But not since Stanley Baldwin, who like Harold Wilson was a master politician of his time, has the political reputation of an ex-Prime Minister slumped so markedly.

History may not judge him so harshly. Personally I feel nothing but gratitude to him for his kindness and good humour to me professionally, especially during my *Panorama* years.

Why Not Get Rid of the Boring Interviewers?

Tony Benn once told me of a theory which classified British Prime Ministers into three categories. This theory was invented by his American wife, Caroline. According to Caroline Benn's 'law', Prime Ministers were either Pedestrians, Fixers or Madmen. I gathered that by 'Pedestrian' was meant dull, uninspiring, colourless, such as Attlee or Douglas-Home. The 'Fixers' were the political wizards, the smart operators, the pragmatists – Lloyd George, Harold Wilson, Jim Callaghan. 'Madmen' was a crude but convenient term for the fanatics and visionaries, those whose conviction was stronger than their judgment. As I understood it, these would include Winston Churchill (but for whose 'madness' in 1940 we would not have survived), Ted Heath (the Euro-fanatic) and, of course, Margaret Thatcher, the iron-willed conviction politician, driven unstoppably by ideological fervour.

I said to Tony Benn, 'If *you* had become Prime Minister, what do you think you would have been – a Pedestrian, a Fixer or a Madman?' 'One of the Madmen. Don't you think so?' said Tony. I murmured my concurrence politely. I forget where Eden, Chamberlain, Baldwin and Ramsay MacDonald fitted into this 'law', which has provoked many enjoyable arguments among students, young and old, of politics. But for myself, I prefer a simpler classification of our post-war Prime Ministers – those who made any real difference and those who did not.

Of all the post-war British Prime Ministers, only two have personally changed the course of British history by sheer force of character and conviction: Edward Heath and Margaret Thatcher.

Heath led this island kingdom, kicking and screaming, into Europe. Thatcher led the social and economic revolution which bears her name. The full consequences of both these historic events, which are still in progress, are yet to be experienced and understood by the British people. By the end of the century we may be better able to judge. But, whatever the outcome, Heath and Thatcher, with their uncompromising commitment, have been individually the driving force in each of these radical breaks with the past.

The other post-war Prime Ministers presided, it is true, over major reforms and important developments. Attlee's Labour government gave independence to India and began the National Health Service. But the momentum for these and other measures had built up during the war and earlier. Attlee was the presiding figure but not the sole driving force. Under the peace-time administration of Winston Churchill (by then in his eighth decade) nothing much happened, unless you count the introduction of ITV. Admittedly that gave me my opportunity, but otherwise the course of British history continued on its tranquil course. Neither of Harold Wilson's two periods at No. 10 produced any great radical advance, even though in 1974 Wilson had come back to power on a manifesto pledged to 'a fundamental and irreversible shift in the balance of power and wealth in favour of working people'. Callaghan's achievement was to cling to office as long as he did with the help of the Lib-Lab pact.

Ted Heath was Prime Minister for less than four years. Yet such was the force of his personality and the strength of his willpower that he achieved his objective – Britain's entry into the European Common Market. He achieved that objective moreover against the wishes of a powerful section of the Tory Party, against the instincts of France, where Gaullism lived on, against the inclinations of the old white Commonwealth, and against the deep-rooted xenophobia to be found among British people.

I interviewed Ted Heath on television at several critical moments in his career: the night he was elected Leader of the Tory Party in 1965, the day Wilson announced the general

DailyMirror 5 Oct 1965

Labour accuses
BBC of bias

ROBIN DAY
INTERVIEWING
TED HEATH
AT
BRIGHTON

FRANKLIN

" WE'RE TRYING TO APPEASE WILSON "

election of 1970, the night Heath introduced his Counter-Inflation Bill to limit pay increases, and on the eve of his 'Who governs Britain?' election of February 1974. And we have had many broadcast encounters in the years, more than fifteen now, which he has spent out of office, as an apparently embittered elder statesman.

Ted denies that he is embittered, but that is the impression which he has given to many of his friends and admirers. What else is the explanation, they ask, for his contemptuous attitude to Margaret Thatcher and her policies, which has seemed to grow more hostile the longer she remains at No. 10 and the more elections she wins? Does he still harbour a grudge against her for challenging him and defeating him for the Tory leadership? If so, fifteen years is a long time to harbour a grudge.

Ted Heath can truthfully claim to have campaigned loyally for his Party in elections since he was thrown out as party

Leader. He has done so despite the many aspects of Thatcherism tnwith which he has profoundly disagreed. These include her attitude to European union, and her 'monetarist' economic policy. It is not 'sullen' or 'disloyal' for Ted Heath to speak his mind on these issues. Politicians have a duty to say what they think in the national interest. But, and this is what some of Ted's most devoted admirers ask, could he not have done his duty as a parliamentarian and an elder statesman in a manner which did not seem so sour or so sulky? More importantly, would not his principled and authoritative indictments of That-cherite policies carry even more weight if they did not seem motivated by personal resentment? It is fair to say that Heath's attendance at the Tory back-benchers' lunch for Margaret That-cher's tenth anniversary as Prime Minister was a graceful gesture which stilled some of these criticisms, if only temporarily.

But his ferocious onslaught during the 1989 Euro-Election campaign against Margaret Thatcher's attitude to European unity ('preposterous', 'insulting', 'patronizing', 'self-serving hypocrisy') caused grave offence. There was even some absurd talk of expelling Ted from the Tory Party, though sharp-eyed commentators noted that he had already been expelled from the pages of the latest edition of its historical reference book, *The Campaign Guide*. The name of the ex-Prime Minister is expunged from the index.

Ted Heath is not a smooth man. He is not a phoney man. He does not specialize in charm. Among all the leading politicians whom I have known, he is one of the most straightforward. This makes him at times seem stiff, awkward and lacking in social grace. But he is in truth a right honourable gentleman. And he has a great sense of humour, though this is not well known to the public. I have heard him speak, sometimes in the House, or at dinners, with consummate wit and without a note. His style is all the more effective because it is one of mock-solemnity. His humour is usually rather aggressive. His banter is not intended to be taken seriously. Or perhaps it is. You are never quite certain.

At an international conference just after his defeat by Mrs Thatcher, Heath was taking part in a session about the media and democracy. He rose to make a pungent intervention. He said the reason political leaders lost elections and were kicked out was that the people got bored by seeing them interviewed so often on TV by the same boring interviewers. 'Instead of getting rid of the boring politicians,' said Mr Heath, looking in my direction, 'I have never understood why we cannot get rid of the boring TV interviewers.' There was loud applause. Ted's shoulders shook and heaved with laughter as they always do when a thrust of his goes down well. The appropriate retort eluded me. I am still working on it.

His humour can certainly be gruff. In 1977, Jubilee Year, Ted was in a TV studio with me preparing for a discussion on events in the Queen's reign. The floor manager, Miss Joan Marsden, known to Ted and many other politicians as Mother, was proudly displaying her Jubilee medal (for BBC services spanning twenty-five years) which she had just received in the post. 'Look,' she said to everyone, 'I have been sent a Jubilee medal.' I and others murmured something appropriate like 'Congratulations,' or 'When will you wear it?' When Ted Heath came into the studio, Joan showed him to his chair and said with obvious delight, 'Look, I got the Jubilee medal this morning.' Ted barked back, 'So did I.' For a brief moment Joan felt a trifle hurt at this apparent contempt for what had pleased her. But being a tough lady of great good humour, she realized that this was Ted's gruff style, and that she had a good story to dine out on. She saw that Ted's reply was really a reaction of amusement to an award which was distributed to BBC floor managers and to ex-Prime Ministers alike.

In the 1970 election, Ian Trethowan and I were sorting the voters' cards for *Election Forum*. Our questions were chosen as usual from those sent in by thousands of voters on postcards to the party leaders. I said to Ian that one of the questions was electoral dynamite. In youthful handwriting it was addressed to the Rt Hon. Edward Heath, Leader of the Conservative Party. It read as follows:

> Dear Daddy,
>   When you get to No. 10 will you do the decent thing and invite Mummy and me for tea?

Now you may think (as a judge will say to a jury), though it is entirely a matter for you, that the words 'Dear Daddy' have only one clear meaning. I heard the voice of Disraeli talking about the ageing Palmerston's sexual indiscretion: 'If this gets out, he'll sweep the country.' But there was another voice (was it Mrs Mary Whitehouse?) saying: 'If a man who seeks to lead this Christian nation behaves like a character in a typical TV play, the voters have a right to know.' What were we to do? Whatever we did could decide the destiny of our country.

I turned to Ian Trethowan for advice. He displayed the cool judgment which was eventually to make him Director-General. He was then, as I still am, a humble worker on the shop floor. Ian Trethowan quietly weighed the considerations in his mind. 'Of course,' he said, 'you must put this crucial question. But only in rehearsal.' Which I duly did. And what was Mr Heath's reaction? As if in gratitude for light relief from pre-transmission tension, his shoulders shook with silent mirth.*

On other occasions, my television encounters with Heath have been vigorous. He never complained, as far as I know, about any question put by me, though some newspapers and some of his supporters did. The night he was elected Leader of the Tory Party, at the age of only forty-nine, Ted Heath was in masterly and good-humoured form. No, he did not see that being a bachelor would be politically disadvantageous. No, he had not taken any personal initiative in that matter. According to Maurice Wiggin, long-time TV critic of the *Sunday Times*, Ted belonged 'to the age of the TV personality . . . He will prove the biggest asset the Tories have had in years.'†

As Leader of the Opposition from 1965 to 1970, Ted Heath was a target of much criticism from within his own party. I remember thinking at this period, how does a man endure what Ted Heath has to endure? Waking up every morning to see himself described in the press, sometimes by his supporters, as inadequate, charmless, wooden, no good on TV, lonely, lacking the comfort of a wife, lacking charisma, lacking the common touch. This was enough to demoralize the strongest character, yet Ted Heath, who is a sensitive man, stuck it out and, to

---

*On legal advice, I hasten to emphasize that the 'Dear Daddy' question was a joke, and entirely without foundation. The above account of this episode is as related by me in an after-dinner speech, heard and enjoyed by Mr Heath himself.
†*Sunday Times*, 1 August 1965.

everyone's surprise, went on to win the 1970 election handsomely.

In one *Panorama* of October 1967 on the eve of the Tory Conference, there was a film of Tories discussing his deficiencies as Leader. This was watched and heard by Ted Heath, who was then interviewed about their disparaging comments. According to the *Daily Telegraph*'s front-page story: 'Mr Heath survived with some credit an ordeal by television possibly never experienced by any politician in Britain.' After that somewhat sensational opening, the *Telegraph* writer, however, went on to describe the questioning as 'tough but legitimate'.*

A question of mine on that occasion was replayed twenty years later in Granada's *World in Action* in 1987 to show how much more independent the BBC was in 1967! The producer of that Granada programme had only to look at my interview with Mrs Thatcher of May 1987. They would have seen that a BBC interviewer was no less independent in 1987 than in 1967. This is the question I put to Ted Heath when he was Leader of the Opposition in October 1967. Michael Cockerell's account is that 'Robin Day went for the kill':†

Q: But how low does your personal rating among your own supporters have to go before you consider yourself a liability to the Party you lead?
   A: Well popularity isn't everything. In fact, it isn't the most important thing. What matters is doing what you believe to be right . . . The question doesn't arise.

There was an unfortunate incident on 18 May 1970. That was the day that Prime Minister Wilson announced the general election. Interviews were arranged with the party leaders in *Panorama*. Though they had equal time, they did not have equal treatment. The Prime Minister was filmed in the sunny garden at No. 10 amid the flowers, puffing his pipe. His interviewer was Peter Hardiman Scott, the BBC's political correspondent. He worked for BBC News, whose style of questioning tended to be

Daily Telegraph, 17 October 1967.
†Michael Cockerell, *Live from Number 10* (Faber, 1988), pp. 137–8.

less vigorous than that in Current Affairs. In this interview, Hardiman Scott's questioning was gentle. Immediately after this relaxed garden scene with Wilson, came Ted Heath in the harsh lighting of the TV studio with me to question him. I did not set out to be 'tougher' than Hardiman Scott. I could not be otherwise. I could hardly tone down my questions to 'balance' Hardiman Scott's gentleness. Apart from the different interviewing styles, the Wilson interview was on his home ground, and Heath's was on my home ground. So the atmosphere of each was different.

In contrast to Hardiman Scott, I looked severe and savage. I was interviewing in the way people had come to expect, especially at election time. When a top politician was questioned, this had to be done in a persistent and challenging manner. But I had not reckoned on the Downing Street performance with Wilson. The effect of the two interviews in juxtaposition was dreadful. It was a bad start for the BBC in that election.

The question from me to Heath which stirred up most criticism was this one:

Q: If you lose a second time, will you resign the leadership of the Party?

A: We are going to win, Mr Day. That is the answer to your question.

My question was unpleasant for his supporters, but it was one which was on many people's minds. More importantly, perhaps, it was a question to which the manner of his answer would show what sort of leader he was. And it did. Characteristically, Ted Heath did not complain, even privately.

But the *Sunday People*, that well-known upholder of civilized behaviour, addressed an entire editorial to me: 'WHO THE HELL DO YOU THINK YOU ARE?' The *People* denounced my questioning of Ted Heath as 'savage', 'insulting', and 'DAMNED RUDE' and in some plain-speaking homes 'BLOODY RUDE'.

When he became Prime Minister, Ted Heath was a formidable man to interview, mainly because his position gave him even greater command of facts and details. There was nothing any interviewer could ask to which he did not have a full and flowing answer. An interviewer simply had to keep his head down and seize any opportunity which might arise of eliciting some new point of spontaneous reaction. On the eve of the February 1974 election ('Who governs Britain?'), I asked Ted Heath whether the stand which the government had taken against the miners was worth the price which the country would have to pay. Heath cut in fiercely: 'We are not against the miners. Let us be quite clear about that. We are not.'

Why did Ted Heath lose the Tory leadership? Perhaps one need look no further than the fact that he had lost two general elections in 1974. But apart from that, what was it about him which had got so many Tory backs up? I asked a former member of his Cabinet. We were having a private chat over a glass of wine at Königswinter on the Rhine during one of those enjoyable Anglo-German conferences. The answer was that Ted had given offence in small but wounding ways. Did Tory MPs, I asked, really resent being talked to straight from the shoulder?

The ex-Cabinet Minister replied, 'Well, to give you just one example, let me tell you what happened to me. I was attending my first Cabinet. I was naturally nervous. My item was called last. I had to make a report on some project. Because the clock was against me, I had to take it quickly. Do you know what Ted, the Prime Minister, said when I had finished, in front of the entire Cabinet? It was terribly wounding.'

'What did Ted say?' I asked.

' "Typical Treasury drivel! Typical Treasury drivel." '

I'm afraid I laughed. Wasn't that what we needed, a Prime Minister who would stand up to the bureaucracy of Whitehall? And was not 'Treasury drivel' a fair description? My companion rebuked me for flippancy. He had been wounded by Ted's cruel jibe, however justified it may have been. I sympathized with him, but I had more sympathy for Ted Heath, trying to galvanize the great sluggish machine of government. Ted liked to quote Disraeli's famous remark about England: 'It is a very difficult country to move . . . a very difficult country indeed . . .' And I liked to remind Ted Heath of what Disraeli said: 'and one in which there is more disappointment to be looked for than success.'* ̄

Is Robin Feeling Rough About It?

Lord Callaghan of Cardiff, writing about his time as Chancellor, paid me a double-edged compliment in his memoirs:

> My favourite interviewer was Robin Day and I would send messages to the BBC asking that he should be given the task. I liked his tough manner of questioning and although he could be a bit of a bully if his victim seemed to flinch, I hardly ever found that he took unfair advantage.†

Does this show, as some of my critics have often argued, that the so-called 'tough' interview is phoney establishment swordplay? If Jim Callaghan (unknown to me) would ask the BBC that I should be his interviewer, does this not show that a TV encounter with me held no terrors for him?

Some myths and fantasies need to be cleared away. First of all, the idea that a parliamentary veteran with years of experience at the despatch box would be in the slightest degree apprehensive about a few questions by me on television is nonsense. That any Prime Minister or other leading politician has ever been subjected to an 'ordeal by inquisition' at my hands is a fantasy created and repeated by writers of silly newspaper articles. What I have always done, or tried to do, is to put vigorous and well-informed questions in parliamentary style. The training and experience of politicians makes them responsible to such questioning. A limp, flabby, ill-informed interview does not stimulate them.

That is why most politicians prefer to be interviewed by an interviewer whose questions are relevant and incisive. That, I hope, is why Jim Callaghan liked me to be his interviewer. But what puzzled me is his statement that he 'hardly ever found that

---

*Disraeli in an interview, a few weeks before he died in 1881, with H. M. Hyndman, quoted in Robert Blake, *Disraeli*, (Eyre & Spottiswoode, 1966), pp. 763–4.
†James Callaghan, *Time and Chance*, (Collins, 1987), p. 180.

I took unfair advantage'. That suggests that on occasion I *did* take unfair advantage. I have searched my recollection ruthlessly and can think of no occasion when it could be said that I had taken unfair advantage. Moreover, those who recall seeing 'Big Jim' being interviewed may find it hard to imagine that he ever let an interviewer get away with anything sharp or below the belt.

Jim Callaghan's remark that I 'could be a bit of a bully' will bring a smile to many people who have had to deal with him in television programmes. He would usually strike a don't-try-any-of-your-nonsense-with-me attitude. If not designed to intimidate, this often did so. He would make it clear that he had had plenty of experience of television. He had been Chancellor of the Exchequer, Home Secretary and Foreign Secretary before becoming Prime Minister. And there was much television expertise in his own family. Margaret Jay, his daughter, was a producer in BBC Television, and his son-in-law Peter Jay was the presenter of ITV's *Weekend World*, the prestige current affairs programme at noon on Sundays.

Jim Callaghan was not an easy man to deal with on television. I was once asked what was the most impossible interview I ever had. My answer was 'one in which Jim Callaghan decides to mix it whatever you try to ask'. There was an interview I did with Jim late at night at a Labour Party Conference at Brighton in 1971. He was in belligerent mood. The question of the moment (some now-forgotten Labour Party rumpus involving 'personalities') was one which he was not inclined to answer. That night Jim was the Party spokesman to do the round of TV interviews. As the evening went on he was on BBC, ITN, several regional programmes and finally, at about 11 p.m., he was on with me for the BBC's Conference report.

I was about the seventh interviewer with whom Jim had sat down that night. The trouble was that we all wanted to ask him about the same point. His previous interviewers had tried their best, but he had brushed them aside. When my turn came, I put the question five or six times courteously but persistently and in a different way each time. Having said at the outset that he was not going to answer, Jim became more angry each time, with 'No, no, Mr Day. Next question.' I kept my cool, just.

A sound-only tape of this interview was leaked from the BBC.

Pirated copies sold like hot pants in Carnaby Street. It became a classic of its kind – the kind where a well-known interviewer is repeatedly told where he gets off by an angry, stone-walling politician.

Jim Callaghan was afterwards asked by reporters why he had reacted so roughly. He replied:

> Robin chanced his arm again and again. Why should the media get impertinent if they don't get an answer to a personal question? But is Robin feeling rough about it? He is much too professional.

I was not 'feeling rough about it' in the least. I explained to reporters:

> It was a question I had to ask, so I repeated it. It wasn't a tough question, because there is no such thing as a tough question; there are only tough answers. But Jim decided to mix it. I interviewed Roy next. He didn't answer the question either, but he used completely different stroke play.

Jim Callaghan was asked what the viewers' reaction had been to his bludgeoning of me. He pulled a letter from his pocket. 'I've had several letters from people who entirely approved. There's this one.' Jim later read it out to me with a beaming smile:

> When I saw your interview with Robin Day I experienced that sheer exultant feeling I get when listening to a fine performance of Mozart's Don Giovanni, or Brahms' Brandenburg Concerto or looking at Constable's Dedham Mill. It was a delicious feeling, a rare moment in life. All I can say is, thank you.

That letter made Jim very pleased with himself. I did not begrudge him his satisfaction. But I thought his adulatory correspondent was from 'Pseud's Corner', if only because I could not recall a Brandenburg Concerto by Brahms.

What did I mean by saying that there was no such thing as a

tough question, only tough answers? I was putting into a nutshell a little-known 'law' of interviewing, that whether a question is regarded as 'tough' is often determined not by the content of the question, but by the tone and manner of the answer. I have spent hours in hopeful preparation of penetrating and incisive questions, only to find they are deflected and blunted by a calm or emollient answer on the lines of 'I'm so glad you asked me that, Robin.' Conversely, the most innocent and unprovocative question can become 'tough' or 'abrasive' if the interviewee chooses to blow his top in reply.

On this night in Brighton, Jim didn't quite blow his top. But his belligerence made my repeated but inoffensive and legitimate questions seem tough and impertinent. Of course I did not 'feel rough' about it. I knew it had provided a moment or two of compulsive viewing on an otherwise dull night.

I had another difficult, but more serious television encounter with Jim Callaghan in 1976. This was his first TV interview as Prime Minister, which he gave to me at the Labour Party Conference of 1976. This Conference will be remembered for two events. It was the Conference at which Chancellor Denis Healey made a dramatic speech from the rostrum after having cancelled his flight from Heathrow to Hong Kong for an IMF meeting. The 1976 conference was also the occasion of the most memorable speech Callaghan ever made. This was written in part by Peter Jay, his brilliant economist son-in-law. Callaghan tells us that this paragraph by Jay 'made the fur fly':

> We used to think that you could spend your way out of a recession and increase employment by cutting taxes and boosting government spending. I tell you in all candour that that option no longer exists.*

That week Prime Minister Callaghan went before the television cameras to steady sterling and the nerves of his Cabinet colleagues. In his interview with me he gave what the *Daily Mirror* called next day a 'stark last-chance warning to the nation'. I had asked him whether failure by the Labour Government to

*Callaghan, *Time and Chance*, p. 426.

overcome Britain's economic difficulties would mean the collapse of Britain's democracy. Callaghan answered gravely:

> You are right. I think this is a responsibility which falls on our government. If we were to fail – and I don't particularly want to make a party point – I don't think another government could succeed. I fear it would lead to totalitarianism of the left or right.

The rest of the interview was a model for the combative manner which Callaghan was to adopt on television during his premiership. I asked him whether the IMF loan conditions would cause the standard of living to fall, but the Prime Minister said this was not so. The interview proceeded thus:

> Q: I ask you the question, Prime Minister, because it has been suggested this morning that, as a result of the loan and tighter money which may result, people should be prepared for higher prices, higher mortgage payments, higher rates, higher VAT to curb spending, perhaps higher unemployment because of spending curbs. Now is this possible?
>
> A: When you say what's said this morning do you mean at Conference . . . ?
>
> Q: No, no, no, no, no, in the press, in the press.
>
> A: . . . or did you mean on the front page of a daily newspaper?
>
> Q: Particularly on the front page of the *Daily Mail* but also in other newspapers.
>
> A: That's right, yes, yes, yes, yes, I saw that, but that I think is pure newspaper speculation.
>
> Q: And no truth in it at all?
>
> A: Speculation.
>
> Q: Is there any truth in it?
>
> A: Speculation.
>
> Q: Is there any possibility of it?
>
> A: Look, the only certainty in life is death. There will be a Budget next April; what will happen I don't know and I think it would help a great deal if the press were not to

speculate about all the worst things that could possibly happen.

Q: I was only asking you, Prime Minister . . .

A: No, and I am not attacking you, Mr Day, on this.

Callaghan's tactic in twice giving 'speculation' as an one-word answer was a new technique for answering awkward questions on television. Michael Cockerell states in his study of Prime Ministers and television that:

> Callaghan had thought long and hard about what his relationship as Prime Minister should be on the screen with Robin Day, who had interviewed him many times over the previous twenty years. Harold Wilson had always attempted a matey approach and called Day 'Robin'. 'Jim decided on "Mr Day" – this was before the knighthood – because he did not want to given the appearance of a cosy old boys' club,' says Tom McNally. 'This was to be the British Prime Minister giving the people the truth about a situation. He was determined that what he wanted to say and how he wanted to say it would dominate the programme: it was not going to be the Robin Day Show.'*

As Callaghan's government moved towards its downfall in the 'Winter of Discontent' of 1979, Callaghan's avuncular style began to show signs of strain. The unprecedented combination of industrial anarchy and appalling winter weather had demoralized the Cabinet. The nightly television coverage made the violence and chaos seem even uglier than it was. According to Lord Donoughue, senior policy adviser to Mr Callaghan in No. 10:

> The Prime Minister was . . . clearly very tired, both physically and mentally. It was equally clear that he was very unhappy at having to control the trade unions.
> His whole career had been built alongside the trade unions

*Cockerell, *Live from Number 10*, p. 231–2.

and he seemed to find it quite impossible to fight against
it.*

Towards the end of February 1979, I interviewed Callaghan
in No. 10 for *Panorama*. It was the day he had reached an
'agreement' with the trade unions. Under this 'concordat', the
unions were to help bring inflation down. Callaghan seized the
moment to talk on television in plain language to the people:

> We have had a basinful this winter, and I've been appalled
> at some of the things which have gone on. I have bitten my
> tongue more than once.

Why did he 'shrink from bringing in the law on industrial
relations'? Jim reacted sharply. He retorted that he would never
shrink from a fight if he thought it was right. He demanded that
I withdraw the word 'shrink'. My spontaneous use of this one
little word had happened to sting him on a tender spot. 'Big
Jim' was sensitive to the frequent allegations that impressive
and strong though he looked and sounded, he would never stand
up to his trade union friends. I promptly withdrew the offending
word in as jovial way as I could manage. At which the PM said,
'God bless you. Thank you.' The benediction seemed a little out
of place, but it was all part of the avuncular personality. Though
there had been nothing improper in the use of the word 'shrink',
I was well aware (knowing what Jim could be like in one of
his belligerent moods) that, had I not withdrawn it, he might
well have declined to continue the interview. As the interview
was live from No. 10, this would have been inconvenient.

There have been at least two occasions when a Callaghan
interview was terminated earlier than intended. Neither was
with me. One was an ITN interview during the '79 election when
he angrily walked out because (he said) the questioning was not
on the agreed basis. Another was after his retirement. Brian
Walden persisted in questioning him about Labour's defence
policy. Jim objected strenuously, so Walden cut short the interview. Music was then played for the rest of the time!

*Bernard Donoughhue, *Prime Minister: The Conduct of Policy under Wilson and
Callaghan* (Cape, 1987), p. 177.

Every Prime Minister and political leader has had his or her own way of dealing with questions and interrupters and hecklers, whether on TV or in Parliament. On television, Jim Callaghan's way was to go on the attack to show the questioner that he, Jim, was in charge and was not going to put up with any nonsense. This often made for good viewing. It was up to the interviewer to look after himself, and to watch his step. The Callaghan technique was good fun and fair enough when the interviewer was impertinent or ill-informed. But sometimes Jim seemed to be 'roughing up' an interviewer because the questions were awkward or difficult.

Jim Callaghan's 'get tough' tactics with television were not confined to ticking-off troublesome interviewers. It is worth recalling how Callaghan proposed to 'reform' the BBC. Those who do not remember will scarcely believe what was actually in the Callaghan government's White Paper on Broadcasting of 1977. Jim himself had decided to chair the Cabinet committee which drafted the White Paper. Like other Prime Ministers, Callaghan was determined to 'do something' about the BBC.

The Callaghan White Paper planned to secure greater government control over the BBC's output by inserting a new layer of managers *appointed by the Home Office*. This would have been government intervention in broadcasting on a scale previously unknown in Britain. The BBC was shocked, and mounted one of its periodic resistance campaigns.

Sir Ian Trethowan recalls that Callaghan's White Paper was greeted by a barrage of hostility from virtually every paper in the country'.* What the Callaghan White Paper proposed was that extra supervisory boards, appointed directly by the Home Office, should be inserted into the BBC at a level below that of the apparently impotent Board of Governors. The absurd idea of these Service Management Boards (one for Television, one for Radio, one for the External Services), whose members would be political appointees, died an unlamented death with the Callaghan government. Whether the plan would ever have been implemented if Labour had won the '79 election is uncertain.

The more serious question is whether this proposal was evi-

*Trethowan, *Split Screen*, p. 176.

dence of an authoritarian streak in Callaghan and his Cabinet, or evidence of the anti-BBC feeling which had grown up among politicians of both main parties. In my judgment it was evidence of both, but the latter was a significant and growing factor. Hostility towards the BBC was later to intensify under the Thatcher government with conflicts over the Falklands coverage, the Ulster terrorist incidents and the Libyan bombing.

I respected Jim Callaghan for his achievements as a parliamentarian. He had entered the Commons in 1945, wearing his Petty Officer's naval uniform. Forty-two years later, he was Father of the House. He was a formidable debater whose interventions rarely failed to impress his fellow Members. He was the first professional trade union officer to become Prime Minister. He was the first politician to hold all the four great offices of state, Chancellor of the Exchequer, Home Secretary, Foreign Secretary and Prime Minister. He had the presence, the stature and the judgment to be a fine Prime Minister. He brought an unpretentious dignity to the premiership. His socialism was not doctrinaire, and he was a patriot.

Yet on two crucial occasions Big Jim proved to be weak where strength was needed. The first occasion was in 1969 when the Wilson government was locked in dispute with the TUC over Barbara Castle's 'In Place of Strife' proposals for legal sanctions to curb unofficial strikes. Callaghan was adamantly against such sanctions, or 'penal clauses'.

As Callaghan admits in his memoirs, the trade unions failed to reform themselves when the withdrawal of 'In Place of Strife' gave them an opportunity to do so. Callaghan, as a lifelong champion of the trade unions, the 'Keeper of the Cloth Cap', would not admit that abuse of trade union power would have to be curbed by Parliament. He was certainly not alone in this opinion. But, thanks in no small measure to Callaghan's opposition, Wilson had to beat a humiliating retreat. Callaghan's reward from the trade unions he had championed was to be turned out of office by their unruly behaviour in the Winter of Discontent.

Then in the summer of 1980 Jim Callaghan and Michael Foot failed to block the plan to have the Labour Party Leader elected by a wider franchise than the Members of Parliament. During

a weekend conference at a trade union college in Bishop's Stortford, the principle of an Electoral College was conceded. Callaghan and Michael Foot were there to represent the Parliamentary Labour Party. As Peter Jenkins brutally puts it, 'Callaghan
and Foot returned from Bishop's Stortford like Chamberlain
and Halifax from Munich'.* That October, the Labour Party
Conference duly voted for the Electoral College. This was a
fateful turning-point for the Labour Party. The defection of the
Social Democrats was brought nearer. David Owen and Bill
Rodgers had seen the conceding of the Electoral College principle as a sign of the lack of fight in Callaghan and the party
leadership. And, but for the Electoral College, Neil Kinnock
would hardly have been elected Leader in 1983.

Again, Jim Callaghan's first priority was to hold the Labour
movement – trade unions and party – together. This concern
was understandable for a man of his instincts and experience.
But it did not help his party, which was to be out of office for
more than ten years.

Callaghan's undistinguished period as Chancellor of the Exchequer had ended in the devaluation of the pound. His premiership must also have been a bitter disappointment to him. He
had no mandate from the electorate, for he had not won an
election. But before long he was governing by courtesy of the
Liberal Party, with whom he had had to make a pact.

Everything, including a worsening economic crisis, was against
him. In the end, his old friends in the trade unions let him down
badly. In these circumstances, Jim Callaghan held the fort at No.
10 as well as anyone could have done. For all his belligerence in
the TV studio, he was always very friendly to me personally.

The last interview I had with Jim was when he announced
his retirement from the Commons. We had an enjoyable and
reminiscent chat with no bellicosity on either side. He took me
by surprise with one answer. I had asked him what he was most
proud to have achieved in his parliamentary career. At once
Jim replied that when he was Parliamentary Under-Secretary to
the Minister of Transport in 1947 he was responsible for the
introduction of 'cats' eyes' on trunk roads. Cats' eyes had been

*Peter Jenkins, *Mrs Thatcher's Revolution* (Cape, 1987), p. 115.

invented before the war and were already in limited use, but Ministry officials were strongly opposed to having them on trunk roads. But Jim insisted, and the inventor of cats' eyes went on to make a small fortune.

James Callaghan was not an intellectual. He did not have a first-class brain as did Macmillan or Wilson or Heath or Healey or Jenkins or Gaitskell. But he had a first-class instinct of what public opinion wanted or did not want, on law and order, on education, on taxation and even (though belatedly) on trade union bloody-mindedness.

In June 1979, towards the end of the general election campaign, Jim Callaghan was travelling in his Prime Ministerial Rover round Parliament Square towards Downing Street. With him was his chief political adviser, Bernard Donoughue, who mentioned some encouraging signs for Labour: 'With a little luck,' said Donoughue, 'we might just squeak through.' But Callaghan turned to him and said quietly:

> I should not be too sure. You know there are times, perhaps once every thirty years, when there is a sea-change in politics. It then does not matter what you say or what you do. There is a shift in what the public wants and what it approves of. I suspect there is now such a sea-change – and it is for Mrs Thatcher.*

Jim Callaghan always knew which way the wind was blowing.

No – Please Let Me Go On

Many are the achievements attributed to Margaret Thatcher's premiership – rolling back the state, curbing the unions, defeating Scargill, Galtieri and Ken Livingstone, defying terrorism, burying Socialism, winning three elections. She is the only British Prime Minister whose name has been given an 'ism'. If these achievements were not enough, she has succeeded in devaluing the setpiece television interview as an instrument of democratic

*Donoughue, *Prime Minister*, p. 191.

dialogue. The adjective 'setpiece' has become the accepted and pejorative word in media circles to describe conveniently the big *Panorama*-type political interview, in which Prime Ministers or other political leaders are closely and vigorously questioned in serious detail for forty minutes. In the sixties and seventies such interviews, on both BBC and ITV, were highly significant and newsworthy events. They made big headlines, with columns of verbatim reports, editorial comment and strong political reactions. I was only one of the interviewers who would regularly be involved.

In the eighties, however, even during general elections, the significance, news value and appeal of the 'setpiece' television encounter greatly declined. The person mainly responsible for this has been Margaret Thatcher, aided and abetted by Neil Kinnock. Both, in their different styles, have been determined to make the TV interview a platform of their own. The interviewer's questions, or attempts at questions, have been treated as tiresome interruptions to the impressive flow of Thatcherite statistics or Kinnockian rhetoric. Interviews have tended to become a series of statements, planned for delivery irrespective of the question which had been put. This technique has gradually brought about the decline of the major television interview. It is now rarely a dialogue which could be helpful to the viewer.

A few years ago, in an after-dinner speech, I cracked a little joke about going to No. 10 and beginning my interview thus: 'Prime Minister, what is your answer to my first question?' Among those who laughed loudest were several members of Mrs Thatcher's Cabinet.

. It is true that these long 'setpiece' interviews have sometimes been boring, unproductive and predictable. This may well have been the fault of the interviewers, myself included. But usually a major political interview has proved less interesting than expected because the politician has decided not to have a reasonable dialogue to help the viewing public, but to steamroller the questioner with prepared answers, whatever the questions.

Margaret Thatcher decided to adopt that tactic early on in her career as a party leader. In February 1976, one year after she had become Tory leader, she was interviewed on *Panorama* by me. The *Daily Telegraph* reported:

Robin Day had no more success than other highly skilled professionals in stemming her practically ceaseless flow of articulate exposition. Time after time he tried in vain to interpolate a question only to be overborne by a relentless determination to complete the previous answer at the length the Conservative leader thought fit.*

And why not? Is not a political leader entitled to address the people on television without an interviewer continually butting in? The answer is that when political leaders accept an invitation to be interviewed on television, that means (or did mean) that there will be both questions and answers. The politician is given the powerful platform of television. The interviewing journalist should be given fair opportunity to ask reasonable questions. As it is, the big interview has been hijacked by the top politicians, presumably on advice from their media advisers.

At this point, I would like to give the reader an assurance. Some readers may find it a difficult assurance to follow. I have absolutely no personal or professional resentment at the decline of the big TV interview. I am *not* protesting because my questions are not answered to my satisfaction, or are not answered at all; nor because critics write that Robin Day has been humiliated; nor because the TV interview, which has been a speciality of mine, has been devalued. My concern is for something infinitely more important than any professional *amour propre*: the right of the people, if they switch on for a TV interview, to see a political leader fairly and fearlessly questioned and challenged.

Who am I, or any TV interviewer, to be the people's challenger? I am merely one of a number of non-elected TV journalists whose professional function is to interrogate those in authority over us, and those who aspire to have authority over us. Nothing would please me more (and I have advocated this for thirty years) than if Parliament were to admit the TV cameras. Then we will see our political leaders questioning and challenging each other. Until that happens (and sometimes even *after* that happens) someone will be needed to ask politicians the

Daily Telegraph, 24 February 1976.

relevant and topical questions, however awkward, embarrassing and painful those questions may be.

The 'set piece' interview has certainly been devalued as an instrument of clarification and information. Such interviews have become more a battle for the interviewer's right to get a question in, rather than a civilized dialogue for the benefit of the watching public. The attention of the viewing audience is inevitably distracted from what really matters (the issues under discussion) and diverted to irrelevancies – the interviewer's desperate attempts to get a question in, or an argument with the interviewee about whether the interviewer is making accusations or merely asking questions.

Here is one small section of my interview with Margaret Thatcher on 8 June 1987, three days before polling day. I had asked her about the criticism that under the government there was not 'one nation' but a divided nation. After her long answer (lasting over two minutes) I tried to ask another question:

Q: Can I get in this question please Prime Minister because –
  A: You asked me the most fundamental thing. I must beg of you.
  Q: I know, but we're not having a party political broadcast, we're having an interview, which must depend on me asking some questions occasionally.
  A: Yes indeed. You asked what I know you call the 'gut' question. Right, it's gone to the gut, it's gone to the jugular. Let me finish it.

And she finished it – in her own time. There was another passage in that interview of June 1987 which illustrates the Thatcher technique of accusing the interviewer of 'accusing' her, when all he is doing, as she knows perfectly well, is asking a legitimate and relevant question. I asked her to answer the charge (made not only by her political opponents) that she was 'autocratic, domineering and intolerant of dissent'. The Prime Minister referred to the 'very, very vigorous discussion' in Cabinet meetings. She went on:

A: It is because we have that that I believe we thoroughly thrash out our problems. I think what you are accusing me of —

Q: No, I'm not accusing you. I'm inviting you to answer criticisms frequently made of you, Prime Minister.

A: I'm so sorry; I don't see how one can be accused of being arrogant when one has in fact tried throughout the whole of the eight years I've been in office to give more power back to the people. We've abolished many controls, because government ought not to have had them, we've taken away —

Q: This is a personal question, this is a personal question.

A: You're asking me a personal question, then I'm afraid I must leave other people to judge. I don't think —

Q: All right.

A: Please may I finish. I don't think oneself is perhaps the best judge of one's qualities. Yes, when I believe in things very strongly, it is then I bend everything to get that policy through. I go to the House, I explain it, sometimes there's a combative way, yes. I decide with others the way we're going then I bend every single effort to get that through, overcoming all obstacles. It isn't arrogance, in my view. It is determination and resolve.

Q: You've referred to your Cabinet meetings, Prime Minister, which I haven't had the opportunity of attending, but Mr Francis Pym is one of those who have, and who was sacked by you, and he said any dissent, *any* dissent, even the admittance of doubt, is treachery and treason. And he went on, after nine years as Party Leader, five as Prime Minister, Margaret Thatcher still asks people the question: 'Are you one of us?'

A: Look. I think you are insulting many in my Cabinet. The Cabinet is made up of people of a wide variety of views within the party, of a wide variety of people geographically and a number of different age groups . . . and if you are saying that every single person in that Cabinet is a 'yes' man, then I think you are delivering a totally unjustifiable insult. Yes, I do put my views combatively. I hold them

combatively. I'm in politics because I want to get them put
into practice . . .

Asked about the possibility of a Tory coalition with the Alliance
to keep out a Kinnock minority government, Mrs Thatcher
concluded her answer thus:

> A: You know, I might, indeed I would, consult my Cabinet
> colleagues, the very thing you have accused me of not doing.
> Q: I did not accuse you of anything, Prime Minister. You
> keep on accusing me of accusing you of things.

It puzzles me if, as in that exchange, a politician accuses me of
doing something which manifestly I have *not* done. My question
about her attitude to dissent in Cabinet was explicitly based on
the public statements of her former Foreign Secretary, Francis
Pym. But some viewers may well have taken the Prime Minister's word for it that I had 'accused' her. So there was no
alternative but to correct her. All of which wastes time and
distracts attention from the issues under discussion.

These recent tendencies in Prime Ministerial political interviews were analysed with more wit than objectivity by Roy
Hattersley in the *Listener*. Labour's Deputy Leader was, however, being entirely fair when he wrote:

> We should not blame the Prime Minister for wishing to
> impose her will on TV interviewers. Her ideal programme is
> quite different from theirs. She wants to demonstrate the
> success of her policies and the strength of her character.
> The interviewers want to provide the politically conscious
> viewer with new and interesting information, to
> demonstrate their forensic skills, and to get a mention . . .
> in the following day's papers.

Hattersley shrewdly observes that:

> the public does not want television interviewers 'to take the
> Prime Minister on', as if the discussion were a contest of

equals. They want sharp but polite questions and (if they are interested in politics) straight and convincing answers.

Hattersley is right, especially about the straight and convincing answers. (Did he send a copy of this article to Neil Kinnock?) He concludes: 'Mrs Thatcher's appeal is to the viewer who observes, "Say what you like, she doesn't stand any nonsense. They don't push her around." '*

'They' – humble interviewers like myself – certainly do not, and do not try to, 'push her around'. In that June 1987 interview, after a Thatcher answer about the City which comprised 171 words, my intervention was:

Yes —

to which the Prime Minister's response was

Can I just finish?

followed by another 84 words. Her next answer began with a plea to be given time to answer. The next attempt at a question by me (357 words later) was:

Let me —

Then, after a final sentence from the Prime Minister, came another contribution from me to democratic debate:

Let me put —

followed by another final sentence from the Prime Minister, at which point I ventured to ask:

But —

Again, I beg the reader to accept my assurance that I am not complaining for myself. The Prime Minister is entitled to adopt

Listener, 25 August 1988.

tactics on television which she feels will be to her political advantage. Her electoral triumphs have vindicated those tactics. But a television interview with a Prime Minister should be a constructive contribution to the democratic process, a dialogue which will clarify and illuminate.

The citizens of today have many opportunities which their forefathers did not have. I think of past generations who never had the good fortune to see in their own homes their political leaders questioned on television. They could never see interviews with Gladstone or Disraeli or Lloyd George or Winston Churchill. Remember also that for the first thirty years of broadcasting in Britain there was no independent vigorous coverage of politics by interviews or discussion. Television has added a new dimension to parliamentary democracy. This most potent instrument of communication should be used reasonably by politicians, and for the public benefit.

My opinions on this subject may not be considered entirely objective or disinterested. I would therefore draw attention to the academic research which has recently been conducted in microscopic detail concerning political interviews such as those by me with Margaret Thatcher and Neil Kinnock in the 1987 election. I knew that interviews may be preserved on videotape. But I did not realize that in our seats of learning there are psychologists with Ph.D.s poring over political interviews, analysing and dissecting them with clinical precision, like pathologists conducting autopsies. Already two learned academic papers have been published by two psychologists at York University. They analysed eight television interviews done during the 1987 election campaign. Dr Peter Bull and Kate Mayer, to whom I am much indebted, presented their findings publicly to the London Conference of the British Psychological Society in December 1988. Their paper was called 'How Margaret Thatcher and Neil Kinnock Avoid Answering Questions in Political Interviews'.

They studied eight TV interviews by four interviewers who each interviewed the Prime Minister and the Leader of the Opposition. My interviews with both were included. The psychologists pointed out that, though it is a commonplace to say politicians don't answer questions, we have no idea how much this occurs or how it is done. Hence this study of evasion in political interviews.

The finding was that Mrs Thatcher and Mr Kinnock evaded more than half the questions put to them. Thatcher evaded 56 per cent, Kinnock 59 per cent. The psychologists distinguish thirty-one different ways of evading questions. These were sub-grouped into eleven main types of evasion, which included:

Ignoring the question
Acknowledging the question without answering
Questioning the question
Attacking the question
Attacking the interviewer
Declining to answer
Making a political point, e.g. attacking opponents instead of answering the question
Giving incomplete answer
Repeating previous answer
Claiming to have already answered the question

The psychologists discovered that, though Thatcher and Kinnock were evasive to a more or less equal extent, they differed in their styles of evasion. Mrs Thatcher would evade questions by attacking the interviewer. Neil Kinnock, on the other hand, would evade by claiming that he had already answered the question, when in fact he had evaded it.

Though the two leaders had their different styles, the conclusion of the psychologists is that Thatcher and Kinnock were strikingly similar in their evasiveness. Both evaded roughly the same proportion of questions, especially by attacking their opponents or attacking the question.

The two York University psychologists produced another fascinating paper called 'Interruptions in Political Interviews: A Study of Margaret Thatcher and Neil Kinnock'. Again, one of those analysed was my interview in 1987 with the Prime Minister. The psychologists make a point which may seem obvious, but it explains how the 'setpiece' interview has been devalued by Margaret Thatcher and, in his different way, by Neil Kinnock:

If the politician continues to talk at length while failing to answer the question put to them, the interviewer has to be able to interrupt effectively in order to address the particular issue which the interviewer wishes to discuss.

From the analysis of interruptions, the psychologists Bull and Mayer note one striking difference between the two leaders. Compared to Kinnock, Thatcher objected much more frequently to being interrupted, 'even on at least two occasions when there is no evidence that the interviewer was actually about to interrupt!'. The psychologists conclude that her protesting at interruptions 'give the misleading impression that she is being excessively interrupted, although the objective evidence . . . clearly shows that this is not the case'.

The indefatigable psychologists of York did a thorough job. They tabulated Mrs Thatcher's every comment on my every attempt to interrupt:

no please let me go on
may I just finish
one moment
I must beg of you
please may I
let me finish it
can I just finish it
will you give me time
may I say something else
may I now and then say a word in my own defence
please may I say
just let me get this
I would love to go on
but can I just go on
yes but one moment
one moment
please there's just one other thing
one moment hold on
no don't stop me
no let me stand up for my own government
but please

Not wishing to leave any stone unturned, the two psychologists note that in my interviews with the Prime Minister I made several explicit references to her tactic of wrongly accusing her interviewer. They also note that I referred to the need for the interviewer to ask questions. The psychologists reach this grave conclusion:

> The fact that such an experienced and eminent interviewer as Sir Robin Day should need to justify his role in this way is a very striking example of the way in which Margaret Thatcher's tactics put the interviewer on the defensive.*

But it is not how Margaret Thatcher (or Neil Kinnock) treated me or any other interviewer that matters. What deeply concerns me is that the very principle of the television interview – the ancient Socratic method of imparting or gathering information by the process of question and answer – has been deliberately devalued.

This is bad for the people, bad for democracy, bad for television and bad, in the end, for politicians. Democracy cannot flourish without fair and reasoned dialogue. In the television age, the television interview is an important element of that dialogue. If television cannot adequately supply that dialogue, democracy will suffer.

I pointed out to Margaret Thatcher in the election interview in June 1987 that no other Tory leaders have had 'isms' named after them. Of Thatcherism there will be many conflicting definitions. It is only right to record for history her own definitive exposition of it – the authorized version, as it were, or the gospel according to Margaret – as it was proclaimed by her on television, three days before polling day in 1987, in answer to this question from me:

> Q: But you have stamped your image on the Tory Party like no other leader ever has before. We never heard of Macmillanism, we never heard of Heathism, we never heard

*Dr Peter Bull and Kate Mayer, 'Interruptions in Political Interviews: A Study of Margaret Thatcher and Neil Kinnock', *Journal of Language and Social Psychology*, vol. 7, No. 1, 1988.

of Churchillism. We now hear of 'Thatcherism'. What is it
– for the help of the undecided – what is it that Thatcherism
means?

A: Sir Robin, it is not a name that I created in the sense
of calling it an 'ism'. Let me tell you what it stands for. It
stands for sound finance and government running the affairs
of the nation in a sound financial way. It stands for honest
money, not inflation; it stands for living within your means,
it stands for incentives, because we know full well that the
growth and economic strength of a nation comes from the
efforts of its people, and its people need incentives to work
as hard as they possibly can. All of that has produced
economic growth. It stands for something else. It stands for
the wider and wider spread of ownership of property, of
houses, of shares, of savings. It stands for being strong in
defence; a reliable ally and a trusted friend. People have
called those things 'Thatcherism'. They are in fact
fundamental commonsense and having faith in the enterprise
and abilities of the people. It is my task to try and release
those; they were always there. They've always been there in
the British people, but they couldn't flourish under
Socialism; they've now been released. That's all that
Thatcherism is.

Margaret Thatcher is a political phenomenon. Not only was she
the first woman to be Prime Minister of the United Kingdom.
Not only was she the first Prime Minister to have been elected
to three consecutive terms for more than a century. Not only
has she led the Tory Party for over fourteen years. But what
has also been phenomenal about her is that she, a bourgeois
Conservative, has proved to be a revolutionary Prime Minister.
In creating Thatcherism, she has buried Socialism, or at least
she has buried 'Clause 4' Socialism. She is driven by conviction
and commitment rather than by intellect or reason. She is
admired for her 'conviction' politics by that left-wing opponent
of consensus, Tony Benn.

From the poor Tory performances in the 1989 Euro-elections
it looked as if Margaret Thatcher's years as an invincible vote-
getter were coming to an end. What with rising inflation and

10 DOWNING STREET

THE PRIME MINISTER

9 March 1985

Dear Robin,

A note to say how
concerned I was to learn of
your operation but so pleased to
know that you are on your way
to full recovery.

Your absence from
broadcasting makes us all feel
a little uneasy — I prefer your

*Letter from Mrs Thatcher to the author after his multiple heart by-pass
operation in 1985.*

presence despite the occasional
pungent comments!

Every good wish
from Denis & me.

Sincerely Yours

Margaret Thatcher

industrial stoppages, no wonder an American TV reporter quipped: 'The Iron Lady is showing signs of metal fatigue.' And after the messy Cabinet reshuffle in which she booted Sir Geoffrey Howe out of the Foreign Office, the Thatchocracy may well end sooner than expected.

But Mrs Thatcher has dominated her Cabinet like no other recent Prime Minister. There is no obvious successor to her. She has achieved all this – and here there is a strange feature of the Thatcher phenomenon – without being a great parliamentarian, without being a brilliant orator, without having a gift for words or memorable phrases, and without displaying a sense of humour. She is probably hated more than any Prime Minister in my lifetime. But she is certainly respected for her guts and determination. Despite many interviews with her on television, and other conversations with her, I have never got to know her as well as her predecessors. I know from many first-hand accounts that she is extremely kind and considerate, and I have experienced this myself. I may come to know her better when she becomes an ex-Prime Minister, if I live that long – which now seems distinctly possible.

14

Terrorism

The Oxygen of Publicity

For many years I have differed sharply from the television establishment on how terrorism should be dealt with on the screen. By the TV establishment, I mean senior BBC people, most TV editors and producers, and most of those who write about television in newspapers and books. For nearly twenty years I have been profoundly concerned about television's responsibility in an age of political violence. Is television's responsibility merely to communicate, to report, to reflect? Or should it be guided by certain values, by some sense of purpose? Does television, for instance, have a duty to uphold the rule of law and parliamentary democracy? Does it have a duty not to encourage violence, disorder and unreason in our society? There is no doubt in my mind as to the answers.

The most difficult question which broadcasters have had to face since broadcasting was invented is this: in a liberal democracy, with a tradition of free and independent broadcasting, how can television ensure that it does not become an ally of terrorism?

My enthusiasm for television as the most vivid and immediate means of journalistic communication is undiminished. But the more television has advanced, the more I have become convinced that television journalists must be careful to use their powerful medium with restraint and responsibility. This meant not doing certain things even though there was no law against doing them. In particular, I could see no justification whatever for interviewing on television a self-proclaimed terrorist, or sympathizer, so that he could explain why some atrocious crime had been committed in this country by him or his associates. Any such interview, no matter how critical and challenging, would serve to imply that there might be some political justification for cold-blooded murder. In our democracy there can be none. Nor could I see any justification for a self-proclaimed terrorist (who may be wanted by the police) being accorded the privilege of appearing on television anonymously and disguised, or with back to the camera, to offer his 'justification' for some hideous atrocity committed here.

Those were the views which I publicly expressed,* and frequently put forward inside the BBC long before Margaret Thatcher called on broadcasters in 1985 to 'starve the terrorists of the oxygen of publicity'. Not surprisingly, my strong opinions on this subject did not endear me to the BBC establishment. I had a stand-up row with Charles Curran, the BBC's Director-General, at a BBC party in the early seventies. I told him it was wrong, utterly wrong, to give a platform on BBC television to anyone who had committed or advocated terrorist crime in this country. Curran argued that it was not so simple and that, anyway, he (the DG) had to be consulted before any such interview was permitted. To which my reply was, with some vehemence, that if he allowed such interviews I hoped his conscience would be clear when a British soldier was murdered. Curran was a hot-tempered man. He turned away from me almost apoplectic with rage.

The television interview which probably did more than any other to bring the BBC into disrepute (and not merely with the Thatcher Government) was screened in July 1979. This was an interview about the murder of Airey Neave MP, transmitted in the final programme of the BBC's late-night current affairs programme *Tonight*. The Editor was Roger Bolton, who was to become a hero in media circles for his repeated readiness to risk

---

*E.g. article by the author, *Daily Telegraph*, 8 August 1980.

conflict with the Thatcher government in what he saw as the cause of reporting the truth, especially about Northern Ireland.

Later that same year, Bolton, by then promoted to Editor of *Panorama*, was the BBC executive at the centre of the Carrickmore incident. A *Panorama* team had, after a tip-off, filmed an armed IRA 'take-over' of a small Ulster village. The film was never transmitted, but reports of the filming led to a blazing row between the Thatcher government and the BBC. Roger Bolton was sacked from the editorship of *Panorama*, but after protests from BBC colleagues was reinstated a few days later.

More recently, in 1988, as Editor of the Thames Television programme *This Week*, Roger Bolton was responsible for *Death on the Rock* about the Gibraltar shooting of three IRA terrorists by the SAS. Once again, Mrs Thatcher was furious. Even Sir Geoffrey Howe raised his voice to demand that the programme be postponed until after the inquest. But Lord Windlesham's enquiry gave Bolton and *Death on the Rock* a vindication which the Thatcher government hotly resented.

These episodes have been exhaustively chronicled or debated in books or articles by Sir Ian Trethowan, Michael Leapman, Michael Cockerell, Alasdair Milne and Roger Bolton himself. My concern here is with the first of Bolton's battle-honours, because I argued within the BBC, unsuccessfully, against the interview being transmitted. This was the INLA interview in the *Tonight* programme on 7 July 1979, the last night of the programme's existence.

At that time my main work with BBC Television was a weekly political item (a short interview or discussion) on Thursdays. In the early evening of Thursday, 7 July, I rang up the Editor of *Tonight*, Roger Bolton, from the Commons press gallery, to ask what had been planned for my weekly item that night. Bolton said that he would like me to chair a discussion to follow an interview which had been filmed with 'a spokesman' for the Irish National Liberation Army. INLA was the extreme terrorist group which had assassinated Airey Neave MP earlier that year.

I was appalled. I could scarcely believe what I had heard. A bomb placed in Neave's car had blown him to smithereens in the entrance to the House of Commons car park. He was one of Margaret Thatcher's closest political friends. He had masterminded her victory in the Tory leadership contest four years earlier. He was her Shadow Secretary of State for Northern Ireland. I had followed Airey Neave's political career closely because we had been barristers in the same chambers at the Bar – No. 5 King's Bench Walk, where Margaret Thatcher had been a pupil. I was familiar with Neave's exploits in the Second World War, as a Colditz escaper and as a secret intelligence officer. He had been much decorated for bravery (DSO, OBE, MC, Croix de Guerre, etc.). All these personal details about Airey Neave flashed through my mind as I was being told that the BBC intended to screen an interview with a 'spokesman' for his assassins. I felt sick with revulsion.

The filmed interview was, Bolton assured me, tough and challenging. That I did not doubt. My argument was that, no matter how tough and challenging, this interview would be a platform for justifying that which is unjustifiable in this country, namely, deliberate murder for political ends. What horrified me was that a self-proclaimed terrorist was to appear, anonymously and in disguise, on BBC Television to offer his justification for a foul murder, the murder moreover of a Member of Parliament in the precincts of the House of Commons. I could not see that any interview with someone who attempted to justify such a crime, and who was presumably wanted by the police, should be broadcast by the BBC. The fact that INLA was not then a proscribed organization did not, to my mind, make the murder of Airey Neave less atrocious or the interview less shameful.

But, whatever I thought about it, the interview had been filmed. Its transmission had been approved at the highest level in the BBC. I could not understand how Richard Francis, the Director of News and Current Affairs, or Ian Trethowan, the Director-General, had approved either the filming of such an interview or its transmission. My immediate instinct was to telephone Ian Trethowan to urge him not to allow the interview to be broadcast, but he was out of London and uncontactable. The Director of News and Current Affairs was also unavailable, at any rate to me.

Sir Ian writes in his memoirs that he had given permission for the interview to be filmed 'clandestinely', and with the INLA man disguised. On transmission day Trethowan agreed 'with some hesitation' that the interview could be broadcast. Because he was away from London that day, he had to make his decision 'on the basis of a description of the interview over the telephone'. In his memoirs Sir Ian asks: 'With the benefit of hindsight, was I wrong to allow the interview to be broadcast? Almost certainly, yes.' He adds after the INLA interview, the BBC stopped the practice of allowing a criminal to appear on the TV screen anonymously. Sir Ian discloses that a few weeks later, after the murder of Lord Mountbatten, he informed the Home Office that 'there could be no BBC interviews with terrorists in the foreseeable future'.*

On the afternoon of 7 July 1979, however, the INLA interview had been approved for transmission that night. Bolton had listened politely to many arguments against its transmission. But my position was weak. I had no editorial standing in the *Tonight* programme. I was not a BBC producer. I was not even the programme's presenter. I was merely an occasional contributor, and not always warmly welcomed as such.

Having made my views known, I had only two alternatives: to decline to take part in the programme (which Roger Bolton said I was free to do), or accept his invitation to chair the discussion between Gerry Fitt MP, leader of the SDLP (the party which speaks for most of the Catholic minority in Ulster), and Robert Bradford, a Unionist MP. I told Roger Bolton I would chair the discussion only if there was no objection to my asking them whether the BBC had been right to transmit the INLA interview which they would have just seen. Bolton agreed.

When the programme was transmitted, the two MPs, who were on opposite sides of Ulster politics, both declared in the most vehement terms that for the BBC to have screened the INLA interview was utterly wrong.

At first, my feeling was that I had done right to take part. I had at least elicited the MPs' condemnation of the interview. But I soon realized my mistake. By being in the same programme, and by immediately following the INLA interview, I was in effect an accessory to what had been done. A typical reaction came from a viewer whose son was a soldier serving in Ulster. He

---

*Trethowan, *Split Screen*, p. 184.

wanted to know why I 'had been involved' in an interview with a terrorist. I had not been involved, but I had appeared to be by taking part in the discussion about it. I ought to have refused to take part. The day after the programme I felt, and still feel, ashamed for not withdrawing, which I had been free to do.

I was not surprised at the outcry against the INLA interview. Airey Neave's widow protested that she had seen her late husband being described as a 'torturer' by the man interviewed on the BBC. Airey Neave had been a close friend of Margaret Thatcher, but when the Prime Minister told the House that she was 'appalled' that the BBC had transmitted the INLA interview, she spoke not only for herself nor for Conservative opinion alone.

Today, ten years later, it is rare to meet anyone in broadcasting circles who does not say that it was shameful for the BBC to have transmitted the INLA interview. But if Roger Bolton has any regrets, his article in the *Listener* of November 1987 does not convey them. Bolton wrote of the INLA interview:

> The organization's claims were put into context, and the nature of their murderous activities was underlined, as was the naivety of their political thinking. . . . *

Other people, of whom I am one, are still unable to understand why, when a vile atrocity is committed in this country, its perpetrators should then be given an opportunity to explain their reasons and their 'political thinking' on television.

Fortunately, the INLA interview did not set a trend. It was a gross error of judgment, which for once, could not be blamed on a programme editor. Roger Bolton had correctly sought permission from the top, and had obtained permission from the top. The error of judgment, I regret to say, was that of the Director-General alone. He permitted the filming. He then permitted transmission. A strange lapse for one whose editorial judgment was normally so sound. It is to Sir Ian's credit, however, that in his memoirs he frankly admits that he was almost certainly wrong.

*Listener, 19 November 1987.

Interviews with terrorists on TV have since been rare. Roger Bolton, writing in his November *Listener* article, said he did not know 'of any interview with a current member of a proscribed organization being transmitted on networked television' since 1979. Bolton added: 'It would take a brave BBC or IBA to mount one nowadays, but I hardly think it likely.'

During the last decade, however, the broadcast coverage of Northern Ireland has included appearances by the political wing of the IRA. In October 1988 Douglas Hurd, as Home Secretary in the Thatcher government, used his powers to issue a notice ordering the broadcasting authorities not to broadcast direct statements made by terrorist organizations or by Sinn Fein or the UDA. This order, though it followed closely the lines of similar restrictions which have been in force in the Irish Republic for some years, was bitterly attacked and resented.

The reader may not be surprised to know that I supported the government in its basic objective of denying the easy platform of TV and radio to those who used it to propagate terrorism. But in my opinion the Home Secretary was mistaken in imposing a ban by ministerial decree, despite his undoubted constitutional power to do so. Such a ban, in my opinion, should have been imposed by Parliament through legislation. The legislation would declare it an offence to broadcast any statement by any person in support of terrorist activity. Whether a particular broadcast was in breach of such a law would be decided by the courts. The broadcasting organization, instead of having to ring up a Home Office official to find out whether a broadcast would break the law, would take advice from their lawyer.

Such legislation would not be arbitrary censorship. It would be extending the rule of law which already applies in broadcasting. For over thirty years, Independent Television has been enjoined by Act of Parliament to include nothing in its programmes 'which is likely to encourage or incite to crime or to lead to disorder'. As Lord Denning has pointed out, that duty, which is in general terms, has often been ignored in practice by the broadcasters. The legislation (which I would prefer to Douglas Hurd's directive) would make the general statutory prohibition more particular and would extend it to all broadcasting organizations, including the BBC.

Propaganda by television is a most powerful weapon in the hands of terrorists and their supporters. That weapon, as Lord Denning has argued, should be taken away from them. But it should be taken away by Act of Parliament. A statutory ban on the lines I have suggested would not prohibit the broadcasting of statements by (say) an elected Sinn Feiner unless the statement was in support of terrorist crime, or the 'armed struggle'. An interview about housing would not be banned, as apparently it is under the Hurd notice. In a doubtful case, the courts would decide.

One objection raised to any such ban, however imposed, is that the government has by it 'declared impartiality to be illegal'. This view was put forward by Dr Colin Morris (BBC Controller in Northern Ireland) at a public BBC seminar on impartiality.* In so far as I understood him, Dr Morris seemed to mean that statements by supporters of terrorism should not be banned from TV or radio because this would be unfair to advocates of terrorism, who are part of the political scene in Northern Ireland, and are often democratically elected. To that it may be said that, just because a man is elected as a councillor or even an MP, this does not permit him to advocate murder or preach the 'armed struggle'. With due respect to Dr Morris, impartiality between murder and peaceful democratic argument has *never* been legal.

Another objection to the Hurd ban is that TV should not be treated differently from the printed press, which remains free to quote Sinn Feiners or whomever it wishes. Is there no difference between a printed report in a newspaper and a personal appearance which goes into millions of homes? Does not television have greater immediacy, greater impact, greater vividness?

If there is no difference in principle between television and newspapers, why have we always had in this country legal requirements, either by statute or in the BBC Charter, to impose on broadcasting certain obligations which are not imposed on the newspaper press? It remains to be seen whether the public interest will still demand different rules for television when there are as many different TV channels as there are different news-

Impartiality: Representing Reality (BBC Publications, January 1989).

papers. I suspect that the public interest, as interpreted by Parliament, will still so demand.

Would it not be infinitely better if broadcasters disciplined themselves, instead of government imposing discipline upon them? That, of course, would be the ideal system for broadcasting, and indeed for the printed press in a democracy like ours. A wise jurist* once said that there were three great domains of human conduct. The first is where our actions are limited or forbidden by law. Then there is the domain of free personal choice. But between these two is a third domain, that in which there is neither law nor unfettered freedom. This is the domain of 'obedience to the unenforceable', where people do right although there is no one and nothing to make them do right but themselves.

The extent to which, in a society, there is this 'obedience to the unenforceable' is the true measure of civilization. Obedience to the unenforceable means self-imposed restraint. It means a sense of responsibility. It means asking not what *can* we do, but what *ought* we to do. That is the spirit which should govern television and should decide its responsibility to society, particularly to a society threatened by unreason, by violence and by terrorism.

This has nothing to do with censorship, which is arbitrarily imposed. It is a matter of editorial judgment by broadcasters exercising their independence with self-restraint. Sometimes the judgment of those with the governing responsibility in television has been wrongly attacked as 'censorship'. There are some TV programme-makers who regard an adverse editorial decision, by those whose duty is to make such decisions, as a denial of human rights.

Broadcasters, rightly, are concerned to maintain their independence. The government, rightly, is concerned that terrorism shall not be propagated on television. These two concerns may come into conflict. The classic case of such conflict was to be seen in the extraordinary episode of *Real Lives* in 1985. The BBC was convulsed. The Board of Governors was locked in open

*Lord Moulton, 1844–1921, Liberal MP, Lord Justice and later Lord of Appeal.

battle with the Board of Management. BBC staff journalists went on protest strike.

The detailed story of the *Real Lives* affair need not be told again here. I was not personally involved. I wish to outline the facts only to refresh the reader's memory and to illustrate my argument, namely that the age of television is also the age of terrorism, which means that those in charge of television should exercise their independence with responsibility and self-restraint.

Real Lives was a BBC TV documentary portraying two Ulster 'extremists'. One of these 'extremists' was Martin McGuinness, the Deputy Chairman of Sinn Fein, the political wing of the IRA, the other was a hard-line 'Loyalist' politician of Ian Paisley's party. Both had been elected to the Northern Ireland Assembly. Whether these two were exactly comparable is a matter for argument, but the central objection to the programme was that it gave a platform to an advocate of terrorism.

The then Home Secretary, Leon Brittan, urged the BBC Governors in a public letter to stop the programme. Significantly, the Home Secretary's letter used the Prime Minister's words about terrorism thriving on 'the oxygen of publicity'.

The ensuing struggle according to Alasdair Milne 'undeniably rocked the BBC to its foundations'.* There was a head-on clash between the Board of Governors (who are in law the BBC) and the Board of Management (the DG and his fellow professionals). Milne's professional Board of Management had unanimously declared the programme to be transmittable. The Governors, much influenced by the Vice-Chairman Sir William (now Lord) Rees-Mogg, vetoed the programme. The DG, Alasdair Milne, who had been on holiday in Finland, returned and clashed with the Governors. BBC journalists, including those in the World Service, then went on protest strike. Eventually the Governors reversed themselves, and Milne transmitted it after only minor alterations.

No one emerged from this shambles covered in glory. The Home Secretary had been heavy-footed and ill-advised in making his original demand publicly, and before the BBC Gover-

*Milne, *DG*, p. 149.

nors had received it in writing. This threw the Governors into an intensely awkward predicament. If they banned *Real Lives*, they would be seen as surrendering the BBC's independence by caving in to government bullying. If they did not ban it merely because of the Home Secretary's public pressure, they would be betraying their governing function, and failing in their responsibility to decide the issue on its merits. Having taken the right decision, with near-unanimity, in the first place, the Board of Governors then lost all credibility by reversing themselves in allowing the programme to be transmitted.

Alasdair Milne, the hapless Director-General, was at fault, as Editor-in-Chief, by having been so out of touch that he did not even know a programme involving Martin McGuinness was in the making.* His top management were also at fault in failing to ensure compliance with the BBC's rule book, which stated:

> Interviews with individuals who are thought to be closely associated with a terrorist organization may not be sought or transmitted – two separate stages – without the prior permission of the DG.

And what of the BBC journalists who went on protest strike against the Governors' decision? Some of those journalists may, in retrospect, endorse Lord Annan's view that their protest strike was 'a disgrace to a great national organization'.† Did the striking journalists think that, just because the Home Secretary had clumsily demanded that the programme be banned, there could be no reasonable grounds for the Governors to ban it?

There was more than one reason why the *Real Lives* programme should never have been approved for transmission in the first place. It was at least arguable that the two Ulstermen (McGuinness and Campbell) were not on a par with each other. Another weakness was that the film had no commentary. Nor were the participants questioned or challenged by a reporter. During the Governors' discussion, it was pointed out that this was contrary to another BBC rule about the coverage of violence.

*Milne, *DG*, p. 140.
†House of Lords Debates, 25 May 1988, col. 919.

This required that propaganda should 'not be allowed to pass unchallenged'. According to one BBC Governor, it was a 'Hitler loved dogs' programme.* The Chairman of the Governors, Stuart Young, thought it made the men of violence out to be 'nice guys, bouncing babies on their knees.'

Milne's Board of Management issued a statement defending the programme. It was in accordance with established BBC policy which included 'the exploration and explanation of the views and motives of those who avow terrorist activity – and their associates.'

The Prime Minister gave her opinion in a TV interview during the row:

> I do not think that any great body like the BBC should do anything which might be construed as furthering the objectives of terrorists. . . . The BBC should never show things which help anyone who wishes to further their cause of violence.†

If those words had been uttered by anyone else except Margaret Thatcher (who is anathema in some circles) they would have commanded almost universal support, even among television people.

Broadcasters naturally believe that the public is entitled to know from television what is going on, to see and hear the truth about why events happen. In an age of terrorism, some broadcasters think they have a duty and a right to explain the motivations and actions of terrorists such as the IRA. Nevertheless, as Lord Annan has observed:

> For the last twenty years Britain has been fighting a war of attrition against the IRA . . . and the broadcasters are singularly insensitive if they do not realize how profoundly this Government are concerned and involved.

The Prime Minister and the Cabinet had very nearly been

---

*Milne, *DG*, p. 143.
†*Newsnight* interview, 17 July 1985.

blown up by a terrorist bomb in their hotel at Brighton. The IRA's plot to massacre the elected government of the United Kingdom had only narrowly failed. But this fact, said Lord Annan, 'seemed hardly to have impinged on the consciousness of the broadcasters'.*

Death on the Rock was transmitted by Thames Television on 28 April 1988 in defiance of the Foreign Secretary's request but with the approval of the Independent Broadcasting Authority. This forty-three-minute programme enquired into the killing by the SAS of three unarmed IRA terrorists in Gibraltar on 6 March – was the killing lawful or unlawful? The inquest had not then been held.

My own judgment about *Death on the Rock* may be summarized as follows: there was no *legal* basis (i.e. contempt of court) for banning or postponing the programme. But since Thames TV would have been legally forced to postpone transmission if the inquest had been in the UK, the *responsible* course for the TV company was voluntarily to postpone *Death on the Rock*.

Another important reason for postponing the programme until after the inquest was that it was unfair and unbalanced, contrary to the Broadcasting Act. Roger Bolton argued: 'Not to have transmitted the programme because of a government's unwillingness to participate would give a government an effective veto on matters of public importance.'†

But it is wrong to say that the government and the SAS soldiers were 'unwilling' to participate. They were not in a position to participate. They *could not conceivably* appear to give evidence in a pre-inquest TV programme while the soldiers faced a possible verdict of unlawful killing, and the further possibility of prosecution for murder. Even if the government's non-participation had led to the programme's postponement, this would not have been a 'veto' because the programme could still have been transmitted after the inquest.

For the above reasons, I respectfully dissent from the conclusions of Lord Windlesham and Richard Rampton QC.

The emergence of terrorism as a constant threat, not only to

*House of Lords Debates, 25 May 1988, col. 918.
†Letter to *Spectator*, 10 February 1989.

the government but to all our citizens and to our way of life, has transformed the conditions under which broadcasting operates. This must be realized. This does not mean that their independence will be in peril if broadcasters fly the flag of moral neutrality. Those who wield authority over television, and are entrusted with its independence, should rekindle their sense of responsibility. Otherwise the broadcasters' independence will be in danger.

Requests or protests from the elected government should not be automatically rejected simply because they come from the government. They should be judged on merit, without fear or favour. That is the way to uphold the independence and integrity of the broadcasters.

A politically independent system of broadcasting is an essential element in a truly free society. It is not so in many parts of the world, even in countries which call themselves free. Politicians of all parties in Britain, if they are in their right minds, have a duty to uphold and not to undermine the independence of broadcasting. That independence will be in danger if the broadcasters fail in their corresponding duty, the duty not only to be truthful and fair, but to exercise responsibility with self-restraint.

15

Question Time

Born Out of a Cock-Up

Apart from the general elections, the last ten years of my television career have been centred on *Question Time*. This programme began on 25 September 1979. At first it was transmitted at the appallingly late hour of 10.50 p.m. on Tuesdays. Before long, the BBC was bombarded with complaints, not about me for once but about *Question Time* being transmitted so late at night. These complaints came not only from the public but from the press. After only a few weeks, the *Daily Express* joined in the clamour:

> A Question for the BBC: Why is this pertinent, lively programme, worth its weight in Parkinson, put on almost as a scheduled afterthought at the fag end of Robin's day?

The TV critic of the *Daily Mirror* begged:

> So please BBC, can we have *Question Time* earlier than 11.12 p.m. I'm not getting my beauty sleep.

An even more important voice was from out of London. The voice of commonsense was heard in the *Yorkshire Evening Post*:

> Why put it on so late? When most people are staggering off

ANOTHER QUESTION FROM THE AUDIENCE

NO, NOT YOU — THE LIGHT-FINGERED GENT SITTING NEXT TO THE LADY WHO HAD A GOLD NECKLACE

with their bedtime cocoa is not really the time to start stirring the brain cells.

These complaints about lateness had no immediate effect. But *Question Time* soon began to catch on.

By February 1980 the programme was moved to Thursday after incessant nagging (she says) by the producer, Barbara Maxwell.* This was much better for the programme because Thursday is often the climax of the political week. By May 1980, when *Question Time* was less than a year old, it was sometimes transmitted at an earlier time, and the *Daily Mirror* declared: '*Question Time* (BBC1 10.10) has become a minor hit.'

This 'minor hit' was to become something of a success. But press acclaim for QT has diminished since the programme won that acclaim originally. For some years now, QT has been treated, and generally ignored, as a routine political show by the critics. The professionalism of assembling and conducting an unscripted, spontaneous, unedited programme is the professionalism which conceals itself. It has not excited the critics' attention (as would, say, a drama or documentary production, about which a would-be Bernard Levin or Clive James could display

*Promoted to Editor in 1983.

his wit and word-power) until I decided to give up the chairman-ship.

Leaving press acclaim aside, how could we tell how successful QT was becoming? Performer's vanity? The flattery of friends? Wishful thinking? No – my awareness of QT's impact came from long and sometimes painful experience as a TV performer. It happens, sometimes suddenly, sometimes gradually, that a TV programme, or a TV series, catches the public attention and becomes a talking-point in pubs or clubs or trains. When a TV programme comes alive in that way, the effect is felt by the TV performer. He can tell by the frequency, the enthusiasm, the anger of the comments and compliments, that the audience of millions in their twos and threes has been moved, amused or angered. He can tell, too, whether he himself has made more than a routine appearance. The performer can tell these things, because he knows how different it is when a programme flops like a lead balloon. He senses the quality of the audience reaction not only from conversation with and comments from members of the public, but from his friends and colleagues. They are an even better guide that the rest of the public, because friends and colleagues, unlike strangers or mere acquaintances, feel no instinctive obligation to lavish praise upon one's TV work. So the praise of friends and colleagues, in whom insincerity would easily be detected, is reliable evidence of a programme's impact.

I am happy to say that my absence from the chair, during sickness or holidays, made no difference to the programme's appeal, except possibly to increase it. If anybody had doubts, it was not a superhuman task to be my understudy, as several gifted personalities proved: Robert McKenzie, Ludovic Kennedy, Donald McCormick, Bernard Levin and Sue Lawley.

There have been other pointers to the success of QT. MPs and other public figures have continually reported that the response from the public, either by mail or in conversation, or by recognition, is greater after they have appeared on *Question Time* than for any other topical programme. Another encouraging sign is that interest in the programme is not confined to one class or kind or age of viewer. It seems to appeal to all ages and races, to poor and rich, to left, right and centre.

The programme's origin was inauspicious. It began as a temporary, six-month 'filler' for a 'gaping hole in the schedules'. That was how it was described in TV circles at the time. The programme was hastily cobbled together in the summer of 1979. Bill Cotton, the Controller of BBC1, found himself with a yawning gap in his late-night schedules. This was because the BBC Board of Governors rejected the professional management's plan for a five-nights-a-week Parkinson chat-show on BBC1. It is not clear what form this would have taken. Objections were that if it included politics and current affairs the new chat-show would not do so adequately, and if it avoided politics and current affairs the BBC would seem to have abandoned public service broadcasting.

I was not involved in these arguments. At the time, I knew of them only from rumours and press reports. The rumours and reports had been about earlier in the year, when a decision was said to be imminent concerning the future of current affairs on BBC1. *Tonight*, a late-night current affairs programme on BBC1, was to be ended. The rumoured plan was that the late-night space was to be given over to a chat-show, possibly with Parkinson cast as Britain's answer to Johnny Carson. Politics and current affairs were to be covered in this new BBC1 nightly chat-show (so the rumours went) and otherwise relegated to BBC2. So strong and so disturbing were the rumours that I decided to write to the Director-General. Being completely outside the Corporation's policy-making process, I did not know whether there was any truth in the rumours. But, in view of all the talk, I wrote to Ian Trethowan to say why I felt the impending decision about current affairs on BBC1 was so important:

It is about whether the BBC's mass channel is to keep a responsible balance between information and entertainment, between serious topical coverage and chat-show triviality.

It is about the long-standing conflict in television between trendy showbiz journalism and informed critical journalism – a conflict in which you and I have always fought on the same side.

It is about whether the BBC's mass channel should increase television's bias against understanding.

It is about whether the BBC's mass channel is to retreat from its duty to provide a strong element of the questioning and controversial coverage of current events which the News cannot provide.

It is about whether the BBC's mass channel is to be run on the basis that politics is a switch-off and must be treated as a minority interest.

It is about the values of public service broadcasting. It is about what the BBC is for.

I would be grateful if these views of mine could be taken into account when the decision is made.

That letter from me to the Director-General was sent on 19 February 1979. Three days later the Board of Governors, under the Chairman Sir Michael Swann, made their long-awaited statement about the future of current affairs on BBC TV. My letter to the DG, which I had copied to the Chairman, was referred to at the Board's meeting. But my intervention was useless for two reasons. It was too late and it was too general. I could refer only to principles because I knew nothing of the actual plans.

According to the Board of Governors' statement, the plans were that there would no longer be a late-night news and current affairs magazine programme on BBC1. There would, however, be a new nightly news analysis programme on BBC2. (Thus was *Newsnight* originated). And it was also proposed (said the BBC Governors):

that BBC1 will end the evening with a programme involving topical interviews and entertainment. This programme should reach a different kind of audience and it is hoped will interest people who are not usually viewers of our more traditional journalism.

That proposal for a new and popular kind of programme on BBC1, combining both topicality and entertainment, was the origin of the Parkinson five-nights-a-week chat-show idea. In essence, the plan outlined by the BBC Governors was that BBC1 (apart from the 9 p.m. news and the weekly *Panorama*) would not cover current affairs and politics except in a more 'popular' way. Analysis and interrogation would be left to the new BBC2 programme. This idea led to the excellent *Newsnight*, but this was to be achieved by denuding BBC1, the mass channel, of any serious nightly current affairs coverage, apart from the 9 p.m. news.

Some of us were of the opinion that this was a step away from the BBC's best public service tradition. No matter how good *Newsnight* is, it wins on BBC2 only a small audience compared to that which a similar current affairs programme would win on BBC1. That is so, even though *Newsnight* now has the fixed time of 10.30 p.m. introduced by the Checkland-Birt regime in the autumn of 1988.

How then did all this lead to the birth of *Question Time* in September 1979? The BBC Governors in the previous February had approved in principle the new strategy – that current affairs should be covered on BBC1 in a more popular and appealing way – but the Board wanted to consider the detailed implications. The Board statement stressed that none of these 'experiments should lead to a diminution of serious journalism, or to trivialization'. That flash of Reithian robustness raised hopes that a Parkinson-Carson-type nightly chat-show was a non-starter. So it proved to be, though whether such a show was proposed in detail was not disclosed.

In the spring of 1979 the battle was reported to be continuing in the BBC to stop BBC1's *Tonight* being replaced by a nightly 'Parkinson'. I was asked by the *Daily Mail* for my opinion. I gave it:

> They ought to have political chat-shows. There are some great personalities in Parliament, good performers, a lot more amusing than some dull little actress. Are they really going to have Moss Evans [Mr Moss Evans was then the leader of Britain's biggest trade union] shoved in between Britt Ekland and Elton John?

But in March 1979, nobody seemed interested in 'a political chat-show'. Yet that, by accident rather than design, is what

Question Time has been for ten years. What is clear is that in the summer of 1979 the Board of Governors dug their heels in and threw out Bill Cotton's plan, backed by Alasdair Milne, Managing Director of BBC TV, for a nightly chat-show, Parkinson-style, beefed up in some way to include topical material.

Hence the 'gaping hole' in Bill Cotton's BBC1 schedules. John Gau, then Head of Current Affairs, was asked by Cotton to fill two of the four slots. Gau asked Barbara Maxwell to produce one of these. She was offered three options, of which 'something with Robin' was the one she took up. That was in July 1979. The idea, simple enough and dirt cheap, which was worked out by Gau and Barbara Maxwell, was to have 'Robin Day with some MPS, and an audience to ask questions'. Thereafter all the production details were worked out by Barbara. She returned from her August holiday three weeks before first transmission. There were no 'pilot' programmes, which is probably unprecedented in BBC history. It was all done in a tremendous rush.

By launching *Question Time*, not only had one gap in the Cotton schedule been filled, but as a bonus the 'Robin Day problem' had been solved. The 'Robin Day problem' this time was not the same as that which had concerned Bob McKenzie in 1964.* That 'problem', it may be recalled, was how to avoid my having too much influence as an interviewer in general elections. The Robin Day problem Mark II, which had developed during the seventies, was the BBC's inability or reluctance to find regular programme work for me. Or as Roy Hattersley explained in a remarkably perceptive *Listener* essay about the origin of *Question Time*:

> Robin Day – his great days . . . behind him – was more than available. He was hanging about with a contract but no adequate way of serving out his time. Indeed, the devil was finding work for Mr Day's idle brain. He complained about the quality of the programmes on which he did not appear and attempted to impose his will on those which employed him. *Question Time* solved all the problems. Now it is a national institution.†

*See above, p. 224.
†*Listener*, 19 May 1988.

So that is how *Question Time* originated. It was born out of a cock-up. It came into being by accident, at the last minute, and accompanied by no great hopes that it would work or would last. Whether it would last depended of course on the whim of the BBC's top brass. Anyway, the gaping hole in BBC1 was filled by *Question Time* on one of the five weekdays. The other gaping holes were also filled somehow, but that was no concern of mine.

Barbara Maxwell had produced items which I had occasionally done for *Tonight*. When she was given the job of producing the new unnamed programme I doubt if she was wildly enthusiastic. She is quoted as confessing to have had some initial reservations about taking on the project, partly because it would be derided as a TV copy of radio's *Any Questions*, and partly because she thought it would be dull work. I don't think Barbara had any great objection to working with me, though she must have known I would have strong views about how the programme should be run. She would not have expected anything less from me. What probably went through her mind were the thoughts which always go through the mind of any able producer who is assigned to produce a programme centred around a well-known TV personality. If the programme flops, the producer is blamed for not 'producing' the TV personality in the right way. If the programme is a success, most of the credit usually goes to the TV performer. If such thought did occur to Barbara Maxwell in 1979, she none the less accepted the challenge. I hope she does not regret it.

Newspaper journalists describe Barbara Maxwell as a shapely red-head. I would never indulge in such sexist language, though I have been known to call her the flame-haired temptress. She is an able and attractive woman with a considerable presence. She is a graduate of Queen's University, Belfast. She joined the BBC in 1967 as a secretary but became an assistant researcher within a week. Before *Question Time* she was a producer on current affairs programmes like *Tonight* and *Panorama*. *Question Time* was her first 'command'. She has been the producer/Editor throughout its first ten years, except when she took maternity leave for the birth of her third child. Her husband is a barrister at the planning Bar. She was promoted to the rank of Editor in 1983. She is forty-six.

When *Question Time* started, Barbara Maxwell and I had several things against us. First, there seemed to be nothing new about the programme. Its presenter was an old (fifty-six years old) war-horse, who was widely thought, in the BBC at least, to be past his zenith. The idea of the programme was old, borrowed from steam radio. The taunts were depressing. 'So BBC Television's idea of novelty is *Any Questions* with pictures,' and 'Is the BBC's current affairs department really so short of ideas that it has to mount a TV version of *Any Questions*?' and '*Question Time* – what a boring, unoriginal title.'

We could, of course, point to several important differences between *Question Time* and *Any Questions*. The QT audience participated, AQ's did not. QT's chairman was different from AQ's David Jacobs. QT was longer (sixty minutes instead of forty-five). But the only effective answer was to demonstrate the difference successfully in action on the screen. This was immediately done.

The title *Question Time* had been chosen because no one could think of anything better. I did not care for it because to me and to many other people *Question Time* is the name, long-established in parliamentary usage, for the hour when ministers answer MPS'-questions in the Commons. It was also too similar to *Any Questions*, from which we had to differentiate ourselves. But no one bothered too much about the title because no one thought the programme would last very long. No one suggested a title with the presenter's name, perhaps because 'Day', by itself, sounds less impressive than 'Wogan', 'Parkinson' or 'Frost'. And the BBC has never shown much enthusiasm for putting my name in a programme title, though there were three brief series with me daringly entitled *Daytime* (in '69), *Newsday* and *Talk-in to Day*, both in the early seventies.

As the programme has advanced in years, the newspapers have christened it *Sir Robin Day's Question Time*. But that was not taken up by the BBC.

Barbara Maxwell achieved one very important victory early on. She succeeded in getting Cabinet ministers to appear on *Question Time*. This was an advance because they had never, for some obscure reason, appeared on radio's *Any Questions*. With Cabinet ministers appearing on QT we stood a better chance of getting other panellists of high political and public standing.

The very first Cabinet minister who was a panellist was Michael Heseltine, then Environment Secretary, in October 1979. He was subjected to some rough and noisy questioning from a small left-wing Labour group about local government 'cuts' which were much in the news. After the programme, Heseltine was furious. The audience, he said, was biased and rigged against him. He would write to the Director-General next morning. We were very depressed and felt that our first Cabinet minister on the panel was our last. The only thing to cheer us was the fact that another panellist, Arthur Scargill of the NUM, had also protested that the same audience had been biased against him.

Three or four days later, at the Conservative Party Conference, I bumped into Heseltine in the Imperial Hotel, Blackpool. I was about to make some inconsequential greeting, unconnected with *Question Time*. But Heseltine got in first:

'Robin, what a *marvellous* programme that was the other night.'
'But Michael, I thought – '
'I've had dozens of letters and telegrams saying how good I was – I mean, *it* was.'

The simple fact was that Heseltine had put up a fighting performance, much better than he would have done without the barrage of left-wing questions. Since then, only one or two Cabinet ministers have refused to appear on *Question Time*; their refusal has not been because of their Cabinet status, but because of personal distaste for the medium.

What else is it that has made QT much more of a success than anyone expected? First of all, there is an unsatisfied appetite among the public for television programmes about topical issues which are both serious and entertaining, which combine information and humour. We have always had broadly two types of topical TV programme: the 'heavy' current affairs programmes such as *Panorama* or *Newsnight*, and on the other hand programmes whose purpose is entertainment, either showbiz chat-show style (*Wogan, Parkinson* and so on) where politicians are dealt with, if at all, as celebrities, or satire (for example, *Spitting Image*) where politicians and others are objects of hatred, ridicule and contempt.

Long before *Question Time* was a TV programme, I had held the belief that political issues and serious current problems should not be dealt with on television only in separate, compartmentalized types of programme – heavy or frivolous, serious or trivial. My view, rooted partly in my own habits of conversation and argument, and partly in the tradition of parliament, was that no subject is so serious or so important that discussion of it must be humourless or devoid of wit. But wit and humour are strands to be woven naturally into the fabric of discussion. That is what happens in the best speech, or parliamentary debate, or television discussion. Humour is not injected separately or artificially. Humour flourishes in the free flow of argument. Wit is not confined to self-contained 'gags' or 'one-liners'. Wit is a weapon of discourse – a poniard to deflate, a rapier to provoke.

Although many subjects of great importance are inherently forbidding and unappealing, my belief has always been that you can present such subjects on television in a way which wins people's interest and even arouses their sense of humour. This is not the wisdom of hindsight. At the very beginning of *Question Time*, when there had been no indication from on high as to what we should be trying to achieve, my aim was simply set out: 'It is a new kind of chat-show, thought-provoking as well as entertaining . . . *Question Time* will bring you an hour of hard-hitting argument and spontaneous humour.' As for the panellists, my views were straightforward: 'I want people of eloquence and wit . . . I expect good argument, controversy and humour.'

This was aiming high. The panels of QT have too often included people with neither eloquence nor wit. The argument around the table has too often been mediocre, the controversy stale and the humour less than brilliant. When this has occurred, I have inevitably felt obliged to pull the programme together and move it along. It has been difficult for me to do this without appearing to throw my weight about too much for some people's taste, and, I may add, for my taste also. Because *Question Time* is not a Robin Day interview with a studio audience. A weak panel forced me to play too big a part.

Because of the wide-ranging topical nature of the programme, panellists who are narrow specialists or inexperienced in public televised debate are unsuitable. I do not care what sex they are or whether they are from politics, industry, journalism or universities, but to do well on *Question Time* they should have proved themselves in public debate. Sometimes I have felt that some members of the audience were better suited to be panellists than the panellists.

Fortunately the audience is rarely unresponsive. That is the second reason for QT's success. The audience participation is not decorative or token. Having watched the programme quite often, they know what is expected of them. They do not only ask questions which they have prepared. They pick up the arguments of the panel.

How is the *Question Time* audience invited? There are about two hundred people in each QT audience. Invitations are sent to two constituency associations of each main political party. Each local party has half-a-dozen tickets. Then there are other groups from minority parties, trade unions, business associations, a school or two, student unions, tenants' and residents' associations, women's groups and various other organizations. And there are about thirty tickets sent to people who write in. Their political sympathies are checked so that invitations may go out in fair proportion to left, right and centre.

Each person has an invitation card with a tear-off section which they can return by post with a question. They can also submit questions on arrival. The audience is not a perfect cross-section, but is invited with scrupulous care and is reasonably representative. When the programme has come from its usual place, the Greenwood Theatre, Southwark, the audience is not only of people from the area around London. Coach parties, especially of schools from far afield, come to see, for instance, the National Gallery, the British Museum and Sir Robin Day in *Question Time*.

If the QT audience has been carefully invited for political and social balance, why does that balance sometimes seem not to have been achieved? There are several explanations. First, the left-wing elements in any QT audience always tend to be angrier, louder and fiercer. Therefore they may appear more numerous. Secondly, the questions raised by the audience are inevitably often critical of the government because the government is in power and has introduced controversial measures. Thirdly, the opponents of a controversial policy are usually more articulate and aggressive than the policy's supporters, who often sit in silence, waiting to hear how the policy (for example, the 'cuts', the interest rates, the ban, or whatever) can be defended.

The perfect socio-economic cross-section could not, in any event, be obtained from only two hundred people. From a thousand possibly, but not from two hundred. You could, of course, make a totally random selection by sticking pins in the electoral roll. Whether this would guarantee to include, among only two hundred thus picked, ethnic or religious minorities, not to mention the main political parties, is doubtful.

After ten years of coping with QT audiences, mostly from the London area, but also from other cities several times a year, I think our audience selection system has provided a reasonably good political and social mix. A member of one *Question Time* audience later achieved fame as a mass murderer. This was Dennis Nilsen, the Muswell Hill killer who was convicted of murdering several young men whose bodies he dismembered and boiled. He worked at a job centre and came to QT in a group from a Civil Service union. Whatever its imperfections, our system has had the advantage of usually producing an audience which includes articulate people of above-average intelligence and knowledge. This is important for a programme whose audience is there to participate and to contribute, not merely to listen and to applaud.

The division of labour between the Editor and myself has been clear. It is the Editor, not I, who has decided on the panellists. I have made suggestions which have often been followed up. I would have much preferred an arrangement which entitled me at least to be consulted about the panellists. I did ask to be consulted, but nothing came of my request. I thought of refusing to continue unless my contract entitled me to be consulted, but I was too preoccupied with other problems to fight that battle.

The Editor and I jointly sift the questions which have been put in, and choose the four or five questioners whom I am to call by name. The other questioners are chosen by me entirely at random. The chairmanship is my responsibility. The Editor can and sometimes does communicate with me during the programme through my earpiece. She does so rarely, first because it is rarely necessary, and secondly because I hate it. But sometimes a word in my ear from either the Editor or the director is extremely helpful. For example when I, in the heat and tension of the programme, forget a name or lose a question-card. Or if I am obviously not going to get through all the questions as planned, the Editor may suggest what to omit. And of course the time signals for the end of the show come through my earpiece. It is a difficult art, which I have not yet mastered, to end a live programme (or as in QT a recorded programme done exactly as if live) precisely on time, without having rudely to interrupt a panellist in full flow.

Question Time is recorded between 8 p.m. and 9 p.m. This is primarily for the convenience of the studio audience for whom 10 p.m. or 10.30 p.m. would be too late a start. Recording also enables us to edit the programme in an emergency, but cuts have been made only once or twice in ten years, and only for compelling legal reasons.

There is, as in any television programme, the person whose function crowns the whole programme operation. This is the director, who is responsible for which pictures taken by which camera are selected to be seen on the viewer's screen. The director of programmes such as *Question Time* is crucial to its success. I never cease to be astonished by, and grateful for, the effect of the director's art. As a programme is being recorded, I form some impression of how it is going, from my standpoint and from a viewer's standpoint. When I watch the transmission, I see a different programme from the one I had imagined. I marvel at the director's magic, the cutting from camera to camera with uncanny anticipation, bringing in reaction shots which add another dimension to the whole thing.

The usual director of *Question Time* is Ann Morley. Unlike

the director of a drama production, she has no script to follow. She does not even know where the speaker is sitting except for the four or five named questioners. She does not know from one second to the next whom I will call on, or how the argument will develop. By her choice of camera shots and camera angles, the director underlines and points up the argument and humour of the programme. She has to follow the back-and-forth of the argument, which is not easy. The skill of the director on *Question Time* is superlative.

In most TV programmes there is conflict or 'creative tension' between the Editor and the presenter. In *Question Time* there has been relatively little between myself and Barbara Maxwell. If there had been any serious conflict, neither she nor I would have endured working together for ten years. The main area of disagreement has been the choice of women for the panel. Not *whether* women should be on the panel – there has never been argument about that. The difficulty has been *which* women. Barbara Maxwell has stated that, because women are so under-represented in public life, she follows a policy of 'positive discrimination' on behalf of women. This means that women are liable to be on the *Question Time* panel not because they are qualified by experience, or reputation, or personality, but because they are women. The problem with this strategy is that it sometimes produces panellists who do not benefit the cause of women's advancement (of which I am a sturdy champion).

The Editor therefore has spent many hours and many lunches over the years seeking, meeting, auditioning and choosing women for *Question Time*. Sometimes she has made a brilliant discovery. Too often, however, the discoveries, though well-qualified in certain ways, have not been up to the task of joining a hard-hitting televised debate with old political hands or veteran parliamentarians. Such discoveries have rarely made more than one or two appearances on *Question Time*.

Barbara Maxwell has been well intentioned. She says she wants to 'exploit the still largely untapped reservoir' of female talent. But I beg leave to doubt whether the regrettable fact that only 6 per cent or so of MPs are women, and other similar injustices, can be redressed by putting unsuitable women on a programme like *Question Time*. My argument has been that it is simply unfair to the 'discovered' woman, who may well be very distinguished in her own field, to cast her among hardened, practised tele-gladiators in front of a mass audience. There are plenty of other TV programmes in which novices, female or male, can be given experience in front of the cameras.

For me personally, *Question Time* has gradually altered what is called my 'image'. Before *Question Time*, the usual epithets attached to me would be gruff, crusty, grouchy, tetchy, crotchety and pompous. These words are regrettably sometimes still applied to me (if only from force of journalistic habit). But, since QT, I have noticed a welcome increase in the use of mellow, witty, charming, polite, avuncular and even flirtatious.

The success of *Question Time*, however, had one retrogressive effect on the professional career of its presenter. As QT became an established success, my work as a political interviewer on TV dwindled away, other than at the annual party conferences and during the general elections of 1983 and 1987. This made me feel less of a journalist than an entertainer.

The real test of QT's popularity is the audience figure, which is often around six million. This is said by experts to be 'fantastic' for a current affairs show after 10 p.m. What is more, the programme sometimes picks up audience, which is rare for that time of the evening.

Perhaps the most professional tribute of all to QT came from Michael Grade, the ex-ITV whizz-kid who was plucked from California to be Controller of BBC1 and went on to become Head of Channel 4. Soon after arriving at the BBC, Grade sent down one of his memos to the workers. It instructed Robin Day to stop saying 'Sleep well' after his goodnight when signing off in *Question Time*. The reason given was that 'Sleep well' could be taken as an insulting comment on the next programme. The audience held by *Question Time* was too good to be lost by me bidding the viewers to sleep well!

There was a minor outcry from the public. The *Sun* newspaper devoted a whole editorial to the issue:

Poor old Sir Robin Day. He's forbidden by BBC boss Michael Grade from saying 'Sleep well' at the end of his popular *Question Time* on Thursday nights.

Mr Grade thought it was unfair to the following programmes to suggest that it's bedtime.

Viewers aren't that stupid. If they want to go on watching the box they'll do so.

Ignore young Grade, Sir Robin. He can't do without you.

But as Michael Leapman records in his entertaining *The Last Days of the Beeb*, 'Day grumbled but complied.' I did grumble a bit because 'Sleep well' was not a gimmick or a deliberate catchphrase, but a normal, natural thing to say at nearly midnight. I thought of offering alternatives, such as: 'If and when you retire for the night, preferably after watching the splendid programme which follows this one, sleep well.'

In due course, 'young Grade' relented and rescinded his ban. 'Poor old Sir Robin' could once again utter the forbidden words.

The regular QT viewer will know that like any unscripted, unedited, spontaneous TV programme, it has been better on some nights than on others. Like any long-running West End theatre hit, *Question Time* has not always lived up to its rave notices:

'Compulsive viewing' – Roy Hattersley.

'The greatest show for all-round entertainment . . . a terrific mixture of humour, sarcasm and stupidity' – *Doncaster Evening Post*

'Hugely successful' – *Glasgow Evening Times*

On giving up the chairmanship of QT, I was overwhelmed by the flood of acclaim in the press, and by the kind letters of thanks and appreciation from viewers.

All very gratifying. But for me, enough is enough. My reasons for giving up *Question Time* at the end of the 1989 season were explained to the BBC in March. I had listed several reasons, some of which were personal. Though my health was good (considering), I did not feel up to continuing a weekly appearance, which was more of a strain than it may have seemed. I wanted freedom to take on other TV work occasionally as a change from QT. Also I had written this book. I knew, what the BBC did not then know, that it contained opinions about certain BBC policies and personalities which might well plunge me into controversy. In those circumstances, would it be right, I asked myself, to continue as a regular BBC presenter? I thought not.

Finally, there was the prospect of the Commons being televised at last before the end of 1989. The *real* Question Time (with Kinnock *v* Thatcher, and Mr Speaker *v* Sillars, and so on) would be on the screen. This was likely to make my version seem out of date. Many people have told me that I am foolish to give up *Question Time*, that I will miss the topical excitement of Thursday nights on the box, that without *Question Time* I will fade away and be forgotten. That is a risk which I have taken. I have gambled once again.

Epilogue

For over thirty years, I have been an enthusiastic practitioner of the new electronic journalism, but have become increasingly critical of television's impact on events. I voiced my growing concern about the inherent dangers and limitations of television as a journalistic medium.* Though my warnings were politely praised as a contribution to discussion, they have been largely ignored in the onward march of television's conquest of society.

I urged that practitioners of television journalism should be governed by principle and purpose and not by the mindless mechanics of the medium. They had a duty, I suggested, to ask themselves not only how this medium *can* be used, but how it *ought* to be used. I had come to feel that television, with its enormous power to project violence and unreason, had a heavy responsibility to present reasoned and civilized argument. The electronic journalism of TV should do more than transmit 'bloody good pictures'.

With its appetite for visual sensation, its tabloid dependence on pictures, television had an inherent tendency to distort and to trivialize. Disaster, violence, disruption, were the staple ingredients of TV's diet. Television's appetite for them was insatiable. This appetite, this lust for visible action and violent happenings, is itself an invitation to create more of the same for TV to project.

*See my *Encounter* article, 'Troubled Reflections of a TV Journalist', May 1970.

Television, ran my argument, thrives on unreason, and unreason thrives on television. Television's dependence on pictures (and the most vivid and bloody pictures) makes it not only a *powerful* means of communication but a *crude* one, which strikes at the emotions rather than the intellect. For TV journalism this means a dangerous and increasing concentration on action rather than thought, on happenings rather than issues, on shock rather than explanation, on personalities rather than ideas, on exposure rather than exposition. I admitted that this meant TV could cover a riot, a war, a revolution, an assassination, more vividly than any newspaper. But TV tended to give much less explanation of the reasons behind these events. Television producers must recognize that the most important developments are not primarily visual.

My arguments did not find favour with those who acquit television of any responsibility for violence and disorder. I pointed out that the civilized order, which is liberty under law and government by consent, has been increasingly threatened by violence and terrorism. My conviction was, and is, that television may well have been, if not the cause, a contributing influence. By reflecting violence, television may have inflamed. By depicting, television may have magnified. By projecting, television may have incited. By accentuating violence, television may have encouraged it.

My conclusion, unpopular in TV circles, was that we should work on the presumption that television is an influence towards unreason and violence. Whatever television touches, it can magnify, inflate, project and spread. Such power should be put on the side of reason and civilized behaviour. Television should be biased in favour of reason.

Index

Roy Hattersley
A Yorkshire Boyhood £3.99

"It was not until he was dead and I was forty that I realized my father was in Holy Orders," Roy Hattersley tells us in the opening pages of his childhood memoirs – setting the tone for an elegant, continually surprising book of unusual wit, eloquence and candour.

A precocious only child, young Roy grew up surrounded by protective adults who were equally determined to expose him to books and to shield him from germs – second hand books were decontaminated by a sharp session in the oven.

Unwavering devotion to Sheffield Wednesday; a ten year feud with the next door neighbours; the hardships of the Thirties and the Blitz – all the pleasures and pangs of a Northern working-class boyhood are magnificently and movingly evoked.

'It has a special sort of charm: a richly idiosyncratic cast of characters, yet a narrator who has the common touch'
BLAKE MORRISON, OBSERVER

'Moving, funny, charming and enormously readable'

LISTENER

Edwina Currie
Lifelines £4.99

'One of the secrets of political success is the resilience normally only seen in cartoons. Drop them, eat them, electrocute them, trample on them , kick them over cliffs and they – the cartoon characters and the politicians – are indestructible. I found it impossible to dislike Edwina Currie. She is professional, chatty, confidential, disarming, genuinely caring, and indefatigable'
LESLEY GARNER, THE DAILY TELEGRAPH

'On the occasion I sat next to Mrs Currie at dinner I must say I warmed to her. The party lost some of its entertainment value when its agricultural lobby decided that she was, after all, not quite fit for human consumption. Now she has written a book which, coming as it does in the twilight of the Thatcher years, might serve as a valuable postscript to that period' JOHN MORTIMER, THE SUNDAY TIMES

'Who will not remember the political storm, the writs, the fury of the farming industry, the gloating jibes from her own party as well as the Opposition? What she went through – even if much of it was self-inflicted – was enough to traumatize even the strongest' ANNE de COURCY, EVENING STANDARD

'Underneath that bright'n'breezy exterior is an essentially well meaning politician . . . as an attitude shifter and leader in public opinion, none can deny the part that Edwina Currie has played in building a more health conscious Britain' DERBY EVENING TELEGRAPH

'No beating about the bush with Edwina . . . in telling her version of events we are left in no doubt that she is still smarting' VAL HENNESSEY, DAILY MAIL

David Owen
Personally Speaking £4.99

Beginning with his Welsh childhood, through his time at university
and in the medical profession, to a career in the Labour Party and
the subsequent formation of the Social Democratic Party, David Owen
discusses his life in revealing detail.

He relates his experiences in a number of government posts – Navy
Minister, Health Minister and, particularly, Foreign Secretary 1977–9
– and provides unique insights into the Falklands, Anglo-American
relations, Africa and the Middle East, Iran, defence and disarmament,
and the European Community. He also discusses candidly his relations
with many prominent politicans including Jimmy Carter, Leonid
Brezhnev, Menachem Begin, Harold Wilson, James Callaghan and the
other three members of the 'Gang of Four' who founded the SDP.

His reasons for leaving the Labour Party in 1981 and the birth of the
SDP are covered in detail, and David Owen tells why, with his belief
that social democracy has a special contribution to make to British
politics, he is continuing as leader of the SDP.

All Pan books are available at your local bookshop or newsagent, or can be ordered direct from the publisher. Indicate the number of copies required and fill in the form below.

Send to: **CS Department, Pan Books Ltd., P.O. Box 40, Basingstoke, Hants. RG21 2YT.**

or phone: 0256 469551 (Ansaphone), quoting title, author and Credit Card number.

Please enclose a remittance* to the value of the cover price plus: 60p for the first book plus 30p per copy for each additional book ordered to a maximum charge of £2.40 to cover postage and packing.

*Payment may be made in sterling by UK personal cheque, postal order, sterling draft or international money order, made payable to Pan Books Ltd.

Alternatively by Barclaycard/Access:

Card No.

Signature:

Applicable only in the UK and Republic of Ireland.

While every effort is made to keep prices low, it is sometimes necessary to increase prices at short notice. Pan Books reserve the right to show on covers and charge new retail prices which may differ from those advertised in the text or elsewhere.

NAME AND ADDRESS IN BLOCK LETTERS PLEASE:

....

Name————————————————————————————

Address————————————————————————————

————————————————————————————————

————————————————————————————————

————————————————————————————————

3/87